ELVIS
HAS LEFT THE BUILDING

Also by Dylan Jones

The Eighties: One Day, One Decade

From The Ground Up

When Ziggy Played Guitar:
David Bowie And Four Minutes That Shook The World

The Biographical Dictionary Of Popular Music

British Heroes In Afghanistan (with David Bailey)

Cameron On Cameron: Conversations With Dylan Jones

Mr. Jones' Rules For The Modern Man

iPod Therefore I Am: A Personal Journey Through Music

Meaty Beaty Big & Bouncy

Sex, Power & Travel

Ultra Lounge

Paul Smith: True Brit

Jim Morrison: Dark Star

Haircults

ELVIS
HAS LEFT THE BUILDING

The Day The King Died

*

DYLAN JONES

Duckworth Overlook

London and New York

First published in the UK and the US in 2014 by
Duckworth Overlook

LONDON
30 Calvin Street, London E1 6NW
T: 020 7490 7300
E: info@duckworth-publishers.co.uk
www.ducknet.co.uk
For bulk and special sales please contact
sales@duckworth-publishers.co.uk,
or write to us at the above address.

NEW YORK
141 Wooster Street
New York, NY 10012
www.overlookpress.com
For bulk and special sales please
contact sales@overlookny.com,
or write to us at the above address.

© 2014 by Dylan Jones

The right of Dylan Jones to be identified as the Author of
the Work has been asserted by him in accordance with
the Copyright, Designs and Patents Act 1988.
A catalogue record for this book is available
from the British Library.
Cataloguing-in-Publication Data is available
from the Library of Congress.

ISBNs
UK: 978-0-7156-4856-8
US: 978-1-4683-0967-6

Typeset by Ray Davies
Printed and bound in Great Britain

For Tony Parsons

From the Roxy to eternity, and back again

"…He lives. We live. He lives."
John Updike, from "Jesus and Elvis"

CONTENTS

Introduction: Exit Stage Left   1

1. God Save The Queen   13
2. The Day Elvis Died   30
3. Real Real Gone   50
4. Punks Vs. Teds   78
5. Elvis Is In The House   119
6. What Happens In Vegas ...   151
7. Are You Lonesome Tonight?   181
8. Don't Be Cruel   214
9. God Save The King   238
10. A King's Ransom   260

Chronological Bibliography   289
Acknowledgements   297
Index   301

INTRODUCTION

Exit Stage Left

*"Elvis Presley is like the 'Big Bang' of Rock'n'Roll.
It all came from there"* – Bono

The phrase "Elvis has left the building" was used for the first time on December 15th, 1956, by the promoter Horace Lee Logan, telling the crowd at his *Louisiana Hayride*, broadcast from the Shreveport Municipal Memorial Auditorium, that the young star had left the premises through the stage door. This night, like so many nights in future, Elvis was accompanied by his police escort. He had played the *Hayride* two years previously, but now he was a massive star, and needed all the protection he could get. What Logan actually said was: "All right, all right, Elvis has left the building. I've told you absolutely straight up to this point, you know that he has left the building; he left the stage and went out the back with the policeman and he is now gone from the building."

Logan was not in fact trying to get the crowd to leave, but to persuade them to stay and see the rest of the acts on the bill. After Elvis had given his final encore and left the stage, the crowd rushed for the exits, even though many other *Hayride* acts were still waiting to perform. Logan didn't want them traipsing round the back hoping to get a glimpse of the new boy.

"Please, young people," he continued over the tannoy, in desperation. "Elvis has left the building. He has gotten in his car and driven away ... Please take your seats." Later, the phrase would be used as a way to clear a room, to encourage people to leave, but this first time that wasn't the case at all.

Even back then Elvis Presley was trouble.

That December night turned out to be the last time Elvis would ever play the *Hayride*. His manager, "Colonel" Tom Parker, had just bought out his contract, and Elvis's show there was never broadcast on the KWKH radio station again.

"Elvis has left the building ..."

Throughout Elvis's Las Vegas years, indeed any time he played a concert, the words would be delivered, matter-of-factly, after the encore, in order to calm the crowd down, or to get them to pick up their bags and their drinks and their posters and go home. Sometimes it was the MC, sometimes a backing singer, and quite often the promoter. But it was always said. It became the punchline to a thousand different jokes, some verbal punctuation, while baseball announcers on radio and television used the phrase as a way to signal a home run. When singing the closing theme to the television series *Frasier*, Kelsey Grammer would sometimes follow the last line with his own version: "Frasier has left the building."

As the *Chicago Reader*'s Straight Dope column once put it, the meaning is clear to all: "the show's over, the curtain has fallen, the sun has set, that's all she wrote, the fat lady has sung, our work here is done, move along, nothing more to see ... so long, hasta la vista, you don't have to go home but you can't stay here ... Scotty, beam me up."

The fateful words were said for the last time at the end of Elvis's final performance, in Indianapolis on June 26th, 1977. On August 16th that year, Elvis left the building forever.

Like the murders of JFK and RFK, or the deaths of Marilyn Monroe, John Lennon or Kurt Cobain, Elvis Presley's death is etched in our collective memory. Whether we're fans or not. Everyone over a certain age can remember exactly where they were when they found out that Elvis was dead. For over twenty years, since the birth of rock'n'roll in 1956, Elvis had been part of the very fabric of American life. He was an object of desire and worship the whole world over. A life without Elvis was unthinkable, unimaginable. Yet the news was incontrovertible: on August 16th, 1977 he was pronounced dead, having been rushed to the Baptist Memorial Hospital in Memphis.

We still feel his death today. A 2004 Samaritans survey of Britain's most emotional memories, for example, placed Elvis's death at No.20, after events such as the fall of the Berlin wall, Neil Armstrong walking on the moon and the 9/11 attacks.

One man, who was barely ten at the time, remembered the moment vividly. "I'd been playing in the garden and when I came inside I found my mother sitting on the stairs, crying. I'd never seen her cry before. I asked her what was wrong. She said, 'Elvis is dead.'"

"My parents sat me down with very serious looks on their faces," recalled a similarly young fan. "My grandfather, who I didn't know very well, was ill so I assumed they were going to tell me he had died. When they said it was Elvis who had died, I was completely distraught and wished it had been my grandfather ..."

In the words of another, "I was working as a lifeguard at an outdoor swimming pool in British Columbia. I was on the deck and another lifeguard, who was [another] huge Elvis fan, came running out of the guard shack waving his arms, yelling, 'Elvis is dead!' I remember the pool, which was very busy, fell really quiet."

According to a British devotee, "I was fixing a TV set and listening to Capital Radio late in the evening. I was just wondering why they'd played several Elvis songs in a row when the DJ announced, 'The King is dead.' All of the pop stations played nothing but Elvis for the rest of the evening."

As for me, I heard the news sitting in the saloon bar of the Nag's Head pub on London Road in High Wycombe, Buckinghamshire, where most of the punk bands in the area played at the time. The Nag's Head was owned by Ron Watts, who also ran the 100 Club in Oxford Street, and everyone who played there played here. I was just seventeen. As the news spread around the bar, a couple of people appeared to cheer half heartedly, although after some stern looks from the barmen, mostly there was hush. Without access to anything other than secondhand information, the rest of the evening was spent in speculation. If it really was true, how exactly had he died? Was he alone? Was he naked? Was it true that it was a drug overdose? Could it have been suicide? I had just finished a dry run of packing for an imminent move to London, to Chelsea, and was about to start a new life. I wasn't an Elvis fan, but this was monumental news, and my friends and I spent most of the evening absorbing its impact. If I recall correctly, that largely involved repeating the fact that Elvis was actually dead, "Fucking dead," over and over again.

"Fuck, Elvis is dead!"

"Fuck me, you're right. Elvis is dead!"

Media speculation about Elvis's wellbeing – his mental state and health – had been so rife that for many his death was a tragedy waiting to happen. However it was no less shocking. After a while we began to feel as though this was our JFK moment, and that we would always remember where we were when the fat lady sang. There were the two Davids, Ross, Julian, and Russell in the bar that night, all of us around the same age, plus a couple of Americans who had just thrashed us at pool. They were more upset than anyone. They went to put some Elvis on the jukebox, but so many people were crowding around it, determined to play Thin Lizzy, Eddie &

The Hot Rods and Dr. Feelgood, that they never got near it.

We were young, but there were people there that night – older men – who were far more affected than us, and their grief for Elvis clearly bound up with mourning their own lost early youth.

Then there was Sid, or "Syd" as he had rebranded himself some time before we all met him, thinking that the Syd Barrett/Pink Floyd connotations would play well in the saloon bar of the Nag's Head. Sid was about twelve or thirteen years older than us – a lifetime when you're seventeen – a light bulb dimmed by excessive drug consumption which, when we first met him, made him appear strangely exotic. He smoked dope all the time, and while this was appealing to sixteen- and seventeen-year-olds like ourselves, even we found his habit excessive.

Being older, and owning a car, Sid became by default our driver. Whenever we were planning an excursion to Beaconsfield or Rickmansworth, or we thought we needed to spend a Saturday night at Skindles in Maidenhead, the Red Cow in Hammersmith, the Marquee in Wardour Street, or indeed the Nag's Head; whenever we decided to spend all night up in the woods above Marlow smoking Red Leb, drinking cider and listening to *The Faust Tapes*, Gong's *Camembert Electrique* or the first Stooges album (Sid *loved* the first Stooges album), Sid would be the designated driver, regardless of what condition he might be in, and regardless of what he intended to consume.

That was the thing with Sid: he didn't outwardly change when he was under the influence of drink and drugs. He appeared to be stoned all the time, which I must admit we found appealing. "Sid's Van," a dilapidated old blue long-wheelbase Transit that had presumably seen better days, became the default response whenever any of our gang asked how we were going to get somewhere. "How? Sid's van." If one of us asked how we were going to get to and from the Reading Festival, Friars Aylesbury, the Hand & Flowers, the 100 Club or the Rainbow – or anywhere, come to that – Sid was immediately appointed our de facto chauffeur. He never volunteered, but it was always assumed that Sid would put down the bong, turn off the Deep Purple and leap up into the cabin.

Sid had a van, Sid could drive, and so Sid would drive us. It was as simple and as effective as that. He could navigate the B-roads of Buckinghamshire and the byways of Soho even when heavily self-medicated, and he would often stop and ask for directions in London with a huge and inelegantly rolled spliff hanging from his lips, attached simply by muscle memory. He was a lovely, sweet man, who went through life assuming that everything would turn out all right as long as he spent every waking hour out of his gourd, smoking roll-ups, listening to Hawkwind on the eight-track in his van and finding the funny side of almost every situation. A carpenter by trade, he would spend hours with a Rotring pen, drawing extravagant speaker cabinets that he would never find the time to make, proudly showing us all while we nodded and asked him to take us to Slough for the night.

Sid was our Gandalf, our guru, our sage, our man who had been there at the beginning. For Sid loved Elvis. Not in a cheap, ironic way, but with a genuine passion. We occasionally teased him about it, but we learned not to; this was one of the few things that would turn his mood, which would cause him to cross the central reservation on the M40 and drive back to High Wycombe. Sid was always good at digging up new music, and whether it was Tom Petty or the new Eagles LP, you could guarantee that Sid would have it before anyone else. He liked all the old head music – Greenslade, Soft Machine, Jefferson Airplane, the first incarnation of Fleetwood Mac – but he was also deep into Iggy Pop and the MC5, and when punk came along he was one of the first of our gang to wholeheartedly embrace it. He felt no desire to dress like a punk – at his age it would have been ludicrous – but he got "where they are coming from." But as we were driving back from some party in the small hours, as we were bickering over what eight-track to play next, squabbling yet again over whether Mike Oldfield's *Ommadawn* or Joni Mitchell's *Blue* was the best thing to listen to when coming down from a massive speed binge, Sid would put on one of his favourites, either *The Beach Boys In Concert,* or an Elvis compilation tape largely made up of songs from his 1968 "Comeback Special," when the King donned black leather and finally rediscovered his mojo. Sid's van had an uncharacteristically sophisticated sound system, his own approximation of what we then referred to as "quad," which was in fact just a bunch of randomly placed mini-speakers torn from several ancient Talbot Avengers.

Sid even had a tiny Elvis tattoo on his forearm, where everyone could see it. We thought it was pretty naff, but rather cool as well (none of us had tattoos at that point, and the whole idea was strange and exotic).

Though he looked nothing like him – Sid wore thick National Health glasses, had dank curly hair and never wore anything other than patchwork denim – he always reminded me of John Milner, the Paul Le Mat character in George Lucas's *American Graffiti,* the cool kid who never left town, the drag racer who never went to college, and who never moved on. While Milner had a Ford Coupe, Sid only had a Ford Transit. But like Milner, Sid would spend every Saturday night with kids five, ten years younger than him, until they too moved on. Sid was destined to never grow up. That was what we liked about him, and why we would eventually feel we could live without him, too.

Sid went to pieces when Elvis died. He turned up in the Nag's Head that night, having heard the news on the van radio, and instead of coming over to talk about it, just ordered a drink – he drank pints of snakebite – and went to sit by himself. We could all tell that he'd been crying, could all tell that while he didn't especially want to be disturbed, he wanted everyone to know just how much he was suffering.

We all knew, even at that tender and callow age, that Sid had been left behind, and that with Elvis's passing he could no longer spend his days in a state of perpetual adolescence. Now that Elvis was dead, Sid would finally have to grow up.

Although Elvis's weight issues had started to turn him into a parody of his earlier self, in essence he had remained the same for so long that when he died it was as though the youthful enthusiasm of early rock'n'roll went with him. And this was written on the faces of all the greasy twenty- and thirty-somethings in the Nag's Head that night. Even though most of the people in the two downstairs bars had long hair and were wearing denim – and most of them were men – you could tell that in their hearts they were seventeen, with big black quiffs and pink peg trousers. At last, this was their James Dean moment.

When Diana, Princess of Wales died almost exactly twenty years later, on August 31st, 1997, there was a national outpouring of grief, as through her immense capacity for empathy had genuinely managed to touch hearts. When she died, that was repaid, and on September 6th, a day of national mourning, three million people lined the route of her funeral procession. As Tony Blair's New Labour government had only recently been elected, it took a form of ownership of the death, and out of tragedy came the prospect of a new political dawn.

Elvis's death was completely different, and had a totally different effect on the US. His death was co-opted by no one. Everyone and their mother would try to exploit the death commercially, but the event and its aftermath were owned by an entire generation, a generation of baby boomers who had watched Elvis grow as they themselves had grown. By 1977 Elvis had been famous for two decades, twenty years in which he had lived his own interpretation of the American Dream, in spite of all the vast political, military and cultural upheaval around him. Elvis proved what might happen if you were a poor, good-looking Southern boy with an innate gift and a winning smile. His success was a manifestation of the national ethos, in which freedom encouraged prosperity, upward social mobility and a reward for hard work. If one were to believe the Declaration of Independence, and that all men are created equal, then Elvis was endowed by his Creator with certain inalienable Rights, including Life, Liberty and the pursuit of Happiness.

This was a dream, however, that ended prematurely, that showed that life was finite, as was success, and that there was a price to pay for living so grandly, so badly, and so publicly. Some thought Elvis's death was the result of divine retribution, and that he was being punished for his sins, which were obviously manifold. He didn't just worship a false God, he was one, and in flaunting himself had paid the ultimate price before God.

If Diana's death signalled the start of something, Elvis's signalled the end.

For me, nearly five thousand miles away, Elvis's death created smaller and smaller echoes, tinier and tinier ripples. After I got over the initial shock – the big old king of rock'n'roll was dead – I got on with my life, and the story quickly disappeared.

Elvis may have passed on, but I was far more interested in my next visit to the 100 Club, in Elvis Costello's next London concert. To me and anyone I knew, Elvis had morphed into the generic, anodyne Fifties shuffle-beat of Showaddywaddy or Mud. I didn't associate Elvis with Sid Vicious's gold lamé jacket or John Lydon's pointed red Robot shoes. I saw him as an old fart listened to by taxi drivers, grandmothers and ageing Teds. For me, he was simply the butt of a hundred jokes, a corny stereotype, a clichéd archetype. By the summer of 1977, Elvis had already become a reductive fancy-dress staple, a crepe-soled joke, a man whose youth meant nothing to the youth of Seventies Britain. Elvis's slipshod teenbeat was the music of TV toilet cleaner commercials, while his mawkish ballads were already Radio 2 staples, the kind of maudlin stuff your mother liked. Elvis's records had been devalued by constant overexposure. By August 1977, there were no hard edges to Elvis's music, only a soft, white underbelly.

By 1977, to me and anyone I knew, Elvis was no different from Jim Reeves, Cliff Richard or Al Martino, a soporific crooner who meant as much to me as Engelbert Humperdinck.

How little I knew.

This is a book about what happened that day, how it affected us all, how it changed our culture, and what it still means today. Elvis's sudden and relatively early death served to fix the iconic status he achieved in his lifetime forever in place. Whether you live in the United States, Europe, Australia, Russia or the Far East, Elvis probably still means something to you.

This is also a book about Elvis's conflicted relationship with punk rock, or rather punk's conflicted relationship with Elvis. Elvis died the month of punk's apotheosis, at a time when his own cultural relevance had arguably never been lower. Yet he was still considered to be rock'n'roll's greatest totem, the lightning flash that sparked a musical, social, cultural, sexual and socio-economic revolution.

Punk set out to destroy Elvis, or at least everything Elvis had come to represent, but Elvis destroyed himself before anyone else could.

However, almost forty years after his death, the man just won't go away. He has penetrated the modern world in ways that are bizarre and inexplicable: a pop icon while he was alive, he has become almost a religious icon in death, a modern-day martyr crucified on the wheel of drugs, junk TV and bad sex. Sure, he could jump from a mellifluous baritone to an imploring tenor in the space of a few bars, yet Elvis's appeal was always about so much more than the way he could sing.

Elvis's journey was the twentieth century's defining instance of the Horatio Alger myth, even if rather than achieving the American Dream by leading an exemplary life, and struggling valiantly against poverty and adversity, Elvis gained wealth and success by catching sunshine.

The story of Elvis possesses the sort of narrative arc to which we all seem hard-wired to respond. It is a cautionary tale, one with no ambiguity: "What you are now, I once was; what I am now, you will become."

Who could deny Elvis? Whenever we catch the melodramatic strains of an old Elvis hit playing on the radio, or in the back room of a downtown bar, who among us begrudges those elemental – if overplayed – cornerstones of popular culture a respectful nod, and perhaps even a secret inner-smile, irrespective of the fact that we have all heard these songs so often their power to move us has long since been diffused?

Who cares? It's Elvis, and no one begrudges Elvis, right? Even if he has long since become Meta-Elvis.

"The death of Elvis Presley in 1977 provoked a gradual blurring of reality and myth that prompted cultural critics to ponder whether he might ultimately become the subject of religious frenzy," wrote pop biographer Peter Doggett, although anyone with a passing interest in popular culture might have anticipated that happening anyway. Elvis may not have been culturally relevant in 1977, but he was still Elvis, and the only man who ever would be. Doggett continued: "By 1992, the BBC's Religious Affairs correspondent could write a book, *Elvis People,* with a blurb that claimed: 'It poses a serious question: are we witnessing the birth of a new religious movement?'"

However the cult of Elvis actually started on August 16th, 1977. Whether it was sharp-featured Elvis you wanted, or the latter-day idol in all his magisterial pomp, the King could supply it all.

There was just so much of Elvis to go round.

According to a 1993 CNN and *Time* magazine poll, one American in five thought that Elvis was, or might be, alive. The survey said that while 79 percent of Americans believed that Presley died in 1977, sixteen percent said he was still among the living, and five percent were not sure. Not only is Elvis the most enduring American icon of the postwar years, he is the pop god by which all others are measured. Elvis was there first, before the Beatles, before the Rolling Stones, before the Sex Pistols or Nirvana.

Elvis was there before everyone; and that's why it felt so strange when he suddenly wasn't there anymore.

CHAPTER ONE

God Save The Queen

"No Elvis, Beatles or the Rolling Stones in 1977 ..."
– Joe Strummer

Until the death of Elvis Presley, the summer of 1977 had belonged to George Lucas, and *Star Wars*. Released on May 25th, the film had instantly become a worldwide pop-culture phenomenon. Produced with a budget of just $11 million, it earned $460 million in the United States and $314 million overseas, easily outstripping the previous year's blockbuster, Steven Spielberg's *Jaws*, as the highest-grossing film of all time.

Lucas, a precociously talented director (and businessman) had made his mark with his own take on teenage subculture *American Graffiti* in 1973 before writing, directing and completing *Star Wars* over the next four. The *Washington Post* called it "A Spectacular Intergalactic Joyride," suggesting that Lucas had supplied 20th Century Fox with a new lease of life. "George Lucas' delightful science-fiction adventure fantasy is a new classic in a rousing movie tradition: a space swashbuckler" while Roger Ebert's review hailed it as "an out-of-body experience," comparing its special effects to Stanley Kubrick's *2001: A Space Odyssey*.

Star Wars started breaking records the moment it was released – even though it was originally only shown on 32 screens. It made $2.8 million in its opening week, but didn't receive a wider nationwide release for another two months, and then only after huge public demand. So idiosyncratic was

Star Wars thought to be that 20th Century Fox didn't know how to market it; in the end it didn't matter, as the public marketed it for them. For months there were lines around the block wherever the movie was shown; people just couldn't get enough of it.

Groundbreaking. Pioneering. Paradigm-shifting. *Star Wars* was 24-carat popcorn, a blockbuster of such power and influence that it changed the nature of cinema completely, ushering in a new era of cinematic behemoths. It was so successful, so quickly, that critics didn't really understand what had happened. *Star Wars* drew a line under auteur-driven cinema, and waved goodbye to the likes of *Easy Rider* and *Taxi Driver*, as Luke Skywalker and Hans Solo jetted off into a galaxy far, far away.

People loved *Star Wars* in a way no film had been loved since *Gone With The Wind*.

In San Francisco, the manager of the Coronet on Geary Boulevard reported that "I've never seen anything like it. We're getting all kinds. Old people, young people, children, Hare Krishna groups. They bring cards to play in line. We have checker players, we have chess players. People with paints and sequins on their faces. Fruit eaters like I've never seen before. People loaded on grass and LSD. At least one's been here every day."

Novelist Jonathan Lethem saw the film 21 times that summer, and only stopped at 21 because the number seemed "safely ridiculous and extreme …"

Whether George Lucas was rekindling mythology in the Homeric tradition, or whether his inspiration lay in the pages of lower-brow Asimovian pulp sci-fi, the pseudo-mythical underpinning of *Star Wars* paved the way for *The Matrix* and *Lord Of The Rings* trilogies, where heroes struggle against the forces of evil. Lucas was no doubt influenced by

Tolkien's labyrinthine mythography in the first place, but pre-1977, moviemakers did not truly think in epic terms. He pioneered a new kind of epic, one that relied on rather old-fashioned ideas of what going to the movies should be like. It was designed as a family-friendly flick, with morally just heroes in whom everyone could believe. Tellingly, when the unfinished film was shown to Fox executives, World War II dogfights were shown where battles between TIE fighters and the Millennium Falcon would be.

Ridley Scott had just released his first film, a stately adaptation of a Joseph Conrad novel, *The Duellists*, which won the Special Jury Prize at Cannes. However the premiere was completely overshadowed by the release of Lucas's film, which Scott queued to see at the Egyptian Theater on Hollywood Boulevard. "The actual air was agog, the air was excited. I'd never seen so many crowds outside a theatre. To me this was what cinema at its best should be. A mass medium, a mainstream audience, and everybody standing outside, having queued for days. We got some pretty good seats, about thirty feet from the front, so I got the best sound and this picture was in my face, and frankly I couldn't believe it. I'd done my little film, which I was happy about, but this film was massive. It actually changed my mind about what I would do next. I'd been developing one thing, and then decided, really, how can I go down that route? I must go in another direction and so instead I made *Alien.*"

Star Wars not only changed what kind of films people watched, but how they watched them. The film made such a fortune for cinema owners that it enabled them to build multiplexes. 20th Century Fox, which had been on the brink of bankruptcy, became a major studio, its stock prices tripling in 1977.

And as you drove to the movie theatre, you were probably listening to Fleetwood Mac's *Rumours*.

Released in February, *Rumours* topped the *Billboard* charts for over thirty weeks, and all three major US trade publications – *Billboard*, *Cash Box*, and *Record World* – eventually named it as their album of the year. By March, it had already sold more than ten million copies worldwide, including over eight million in the US alone. If you drove down any main street, in any town, in any city, the songs you would hear pouring out of the stores and the malls were all from *Rumours*: "Go Your Own Way," "Don't Stop," "Dreams," and "You Make Loving Fun." It was almost as if the harmony-driven sound of Fleetwood Mac had taken over the whole country.

During the late Seventies, Fleetwood Mac's only rivals in bottling the musical essence of Los Angeles and southern California were the Eagles, who had spent the best part of the decade working up to it; with Fleetwood Mac it sort of happened by accident. Before Stevie Nicks and Lindsey Buckingham joined, Fleetwood Mac was a middle-ranking British blues band that had recorded a handful of already classic songs – "Black Magic Woman," "Albatross," "Man Of The World," "Oh Well" – all written by the now-departed guitarist Peter Green.

Fleetwood Mac 2.0 were a different proposition altogether, able to fuse the singer-songwriter pretensions of the early Seventies with a slick pop sensibility (and a great drum sound) that sounded just fine on FM radio. Especially in your first car, with the top down, and four or five friends in the back, passing beers and smokes between them. Visually, the group played it safe too, their image synonymous with the leather and lace of singer Stevie Nicks – a look that originally consisted of a chiffon dress, a leotard, a small jacket, a pair of suede platforms and a top hat. All black.

Rumours cost over a million dollars to produce, was

recorded in seven different studios, and took over a year to finish. Yet it turned out to be a bona fide classic, not so much a concept album as a soap opera, chronicling the convoluted romances of the band's five members. The artists' real lives became virtually indistinguishable from the songs they were singing, and in some respects the album was the apotheosis of confessional pop writing. The making of *Rumours* was tortuous as Lindsey Buckingham and Stevie Nicks' relationship broke down during its recording, as did the relationship between John and Christine McVie. Then there were the drugs, which fuelled the band's work ethic. "It was the craziest period of our lives," according to Mick Fleetwood. "We went for four or five weeks without sleep, doing a lot of drugs. I'm talking about cocaine in such quantities that, at one point, I thought I was really going insane."

As one critic put it, *Rumours* articulated the conflicting morass of love, possessiveness, freedom and reflection that the end of a relationship brings. It had some great harmonies too, harmonies that suggested the Californian coast, even if you were actually just driving along the M40 after an evening spent at the Hope and Anchor.

In Britain, bands like Fleetwood Mac were meant to be on the way out in 1977, banished to the margins by the likes of the Sex Pistols and the Clash, but though the zeitgeist might definitely be elsewhere, *Rumours* was as perfect a pop record as anyone could hope to hear.

Bossa nova also had an unexpected renaissance in 1977, in the form of Joao Gilberto's extraordinary *Amoroso* album. The Brazilian "new trend" had been at its most fashionable in the early Sixties, yet Gilberto's LP used lush orchestration to move the genre a little further towards the mass market. And in 1977 it was nothing less than a revelation. In particular his version of the Antonio Carlos Jobim classic "Wave" could be heard on beaches from Miami to Rio, from Puerto Banus to St. Tropez.

Woody Allen also owned 1977, propelled by *Annie Hall* into the mainstream as a writer, actor and, most importantly, a director. The movie turned his nerd alter-ego into a sex symbol, a man who was finally saying goodbye to the Sixties. Diane Keaton's Annie Hall may have kick-started a fashion for big hats, baggy trousers and waistcoats, but Allen's lovable loser became the archetype with whom most people identified. The film won four Academy Awards, was adored by critics, and managed to convince its audience that New York was the most sophisticated city in the world. It was pretty funny, too.

Elsewhere, in Michigan to be precise, Led Zeppelin set a new world record attendance for an indoor solo show at the Pontiac Silverdome when 76,229 people attended a concert there on April 30th. On March 10th, five days before Luciano Pavarotti made his first appearance on American television, the rings of Uranus were discovered. This was the year when music went truly universal: when NASA launched their Voyager unmanned probes, each spacecraft carried a golden record containing sounds and images representing life and culture on Earth, including the first movements of Bach's Brandenburg Concerto and Beethoven's Fifth Symphony and Chuck Berry's "Johnny B. Goode." *American Bandstand* celebrated its 25th anniversary with a special hosted by Dick Clark, including an all-star curate's-egg of a band, made up of the Pointer Sisters, Booker T and the MGs and Gregg Allman among others, performing another Chuck Berry song, "Roll Over Beethoven." Elvis wasn't anywhere to be seen, but then he never was, unless he was performing alone.

1977 was also the year in which Spain held its first democratic elections for over forty years, General Franco having died in 1975; the US Supreme Court ruled that states were not legally required to spend Medicaid funds on elective abortions; and South African anti-apartheid activist Steve Biko died in police custody, aged just thirty.

The United States was still recovering from Watergate, keen to see their new president, Jimmy Carter, wash away the paranoia and indignity of Richard Nixon's reign. Carter offered a new dawn, a new hope. And then just as the country appeared to be forgetting its troubles, and indulging in some good old-fashioned American science fiction, one of its most revered, most treasured folk heroes went and died.

Elvis had left the building.

There were two enormous television events in 1977. In January, the twelve-hour, eight-episode TV adaptation of Alex Haley's novel *Roots* was screened on consecutive nights. Among the most emotive series ever made, it traced the capture and enslavement of Kunta Kinte, a Mandinka born in Gambia in 1750, and the emancipation of his descendants after the Civil War. It was an enormous hit, breaking US audience-rating records and winning nine Emmys and a Golden Globe.

Later, in an extraordinary journalistic coup, David Frost broadcast four ninety-minute interviews with disgraced former President Richard Nixon in May.

In March, KLM flight 4805 crashed into taxiing Pan Am flight 1736 as the KLM jumbo jet attempted to take off from Los Rodeos Airport in Tenerife, killing 583 people. The airport was crowded with diverted planes following the detonation of a terrorist bomb at Las Palmas' main airport for the Canary Islands. Fog had made the runways unmanageable, and not only could the aircraft pilots not see each other, neither could the air traffic controllers. At the time it was the world's worst air disaster, and remains so to this day.

In the fashion world, the TV show *Charlie's Angels* was all enveloping. The principal star was Farrah Fawcett, whose long feather-cut and big flicked hair, as well as her well developed body, made her a pin-up for both men and women. Other big hairstyles of the day included the pageboy and Vidal Sassoon's wedge.

On June 5th, Apple launched its first personal computer, the Apple II.

Britain, meanwhile, had by 1977 appeared to lose not only its pride but even its ability to manage itself, after over half a decade of unwieldy inflation, strikes, flip-flopping governments and even a three-day week. After all but running out of money in 1976, and having to negotiate a loan from the International Monetary Fund, the country was perceived to be the sick man of Europe, a term once reserved for the Ottoman Empire. What it needed was a massive celebration, a year-long street party – and it got one, in the form of the Silver Jubilee.

A couple of months before Elvis's death, the week of festivities celebrating the Silver Jubilee of the Queen's accession to the throne began when she lit a bonfire in Windsor Great Park. That was the first of a hundred beacons that lit up the sky all over the country. There were street parties everywhere, even in places that didn't strictly have streets. On June 7th, more than one million people lined the streets of London to watch the Royal Family make their way to St. Paul's at the start of the official celebrations. The Queen, dressed in pink and accompanied by Prince Philip, led the procession in the golden state coach. At St. Paul's, 2,700 selected guests joined in the ceremony. It started with Vaughan Williams' arrangement of the hymn "All People That On Earth Do Dwell," which had been played at the Queen's coronation in 1953.

For a while, people in the UK discovered a new sense of belonging, and while the economy was still in disarray, and the unions still playing up, the anniversary was a much-needed fillip.

However, in the UK, above all else, 1977 was the year of punk, the anti-Jubilee cult. Punk was an oratorio of aggression, with everything calibrated to annoy. Although opinions differ as to the precise provenance of punk, the *Economist* got things pretty much right in its obituary of Johnny Ramone: "The counterblast began on August 16th 1974, in front of a tiny crowd in a seedy New York bar called CBGB. Four young men – Johnny, Joey, Dee Dee and Tommy Ramone – walked on stage. The concert they gave was shambolic; they spent as much time shouting at each other as playing. But they improved rapidly, and it soon became clear they had hit on something."

Punk, basically.

Predecessors had included the Velvet Underground (1966), the Stooges (1968), the MC5 (1969), Jonathan Richman, and Richard Hell (whose "Blank Generation" was written in 1974), while Patti Smith soon followed with *Horses* (1975), but it was the Ramones who first made punk flesh, who ushered in a sense of the Zeitgeist. The Ramones' first album was released in 1976, and a fusillade of British records swiftly arrived in its wake, namely the Damned's "New Rose" in November 1976, the Sex Pistols' "Anarchy In The UK" the same month, and the Buzzcocks' "Spiral Scratch" in January 1977.

While it was rooted in garage rock – these new bands were happy to use the familiar tools of rock – punk's determination to eschew the musical and lifestyle excesses of the previous generation resulted in a "Year Zero" mentality. Punk bands made accelerated, hard-edged music, with aggressive lyrics and stripped-down three-chord instrumentation. There was a

DIY ethic, with most bands turning their backs on the multi-layered, overdubbed pop symphonies favoured by the likes of Fleetwood Mac. Punk served as an apocalyptic catalyst to so many Seventies teenagers; it shook them around, threw them up in the air, and – when they bounced back down again – forced them to confront their preconceptions about life, the universe and everything in it. Well, at least the records they bought and the clothes they wore.

Though the music may have originated in the US, it was the UK where the youth cult started. By early 1977 the centre of each and every British city, town and village was full of young people dressed as the Sex Pistols' Johnny Rotten (real name John Lydon) or Johnny Ramone – complete with a floppy pudding-bowl haircut, drainpipe jeans, plimsoles, a matelot top and a (plastic) leather jacket. Overnight thousands of young men turned from being neurotic boy outsiders in oversized overcoats and hooded brows (clutching their Genesis, Bob Dylan and Joni Mitchell albums under their arms), into the personification of Soho yobs or Bowery punks. The Johnny Ramone option was certainly less confrontational, and actually quite appealing: how could you not fall in love with a group who displayed such a blatant disregard for sophistication as the Ramones? Whose bare-boned playing was matched only by their idiotic singing – the lyrics to their song "I Don't Wanna Walk Around With You" were four lines long, three of which were the same. When Joe Strummer, the frontman of the Clash, as *The Economist*'s obituary of Johnny Ramone relates: "approached the Ramones after seeing them play in London in 1976, he was worried that his band's musicianship was still too rough for them to start recording. 'Are you kidding?' said Johnny. 'We're lousy, we can't play. If you wait until you can play, you'll be too old to get up there. We stink, really. But it's great.'"

In the UK, London was the epicentre of punk, as the city became a metaphor for the whole movement: urban decay, anarchic fashion (safety pins and monochromatic severity), backstreet violence, fast drugs, silly hair. The town became vaguely mythical, a magnet for future punk royalty: the Jam's Paul Weller was so obsessed he would travel up from Woking to the West End just to record the traffic (one of the band's earliest songs was called "Sounds From The Street," and their first two albums are so poorly produced they don't sound much better than Oxford Circus at rush hour). The Jam's urban fixation showed in "Down In The Tube Station At Midnight," "In The City" and "A Bomb In Wardour Street," each of them a little snapshot of tough city life. Pop has always needed the city's shroud to make it cool – how could you be a market-town punk or an East Anglian mod? – and the urban backdrop of London in 1977 was the most perfect shroud of them all. One of punk's defining rationales was reinvention; nobody who'd made it in London wanted to admit they had actually been brought up in Henley or Swindon. And Woking? Puh-lease …

The Clash also made a point of writing about London. In fact they seldom wrote about anything else, although they tended to concentrate on Notting Hill and points west. Pop archaeologist Jon Savage once called their debut album, *The Clash*, "virtually a concept album about North Kensington and Ladbroke Grove," which contained "White Riot," "London's Burning" and "48 Hours." While they went on to cast their concerned eyes over the Middle East, South America and any imploding quasi-Stalinist state they could find, for a while London was their world, inspiring their two finest songs: "White Man (In Hammersmith Palais)" and, of course, "London Calling" (of which Joe Strummer said, "I want it to sound like it's coming through fog over the Thames").

As I have said before in my *Biographical Dictionary of Popular Music* the early days of punk were analogous to present-day activity on the web – scattershot releases, limited edition rather than viral, but still with an urgent guerrilla sensibility. Records were released without great fanfare, and often you only knew where to buy them… if you knew where to buy them. You needed to read the right papers, know the right people, and shop at the right stores.

Singles were the only recognized currency. Oddly, albums, LPs, were for a while considered to be distinctly "old wave," an indulgence too far. It was decreed by the cognoscenti that everything had to be short, Spartan, and almost devoid of adjectival subjectivity. Pop culture appeared to be moving so quickly that each new release came complete with its own promise of Zeitgeist-defining authority.

The British punk scene was the result of many things – the influence of the early American groups, a generational rebellion against aging pop-cultural forces, and the natural cycle of fashion. There were also various calls-to-arms in the media, one of which appeared in the *NME*. At the end of January 1976, the music paper felt compelled to run a cover that asked the question, "Is rock'n'roll an old man's game?" The accompanying feature, by Max Bell, included the likes of Paul McCartney, Rod Stewart and Keith Richards and lots of other "aged" members of the rock aristocracy whose lifestyles involved limousines, private jets and unimaginably expensive recording studios (where, the paper said gleefully, they would make lavish-sounding *double* albums).

"It's about time 1976 launched a few more of its own teenage heroes," wrote Bell, "instead of leaning on the main men of an earlier generation."

Punk was a world away from Elvis. Hell, Elvis didn't even get the Beatles, so how on earth was he going to understand the Sex Pistols, the Clash or Elvis Costello? Punk was all about connecting, all about the guy on top of the speaker stack or in the middle of the crowd who runs up on stage. Elvis may have said that going back to live performances in Las Vegas was all about connecting with his fans, but after a while he was simply going through the motions. Everything he had done since becoming famous involved some form of repetition. As soon as he left Sun, each of his RCA records started to sound similar to the next; his movies became interchangeable after a while; and his Vegas concerts were all versions of the same performance. Elvis wasn't inquisitive in the usual way for a performer, or at least one with his monumental powers. He was the co-custodian of his own downfall, much of which was caused by his inability to stretch out, whether by working with better record producers, better writers, better movie directors or better orchestral arrangers. Of course, everything might have been different had he worked with a more considerate manager than the notorious "Colonel" Tom Parker – the other custodian of Elvis's career – but then if that had happened we would all be living in a parallel universe.

So much has been written about punk that it has become almost impossible to imagine what it was really like at the beginning. It has been decoded and mediated in such a way that it doesn't really mean anything any more. "Punk" as an idea was gelded long ago; it has been emasculated in the same way that Motown once was – devalued through heavy rotation on commercial radio, kick-started by its repositioning in the Eighties as acceptable music for television advertisements.

Yet punk remains the most vibrant, most divisive cult of them all. Back in 1975 it was possible to tell that things might be going to change, that something might be about to happen, even though no one knew exactly what it was going to be when it eventually arrived. The first group who indicated the approaching storm to me was Dr. Feelgood, who I saw that summer at the Nag's Head in High Wycombe. Although it took a while for this to alter how I consumed music, when it came, it came like a tsunami: the Clash, the Jam, Adam and the Ants, the Damned, Slaughter and the Dogs, the Slits, the Buzzcocks, Wire, Elvis Costello, Deathwish and so on – dozens and dozens of bands seen in sweaty basements in a two-year period that pretty much changed how my generation viewed the world.

Everything was about connection, about intimacy. We were encouraged to hate Pink Floyd and the Rolling Stones because they played huge pop warehouses like Wembley Arena and Earls Court. The new doctrine required us to see bands in clubs above pubs that were the size of wardrobes. Back then, small was good, and big was most definitely bad. Who wanted to see a band in an aircraft hangar? Who wanted to see a band from the last row in the stalls, when they looked so small they could have been anyone? No. Back in the day, small was cool.

One of my favourite memories from that period is of a concert at Friars in Aylesbury in the spring of 1977. We had come to see the headliners, the Ramones, and had never heard the support act, Talking Heads. We'd read about them in the *New Musical Express* – everyone read the *NME* at the time – but didn't know what they would be like. At all. Obviously they were extraordinary, dressed as preppies, playing like lab technicians, and introducing every song thus: "The name of this song is …"

The Ramones, who came on after them, attempted even less communication with the audience, simply diving into each song as though it were a fait accompli, with a simple "One-two-three-four!" Watching the Ramones on stage was to witness a barrage of sound, and songs played so fast and with such little fanfare that you couldn't put a cigarette paper between the end of one tune and the start of the next. It remains the most extraordinary concert I've ever seen, and one that was summed up when Graham Lewis of the punk band Wire described seeing the Ramones perform at Dingwalls, then one of the coolest venues in London: "I couldn't believe it. It was glorious. They came on stage and it was semi-lit, and they just stood there for what seemed like an age. Joey Ramone said, 'Woman, shut your mouth.' And it all started, and it didn't fucking stop, this delirium of noise, you walked in and out of it, a physical environment of noise."

That was what punk was like for me, as it was for many: a physical environment of noise.

To Elvis, it would have been just noise, and noise only. Of course, he appeared to understand the finer elements of certain types of American music, and he certainly liked, and knew a lot about, rhythm and blues, country and gospel. Insurrection, anti-establishment behaviour, and anything to do with the counter culture were all beyond him, though, as they were anathema to his understanding of the world. Punk's *raison d'être* was nihilism, plain and simple, regardless of how some of those involved like to dress it up with politics or bondage trousers. Being *for* something would have been against its principles; at this point in the arc of post-war popular culture, being against something – anything, frankly – was far more fun.

Punk harked back to the time when the idea of the teenager was just beginning, at least in its modern sense. The distillation of punk could be traced back to a line in *The Wild One*, the Marlon Brando outlaw biker movie from 1953, a time even before Elvis. When a girl asks the Brando character – Johnny Strabler, the leader of the Black Rebels Motorcycle Club, who is dressed in blue jeans, leather jacket and cap – "What are you rebelling against, Johnny?," he answers, "Whaddaya got?"

Johnny Strabler was the first popular rebel of the decade, and, like a lot of boys, Elvis was smitten with him. He loved Brando – loved the way he spoke, the way he looked, and the way he dressed. The actress Jan Shepard played Elvis's sister in 1958's *King Creole*, and was responsible for Elvis meeting his hero that year in the Paramount commissary. She and Elvis were taking lunch together one day when Brando came in and made a beeline for a table just behind Elvis, who didn't notice him. She continued the story: "I said, 'Elvis, Marlon Brando is sitting right behind you,' and he almost put his face in his sandwich, he was so shy. He wanted to hide. I said, 'Keep it cool, but when you get up, your chair is going to hit his chair, and he's going to get up because I know he wants to meet you as much as you want to meet him.' And that's exactly what happened. Elvis played it cool, very cool, but when we got out of the cafeteria, he jumped about four feet in the air, and said: 'My God, I met Marlon Brando!'"

Brando didn't turn out to be the biggest Elvis fan. Never worried about speaking ill of the dead, Brando commented long after Elvis's death that "It seems to me hilarious that our government put the face of Elvis Presley on a postage stamp after he died from an overdose of drugs. His fans don't mention that because they don't want to give up their myths. They ignore the fact that he was a drug addict and claim he invented rock'n'roll when in fact he took it from black culture; they had been singing that way for years before he came along, copied them and became a star."

By 1977, even if Elvis was still a fan of Brando, the original punk, he wanted absolutely nothing to do with his progeny. Cocooned and separated from his audience, Elvis had slunk back into a world that felt safe and warm. He had no interest in embracing anyone with a curled lip and a floppy quiff, or indulging anyone with a pink drape jacket and quilted gold winklepickers. Elvis had broken the mould himself, and the last thing he needed was a bunch of copycats to come round the mountain after his hide.

What Elvis had done felt special and particular. All the girls out front were his. He didn't need anybody queering his patch, didn't need anyone shaking their pelvis and thrusting their groin into the faces of all those pretty young girls. That was his job, Elvis's job, and it should be done by Elvis and no one else.

Far from being a talismanic rebel, an iconoclast who wouldn't suffer fools gladly, by 1977 Elvis had become a good ol' boy, a man who liked to be surrounded by men, and who knew the importance of the Confederate flag. Elvis didn't like competition.

Back in the Fifties he had taken a dislike to the wannabes thrust in his face by rival record companies – after all, why on earth would Elvis warm to the likes of Fabian, Frankie Avalon or Guy Mitchell? Who was Pat Boone? And Tab Hunter? Seriously, which one was he? Was he the one with the puppy dog smile and the party shirt?

In the Sixties Elvis had been circumspect about the Beatles and the Rolling Stones and all the British beat groups who had arrived in America to try to steal his crown.

And in some respects the Seventies seemed to have passed him by completely.

In 1977, Elvis knew exactly what Elvis was doing, but he had no idea what was happening in the rest of the world.

CHAPTER TWO

The Day Elvis Died

"Why, I'll go right on managing him" – "Colonel" Tom Parker

Elvis Presley died aged forty-two on August 16th, 1977, in the bathroom of the star's own Graceland mansion in Memphis. Sitting on the toilet, he had toppled like a toy soldier and collapsed onto the floor, where he lay in a pool of his own vomit. His light blue pyjamas were around his ankles. Elvis was rushed to nearby Baptist Memorial Hospital, where he was pronounced dead at 3.30pm CST. The announcement was made to the public at 4pm, and his autopsy was performed at 7pm.

Until Elvis's death, August 16th had been an inconsequential date in the rock'n'roll calendar, notable only as the birthday of Soft Machine member Kevin Ayers, singer Eydie "Too Close For Comfort" Gorme, and, in 1958, Madonna Ciccone. Strangely, Elvis shared his death date with blues legend Robert Johnson, who died in mysterious circumstances in 1938, having "sold his soul to the devil."

On August 15th, Elvis had entertained friends, playing the piano and getting himself ready to fly in his four-engined private jet to Portland, Maine, where he was scheduled to perform the first concert of a twelve-city tour at the Cumberland County Civic Center on August 17th.

At around 8pm, wearing a Drug Enforcement Agency sweatshirt under a ruffled white shirt and his trademark metal-framed sunglasses, and with two guns in his waistband, he visited his dentist. The temporary crown he had fitted was later knocked out of his mouth when the ambulance crew tried to put a breathing tube down his throat. Elvis specifically asked for, and was given, codeine. He had suffered allergic reactions to the drug in the past, and some have suggested that it caused an anaphylactic shock that contributed to his death.

The last picture of Elvis alive, taken on his return from his dentist at 12.28am on the morning of August 16th, shows him waving to fans from the driver's seat of his Stutz Blackhawk. The photo distinctly resembles Richard Hamilton's 1968 screenprint, *Swingeing London 67*, depicting Mick Jagger handcuffed to the art dealer Robert Fraser in the back of a police van as they were being taken from Lewes prison to Chichester Magistrates Court following their June 1967 arrest for possession of amphetamines. Author and critic Andrew Wilson interpreted Hamilton's picture as a historical polemic: "the subjects are holding their hands over their faces, highlighting the struggle against the British state's attempt – aided by the popular press – to repress any expression of personal liberation." Although Elvis rarely shielded his face from his fans or the media, and in this picture he's actually holding his open hand up, almost as a greeting, there's a similar sense of isolation and distance. Given it was also the last photograph taken while he still had some control over his body, it is also filled with pathos.

The last meal Elvis ate was a plate of peach ice cream and Chips Ahoy chocolate chip cookies, eaten in bed at around 3am. After a few games of racquetball around 4am, and a brief stint on the piano he kept by the court, he finally went to bed around 8am, having his drugs administered as usual.

Elvis's outsized and luxurious en-suite bathroom was located on the first floor of Graceland, just next to his bedroom.

By knocking through two large rooms, he had transformed it into a combination bathroom-office-study-lounge. The top half of one entire wall was covered with a huge mirror surrounded by the kind of megawatt bare lightbulbs you find in theatre dressing rooms. Under the mirror a large Formica dressing table held a purple sink on which were strewn all of Elvis's "attacks."

Around 2pm on the afternoon of August 16th, Elvis was discovered in his bathroom by his twenty-year-old fiancée Ginger Alden. He was slumped in front of the toilet bowl, all nineteen stone of him, with his face buried in the carpet and a copy of *The Shroud Of Turin* by Ian Wilson lying in front of him. Around his neck was a cross, the Hebrew letter chai, and a Jewish Star of David – he used to say that he didn't want to miss out on Heaven due to a technicality. His body had turned purple, and his muscles had already stiffened. His eyes were rolled back, and his tongue was sticking out, half bitten off and already black. Elvis was surrounded by syringes. He had been dead for at least two hours.

Summoned to the scene, Elvis's assistant Joe Esposito pulled the body over, whereupon Elvis released a small breath of air. Esposito made a desperate attempt to revive him by giving him mouth-to-mouth resuscitation, and pounding on his chest in the hope of restarting his heart. But he knew it was futile. Ginger slapped his face a few times, trying to rouse him. But to no avail.

So they called for an ambulance.

Until that moment, Graceland was alive with its traditional daytime activities. Its cooks were cooking, its maids were cleaning, and the support staff were fixing lightbulbs and washing cars. Elvis's nine-year-old daughter Lisa Marie, who was visiting from the West Coast, where she lived with her mother Priscilla, was sleeping soundly right next door to the bathroom, oblivious to all the commotion.

Phones were being answered, mail was being sorted, and clothes were being washed and pressed. The usual fans were crowded outside the gates, but none knew that upstairs, on the first floor, their hero was dead.

And then, suddenly, the house was thrown into turmoil. As ever with domestic emergencies, everything and nothing happened at once. Some staff were called upstairs to help; others were shooed away downstairs, and Graceland took on the air of a grand townhouse in Edwardian London, complete with the Tennessee variants of authoritarian butlers and pragmatic parlourmaids ordering around the dutiful, the slow-witted, the mischievous and the devious. Cleaners were given dirty sheets, maids were told to prepare the bedrooms, and bodyguards scurried around the house like footmen. The house was noisy and quiet all at once, with those trying to revive Elvis, those sent to calm Lisa Marie, those removing drugs from the scene, and those on the phone to the emergency services. People were busy and they were stationary, some knowing what to do, and others simply standing stone still, scared of doing something wrong, scared of making a mistake. Some had only ever moved at Elvis's behest; now that he was lying dead on the floor, from whom were they going to take orders now? How were they going to take care of business now that the King was dead? Not only that, but soon everyone would know it, know they didn't have a job anymore! At one point there were a dozen people in the bathroom, screaming and crying for someone to help Elvis: there had to be something that could help him? *Jesus. What would happen now? Was this really the end? If Elvis died, where were we all going to live? Who was going to pay us? Would*

Vernon keep us on, would the Colonel fire us all? Oh my good God, what would we all do now? Things surely couldn't carry on as they were, could they?

So many questions, and Elvis wasn't even at the hospital yet …

Here, amid the bright red velour, the golden tassels, simulated waterfalls and shiny polyurethane finishes so meticulously catalogued by his many biographers, Elvis was gone. No longer would he sit up in bed staring into space, his gaze bouncing off the black suede walls onto the crimson drapes. No longer would he glance at the huge mounted portrait of his mother Gladys that nestled on a wooden easel by his bed. No longer would he wander his halls dressed only in his Hefnerland robe and slippers, an unlit cigar poking from his fingers.

The gilded hillbilly was gone.

Here lay the man-boy who had sounded the clarion call of white rock'n'roll. The young Elvis was a rogue energy, the manifestation of a mutant beat, a frenzied expression of teenage lust … and yet here he was, twenty years later, bloated and over. Every dream he ever dreamed had come true a hundred times, and this is where he had ended up. No longer trapped in an endless exhibition of his power and influence, no longer standing on stage building his deliberately melodramatic accretions, no longer the overlord of Memphis, the Burger King was well and truly dead. Having gone from being a truck driver without prospects to pretty much the most famous man in America, Elvis had slipped off the mortal coil in the most undignified fashion. In twenty years Elvis had gone from being the avatar of US cool to the embodiment of American excess, his life a metaphor for the post-war consumer American dream.

What were his staff going to do now? Stand around and sing "What A Friend We Have In Elvis"?

Things immediately started to disappear from the house. Whatever wasn't nailed down was game. Ornaments were stuffed into bags, watches stolen from Elvis's dressing table and wardrobe. Gold discs were snaffled away, as were clocks, ties, sunglasses, guns, hats, silverware, ashtrays, jumpsuits, pens, sheet music, cash, jewellery and statues of the Venus de Milo (Elvis had started collecting them, and owned hundreds). Scraps of paper on which Elvis had scribbled were hastily shoved into pockets, even soiled tissues from the small wicker wastebaskets in the bedrooms. The death scene was soon secured by the police, but by then it was futile – so much evidence had vanished, and a lot of it was already sold.

When the emergency services were first notified that someone at 3764 Elvis Presley Boulevard was experiencing difficulty breathing, no one was especially concerned. There had been frequent similar alarms in the past, most prompted by fans fainting in the crowd outside the gates. The two medical technicians who drove to the scene, Charlie Crosby and Ulysses Jones Jr., had no idea that this time the patient was Elvis himself. They were ushered directly up to Elvis's bedroom, however, where they found the King unconscious on his bed, surrounded by Graceland employees and his personal doctor, George Nichopoulos. During the ensuing seven-minute ambulance ride to Baptist Hotel, they struggled in vain to revive him.

Alerted by the emergency call, the press had already reached the hospital by the time Elvis arrived. Even as he was being rushed into the trauma room, journalists were crowding the reception area. Elvis had been fast-tracked in before, but this time the press could tell that there was rather more urgency.

Rumours were swirling as to why he had been admitted.

Elvis had been hospitalised in Memphis at least five times in the previous four years. Despite suggestions that the illnesses were drug related, his physician, and the two hospitals concerned had variously attributed his condition to fatigue, colon obstruction, eye problems, intestinal flu, hypertension and high blood pressure. During his most recent stays at the hospital, he had been ensconced in an 18th-floor suite in which the windows were covered by aluminium foil.

Elvis's personal doctor George Nichopoulos, who had spent a decade helping to prescribe the cocktail of drugs – from uppers to downers, and narcotics to laxatives – that kept him going, struggled one last time to revive him. "Come on Presley, breathe for me," he pleaded, but the spirit never returned to the body. At 3.30pm, he finally pronounced Elvis dead.

Then he walked back into the anteroom where Vernon and some of the Graceland staff were waiting, and announced simply, "Elvis just left ..." Half an hour later, on the steps of Graceland, Vernon Presley in turn told the world, "My son, Elvis, is dead."

The Presley family consented to an immediate autopsy, which was performed that same evening at Baptist Memorial Hospital. According to medical examiner Dr. Jerry Francisco, who signed Presley's death certificate, the autopsy diagnosed cardiac arrhythmia, or irregular heartbeat. He added that "There was no indication of any drug abuse of any kind." His pathologist colleague Dr. Eric Muirhead, on the other hand, reported that Elvis's body contained more than a dozen different drugs, including codeine, antihistamines, Quaaludes, painkillers and tranquillisers.

Elvis's heart was found to be fifty percent larger than normal, a classic symptom of heart failure that explained the dizziness, shortness of breath and high blood pressure that had plagued him during his final years. He was just forty-two. Bloated with painkillers, sleeping pills, sedatives, junk food, his end was as ignominious as his rise was glorious.

Elvis's stepbrother David Stanley has repeatedly stated that on the evening he died, Elvis deliberately took all three of the nightly drug cocktails that he called "attacks" at once, and had thus committed suicide. All the other witnesses who were present dispute the claim, but Stanley insists that he found all three "attack" envelopes, and several Demerol syringes nearly empty: "I looked and saw Elvis in the fetal position and knew he was gone. The first thing I said was, 'You son of a bitch!' I knew right there and then at that time that Elvis said, 'I am out of here.' I'm telling you what I know. And the fact is, that much medication will kill you. And Elvis knew that. Elvis Presley woke up on the 16th of August, premeditated, planned, took, and killed himself deliberately."

Suicide was also the major thesis of Albert Goldman's second Elvis book, *Elvis: The Last 24 Hours*, published in 1990. However, the idea didn't create as much traction as Goldman hoped – probably because his original book had been so unremittingly nasty.

Then the business of organising the funeral got underway. As both an official funeral director at the Memphis Funeral Home and Elvis's unofficial limo driver, Robert Kendall was a strange kind of hyphenate. When he arrived for work at the funeral parlour on August 16th, he was expecting just another routine day. At around 4pm, however, when his colleague C.D. Smith raced into the reception area to announce that he'd just had a call from his police-officer son, saying that Elvis was dead, Kendall's life changed forever. There were no details, no background, just that one blinding fact. Elvis Presley was dead.

Three hours later, Kendall received a call from Joe Esposito, asking if he would handle the funeral arrangements, followed by another from the hospital, saying the autopsy had been completed and the body was ready for collection. When the white Cadillac funeral coach reached the hospital at eleven minutes past eight, there were people everywhere. One teenage girl, with tears streaming down her face, clutched a rosary in her hand, while others carried home-made signs bearing Elvis's name, or wore T-shirts emblazoned with hastily copied photographs of the dead star. A middle-aged woman carried a portable record player, which pumped out one of Elvis's old ballads. By the time Kendall and his two assistants returned to the funeral home, the crowds around Union Avenue had swelled even more, boosted by hundreds of television and radio crews with their microphones, cameras and lights.

As they started to prepare the body for the viewing the next day, one of Kendall's assistants lifted the edge of the sheet covering Elvis to look at his face. "Now I believe Elvis really is dead," he said. The low strains of Elvis singing "Heartbreak Hotel" could be heard from a radio in the adjoining room. "The King is dead," said Kendall's other assistant. "Long live the King."

Elvis was then laid in a hastily ordered 900-pound steel-lined copper coffin. His face was bloated and his sideburns reached his chin, while even in death the left side of his upper lip was slightly curled upwards. Not only did he not look like Elvis, he didn't really look like anyone. He had created another archetype, one that would be copied by truck drivers, good old boys and ageing Teddy Boys in perpetuity.

Meanwhile, following the official announcement, all hell had broken loose at Graceland. Dozens of people were running around with nothing to do. Vernon was shaking, and couldn't sit still. He didn't know what to do with himself. Lisa Marie was running all over the house crying, screaming, "My daddy is gone" at the top of her voice. Ginger was walking around in a daze. There wasn't just short-term grief to deal with, there were long-term plans too.

In Los Angeles, Priscilla Presley had been due to meet a friend for lunch at a restaurant on Melrose Avenue. "I left the house knowing something was wrong. The air was wrong. The sky was wrong. I had a meeting earlier that morning during which I felt like the world was wrong. Something was putting me on edge. Something grave." When she reached the restaurant, and her friend told her that Elvis had been rushed to the hospital, Priscilla jumped in her car and raced home. "I ran every red light and nearly ran off the road before reaching my house. Inside I heard the phone ringing. I fumbled with my keys, I screamed inside, I finally got the door opened and raced to the phone. My worst fears were confirmed."

She had them send the plane.

The scene outside Graceland resembled Hitchcock's movie *The Birds*. First there was one fan, then another arrived, and then another. Suddenly they were everywhere, crowding the sidewalks, the lawns and the traffic intersections, looking forlorn, bewildered, yet morbidly excited. This was a little bit of local history that was already national, international, global news. Many just happened to be in the area; some had turned up in the same way that people flock to a crime scene, or slow down to study a motorway pile-up. Many more were true believers.

They came in their hundreds, then thousands, driving in

from the suburbs, from Nashville, Tupelo or Greenville, from cities in the north, from all over, climbing into their cars and weaving through the Marlboro signs, gas stations and fast food restaurants. Some rolled in from the cotton country of Arkansas, having sped by the pines and unpainted cypress shacks separated from the road by mud flats. Others arrived from Macon, Mobile, Shreveport, Texarkana and Fort Smith, just to be there, just to say they were there, just to show they cared. There were bikers, too, some of the meanest looking bikers you could ever see, speeding down to Memphis with tears in their eyes. They'd say it was the wind that made them cry.

Three hundred National Guardsmen were called in to maintain order, and there were cameras and lights everywhere. There was an overwhelming sense of disbelief, as though everyone would eventually wake up to find that things had returned to normal, with Elvis still very much alive. The area in front of Graceland had the hopeful, overlit look of a sport stadium. But there was nothing hopeful there at all.

As they flocked towards Memphis, Elvis's fans listened to the radio – to hear his songs, to hear more news about the autopsy, the funeral arrangements, and press statements from the Presley family. Anything, in fact, that was Elvis-related. Of course what they really wanted to hear was that the whole thing had been an exaggeration, and that he was lying in his hospital bed in the intensive care unit slowly recuperating. But then a DJ would come on and announce another classic Elvis ballad, and introduce it with the words: "One of the great ones, by the late Elvis Presley."

The late Elvis Presley.

A witness who was working in Seessel's Grocery Store across the street from Graceland remembers people stopping their cars in the middle of the road, kneeling on the tarmac in front of the mansion and praying that the news was not true. People fell out of the aisles of the grocery store in tears. The supermarket was full of Elvis postcards, which others grabbed as though they had some kind of talismanic quality. Some postcards were framed, but they'd just smash the glass and snatch the pictures. Traffic outside Graceland was backed up for five miles in both directions. You had to drive nearly thirty or forty miles to get home, for a journey that would normally take five minutes. But nobody could say anything, nobody could ask anyone to move, because everyone was in shock. It was blasphemous to say you didn't love Elvis, so you just shut up and put up.

The mayor of Memphis announced that flags on all city buildings would be flown at half-mast until the funeral, two days later. Overnight, the city became a raggedy gypsy camp, as its hotels, motels, boarding houses and B&Bs filled with Elvis fanatics from all over the country.

That night there was a candlelight vigil outside Graceland. Along with flowers, items left at the gates included poems, photographs of Elvis torn from magazines, album covers, dolls, toys, handwritten messages, dozens and dozens of teddy bears, and a fair number of women's panties.

Souvenir hunters were snatching rocks and twigs from just inside the mansion grounds.

Also that night, church services were held in villages, towns and cities all over the US, and especially in the southern states. There was wailing and grieving and such outpourings of emotion it felt as though the whole country was in mourning. Here was America's only son, a teenage iconoclast who had been tamed by society, by the church and by the Army, and had gone on to build himself his own American dream. And now he was gone, and the country couldn't quite believe it.

Couldn't quite believe that his dream had been taken away from him, and them.

On the next day, August 17th, Elvis's body lay in state at Graceland. The public viewing was originally scheduled to last from 2pm until 4pm, but with a huge crowd lined up outside, the mansion gates eventually remained open for an extra ninety minutes. A white linen carpet had been laid under the casket, to protect the Graceland rug from the thousands of scuffling feet.

Elvis was dressed in a cream coloured suit, a blue shirt and a striped silver tie. According to his father Vernon, "I bought that suit for Elvis at Nudie's not long ago when we were in California. It didn't get here until about two weeks ago. You know, he never got to actually wear it."

Elvis had always had a mother fixation, and he would often say that he wanted to die on the same day as she did, August 14th. He missed by just forty-eight hours. He may also have died at the same age, although her claim to have been forty-two at the time of her death in 1958 is disputed by those who insist that she was actually four years older.

Concerned that the make-up on Elvis's hands and face might start to melt and streak, Kendall was worried about how long the body would be on display at Graceland. Elvis had also been given a thin coat of tint on his lips, and his fingernails had been manicured. "Everybody said it didn't look like Elvis in the casket," said Marty Lacker, one of the Memphis Mafia. "But he'd laid on his face so long that the undertaker had to put all kinds of stuff on him to make him look flesh-coloured again. That's how all these rumours got started that it wasn't Elvis in the casket but a wax dummy. Joan Rivers said they didn't bury Elvis at all – they buried a fifty-two pound candle."

"People said he looked so fat in the casket," said fellow Mafia member Billy Smith. "We'll argue about that forever. Elvis was swollen and sick, and he was overweight, but not to the point they were talking about. But I was worried how he was going to fit in that suit. And Dr. Nick said, 'It won't be a problem. Because there won't be all that there. We can put him in anything.'"

August is an insanely hot month in Tennessee, with temperatures way up in the nineties. It is usually incredibly humid, too, and that day was nothing if not humid. People were fainting all over the place. In deference to the heat, the public were told they could wear what they liked.

As for Colonel Parker, he was sporting a Hawaiian shirt, a baseball cap and baggy brown trousers and scuffed loafers. When film producer and concert promoter Jerry Weintraub dropped in at Graceland, he found Parker engaged in a heated discussion with Vernon Presley as to whether they should sell commemorative T-shirts to the fans outside.

In the end, out of more than 75,000 people present, around thirty thousand were able to pay their respects, including Caroline Kennedy and James Brown.

Unlike Chuck Berry, Brown thought Elvis deserved all the plaudits coming his way: "Some people say Elvis stole black music," he said. "Those people are fools, Elvis gave black people a voice. I wasn't just a fan, I was his brother. He said I was good and I said he was good; we never argued about that. Elvis was a hard worker, dedicated, and God loved him. Last time I saw him was at Graceland. We sang 'Old Blind Barnabus' together, a gospel song. I love him and hope to see him in heaven. There'll never be another like that soul brother."

Once the public viewing was over, Elvis's family and

friends had their own private time with the deceased King. Priscilla and Lisa Marie placed a silver bracelet depicting a mother and child's clasped hands on his wrist. Vernon was the last to kiss the coffin. He placed his hand on it, and had to be helped away.

Memphis was sad and heavy, as though a huge tarpaulin had been draped across the sky. People went about their business, but no one could ignore the fact that the city's most famous resident, the most famous man in America, was dead. The driveway in front of Graceland was banked with wreaths, hundreds on each side. One floral tribute was a huge pair of blue suede shoes, Brobdingnagian in their scale and ambition. Another was an enormous wreath in the shape of a hound dog.

The crowd outside Graceland could have come from the mind of Cecil B. DeMille. In some respects it looked like a nightmare, as no one was smiling. The faces were twisted, grieving. People were lining the streets, sitting on the kerbs, lying in the grass, tuning in to their transistor radios and using umbrellas to shield themselves from the ninety-degree heat. Some were trying to climb the Alabama fieldstone wall that surrounded the property. Some had brought candles. Many more had brought cameras. Some had thought to bring food, but most relied on the fast-food trucks that were now circling the perimeter, selling glazed doughnuts and piping hot dogs, Cokes and Seven Ups. Someone was selling cotton candy, but it felt inappropriate, and trade was slow.

The "coffin riders," as hawkers of Presley tat were called, made their first appearance that day, setting up stalls along the sidewalk. Along with commemorative shirts, mugs and baseball caps, you could find Elvis charm bracelets, statuettes, pencils, songbooks, photo albums, lipstick ("Hound Dog

Orange" or "Tutti Fruitti Red"), even rapidly produced costumes of multi-rhinestoned complexity fashioned from the cheapest satin money could buy. Someone even tried to hawk a copy of his "last will and testament." Another sold empty vials of pills, purportedly found next to his dead body.

The flat, bright blue sky was slowly turning peach as the sun disappeared into the west. On the lawns within the wall, a paramedic station was offering aid to hundreds of distressed fans; some had been overcome by the hundred-degree heat, others simply needed their grief to be acknowledged. Many had been waiting without food or drink since the previous evening, and were crawling along the sidewalk like sullen lizards.

People had been writing on the wall since Elvis had had it erected when he moved into Graceland, in 1957. But as soon as he died the graffiti became more strident, more impassioned. In the days following his death the wall was regularly hosed down, as many of the messages were quite ribald; most were in tribute, but others simply offered sex, even in death. One piece of graffiti just said: "My heart stopped on 8-16-77".

One fan, who was turned away when he tried to enter the grounds, observed "The wall around Graceland is low enough. I could jump over." Then he looked into the crowd, shook his head and seemed almost embarrassed that he had considered it. "I could never do that to Elvis, he means the world to me." Then he walked home with his girlfriend.

Another fan told the BBC "I'll tell you what, something that I feel real deep about, whether you're black or white, whether you're country, redneck or freak, young or old, from Moscow to London or Memphis, Elvis Presley will still be the King of rock'n'roll to me."

There were many children among the crowd. Nine-year-old Mary Mauck picked a handful of grass, and kept staring at it, as though it had some magical qualities. She and her family were in Memphis on vacation, visiting from Virginia. Mary had obviously never met Elvis, nor seen him in concert, but she had heard his songs and, being a child, the news of his death made her cry. "This is Elvis Presley's grass," she said, clutching it up in her tiny hand. "And he'll never be dead in my heart."

One Illinois woman was charged with child neglect when she returned home, having left her two, four and five-year-old children with a twelve-year-old babysitter so she could join the mourners at Graceland.

Some of the faithful stayed up all that night. They had driven, in cars, camper vans and motorcycles, to be there, for reasons few could articulate. Many would have been teenagers in the Fifties, but many too had been young in the Sixties, and were the children of those who had made Elvis the Sinatra of their time. "I'll always love him," said Nancy Childers, a mother of six, who had driven all night from Atlanta. "I'll just never get over it."

Dorothy Smith, who lived near Memphis, said, "I wonder now what people will do now that he's gone. What will they have their hopes, their dreams on. I know my dreams have just gone. It's like someone just snatched the world from under me."

At 3.30am on August 18th, in a dreadful prelude to Elvis's funeral, a drunken driver careered into the crowd outside Graceland, and killed two teenagers.

On the morning of the funeral, it took one hundred vans about five hours to remove the flowers from Graceland, to Forest Hill Cemetery, where Elvis was to be interred.

Mourners included Farrah Fawcett Majors, John Wayne,

Ann-Margret, Cher, Burt Reynolds, Sammy Davis Jr., Ringo Starr, Chet Atkins and George Hamilton. Despite the summer heat, Elvis's nurse, Marian Cocke, was wearing a full-length mink coat that Elvis had given her a few years previously, when he had been admitted to Baptist Memorial Hospital, where she was working at the time, with stomach problems. Cocke was appalled by George Hamilton's appearance. "Who in the heck is that turkey that doesn't have any better sense than to go around with his shirt unbuttoned, showing his chest, and his sleeves rolled up," she thought to herself. "Needless to say, he didn't impress me in the least." (This from a woman who wrote a book that detailed the gifts Elvis gave her, and those that were yet to come: "A few days before he died, he told me that he was going to have a diamond 'TLC' chain made for me ...")

The service itself took place in the music room in Graceland, starting at 2pm in front of 150 people. First, Kathy Westmoreland, one of Elvis's favourite back-up singers, sang "My Heavenly Father Watches Over Me," and then Jake Hess – cited by Elvis as a major influence – sang "Known Only To Him" with two members of the Statesmen gospel quartet. Gospel singer James Blackwood then delivered the title song of one of Elvis's albums "How Great Thou Art" before the Stamps' renditions of "His Hand In Mine" and "Sweet, Sweet Spirit." The songs were followed by short eulogies from pastor C. W. Bradley, a longtime friend of the Presley family; television evangelist Rex Humbard; and comedian Jackie Kahane, Elvis's regular opening act in Las Vegas.

Bradley's main eulogy was surprisingly frank: "Elvis was a frail human being. And he would be the first to admit his weaknesses. Perhaps because of his rapid rise to fame and fortune he was thrown into temptations that some never experience. Elvis would not want anyone to think that he had no flaws or faults. But now that he's gone, I find it more helpful to remember his good qualities, and I hope you do too."

Elvis's body was then driven to the cemetery, accompanied by a cavalcade of white Cadillacs. A further 150 cars followed the funeral cortège. As the casket was extracted from the hearse, a man stepped forward with a camera, snapping away at the casket. The camera was snatched by the police; its back was opened, and the film exposed to light.

After a brief ceremony, Elvis was entombed in the white marble mausoleum. Before the casket was interred, Kendall placed an ID vial between Elvis's feet. It contained a piece of paper on which was typed: "Elvis Aaron Presley, Born January 8, 1935; Died Aug. 16, 1977; Funeral, August 18, 1977 at 2 p.m. in Graceland; Interment same day, Forest Hills Cemetery (Midtown, Memphis, Tenn.)." When he finally closed the casket lid before sealing it, Kendall had a startling revelation: he was going to be the last person on earth ever to look at the face of Elvis Presley.

According to writer Chet Flippo, who was at the funeral, what most amazed him was the emotional intensity. He had no idea there were so many people, so fiercely devoted, who felt such a devastating loss and emptiness. "In many ways, Elvis's death is best compared to that of Robert E. Lee," he said, "both because of the cultural similarities and the extraordinary degree of public grief. Both Lee and Presley were identified by Southerners as ideal Southern boys who were sullied or brought down by outside forces beyond their control." In this respect Flippo was right, as Elvis was martyred overnight. He reflected that the silent intensity among the crowds was so overwhelming that it could have levitated an unbeliever.

David Stanley – Vernon's stepson, and Elvis's stepbrother – later recalled that: "After the funeral I remember coming out of Graceland and looking down the hill at this enormous sea of people. All kinds of people, some crying, some screaming, others just solemn and sad. It was like a Presidential funeral, a universally shared grief. When we got into the limousines, I remembered one of Elvis's favourite songs called 'Long Black Limousine.' It was a song about life's last long trip, and here Elvis was doing just that at last. The show was finally over."

The next morning, August 19th, over fifty thousand people flocked to the cemetery to pay their respects. Within days, however, an abortive attempt to steal Elvis's body prompted a family decision to move he and his mother away from Forest Hill. Following a special dispensation, they were reburied in the Meditation Garden at Graceland. As for Colonel Parker, Elvis's low chamberlain, he was quiet throughout the entire day of the funeral, and refused to ride in the lead mourners' car. He wasn't even at the service, saying he preferred to mourn his boy "in private." Asked why he didn't wear a suit and tie to the funeral – he opted for a Hawaiian shirt instead – he replied "I couldn't wear a suit. Why, if I did, Elvis wouldn't have spotted me in the crowd."

When Esposito first called Parker to tell him Elvis was dead, about an hour after his body was discovered, the Colonel had simply responded: "Nothing has changed. This won't change anything." Reporters later enquired what he would do now that Elvis was in the grave. He replied "Why, I'll go right on managing him."

CHAPTER THREE

Real Real Gone

*"When I first heard Elvis's voice I just knew that I wasn't going
to work for anybody; and nobody was going to be my boss"*
– Bob Dylan

Elvis's death prompted an outpouring of very genuine, very specific grief. Among the thousands of messages of condolences Vernon Presley, Elvis's father, received in the hours and days after his son's death were telegrams from B.B. King ("… the loss of one of the world's greatest musicians and humanitarians"), Little Richard ("Words are inadequate to express the shock I feel …"), and Johnny Cash ("We share your grief").

Cash had co-existed with Elvis for over twenty years, although there was never that much love lost between them. Elvis felt that Cash was a bit like a mean older brother, while Cash begrudged the younger man's success. A short while after Elvis died, Cash said, "June [Carter, Cash's wife] and I loved and admired Elvis Presley. We join his family, friends and loved ones in mourning his death. He was the King of us all in country, rock, folk and rhythm and blues. I never knew an entertainer who had his personal magnetism and charisma. The women loved him and the men couldn't help watching him. His presence filled every room he walked in. He, of course, will never be forgotten, and his influence will always be felt and reflected in the music world."

Carl Perkins was even more effusive, saying "We've lost the most popular man that ever walked on this planet since

Christ himself was here." He later reflected that "Elvis was a victim of his own success. He had a little too much. But thank God for him. The world attention that came upon him so fast opened the door for most all of us. This boy had everything. He had the looks, the moves, the manager, and the talent. And he didn't look like Mr. Ed like a lot of the rest of us did. In the way he looked, way he talked, way he acted … he really was different."

Bob Dylan fell into an immediate depression when he heard the news, as Elvis had been largely responsible for his own self-invention. As he put it on the tenth anniversary of Elvis's death, without a hint of hyperbole, "When I first heard Elvis's voice I just knew that I wasn't going to work for anybody; and nobody was going to be my boss. Hearing Elvis's voice for the first time was like busting out of jail."

Someone once said that when Bob Dylan first started his career he wanted to be Elvis Presley much more than he wanted to be Woody Guthrie. The trouble was that there was an opening for a Guthrie and not for an Elvis, so Dylan went down the folk road instead.

Who wouldn't want to have been Elvis?

No matter how ambivalent they felt about Elvis as a person, everyone was shocked by his death.

Frank Sinatra told an audience at a performance in East Troy, Wisconsin, that night, "We lost a good friend today." This from a man who had once described Elvis's music as "deplorable, a rancid-smelling aphrodisiac."

"There's no way to measure the impact he made on society or the void that he leaves," said Pat Boone on the television news, while Sammy Davis Jr. added: "There was something just bordering on rudeness about Elvis. He never actually did anything rude, but he always seemed as if he was just going to.

On a scale of one to ten, I would rate him eleven." A few hours later, the DJ Wolfman Jack announced on-air in Toronto that "Two thousand years from now, they'll still be hearing about Elvis Presley."

Paul Anka got to know Elvis when they were both performing in Vegas, and would hang out after each other's shows. For years before his death, Anka could sense that Elvis was out of control. "Life is about construction and destruction," he later recalled. "It's all in the balance, everything we see when we can look far enough. When you lose track of that, you self-destruct. And that's what happened to my talented friend.

"I was in Vegas, got up, turned on the news. Elvis Presley – gone. I cried that day. He was a cool guy, a nice man, but was too young to go. Really blew it … so locked in that prison of celebrity, of who he was, and his image, the person inside shrivelled up. Sometimes you sat and talked to him and it was as if he were already gone. You couldn't save him. Elvis imprisoned himself, and lived in a perpetual night. And then there were the guns. He hated Robert Goulet, and every time he was on TV, Elvis would shoot the television. There were bullet holes all over the room. He was shooting at ghosts and in the end he became one himself."

Pressed for a comment, John Lennon, who was in Japan with Yoko Ono at the time of Elvis's death, simply said, "Elvis died when he went into the Army." Lennon was asked again about Elvis just before his murder in 1980. He grimly quipped: "It's the courtiers that kill the King."

Rod Stewart observed: "Elvis was the King, no doubt about it. People like myself, Mick Jagger and all the others only followed in his footsteps."

T. Rex's Marc Bolan turned to his girlfriend Gloria Jones on hearing the news and said, "I hope I don't go this week because I'd only get a few lines on Page Three." He was to die exactly four weeks later …

Fleetwood Mac's Mick Fleetwood was driving back from the hills around LA when he heard the DJ announce he was going to play an Elvis medley. "I thought 'Great,' and then they came back with the news. I learned music listening to Elvis's records. His measurable effect on culture and music was even greater in England than in the States."

Glam rock star Suzi Quatro, who at the time had just had half a dozen top ten hits in the UK, was also in Los Angeles. "I was auditioning for a two-part episode of *Happy Days* with Fonz. They asked me, after I had read for the part, to go back to my hotel and wait for the call. The call came. I was excited because they wanted me to do fifteen episodes, not just two. I was to play the role of Leather Tuscadero. The moment I received the news over the phone, I happened to glance at the television. It said: 'NEWS FLASH. THE KING IS DEAD.' I was excited and devastated at the same time."

Joanna Lumley was filming the last-ever episodes of *The New Avengers* in Toronto when the news came through. "To my horror and disbelief no one on the set seemed remotely touched by an event which was for me a seismic sorrow. The attitude was, 'He was too fat,' 'Man, he took so many drugs,' 'His records had been shit for ages.' The usual ghastly, coarse jokes about the nature of his death did the rounds. It seemed that they had all gone deaf in their memories of 'Heartbreak Hotel' and 'Are You Lonesome Tonight?' They were pygmies, scuffling and sniggering around the fallen hero, kicking his reputation into the dirt to get a cheap laugh. No one cried but me."

Lumley had fallen for him when she was ten years old. She read all the magazines and was worried that his mother didn't smile enough, wasn't proud enough of this legend who was always trying to please her. She gasped when his hair was GI shaved, and swooned when he sang in his black leather jumpsuit in the boxing ring. She sweated with him in his rhinestone suits, and thought that if she could just meet him, she could be his special friend, and help him get well. She forgave him his films, but knew he could have been a fine actor. She planned to sever the control wielded by the arch-enemy Colonel Parker: she would arrange for Elvis to visit England, where he was so adored, where he would have stayed at her place.

David Bowie was as shocked as anyone. He even briefly considered recording a tribute album, arranging classic Elvis songs for his friend Iggy Pop to sing (he had just produced two albums for Iggy, *The Idiot* and *Lust For Life*). Bowie had been a fan all his life. His first-ever performance, aged eleven, was an Elvis impersonation for an audience of boy scouts in Bromley. Years later, he would paint Elvis's TCB – "Takin' care of business" – lightning-bolt logo onto his face for the cover of *Aladdin Sane*. His Ziggy Stardust concerts usually closed with the melodramatic "Rock'n'Roll Suicide," which Bowie sang wearing an Elvis-style jumpsuit – copied by Bowie's designer friend Freddie Burretti from one of the King's – before departing the stage. This was immediately followed by the announcement, "David Bowie has left the building." Bowie's manager at the time, Tony DeFries, was a big fan of Colonel Tom Parker, and would quote his apocryphal maxims to anyone who would listen.

Bowie had even written a song for Elvis, "Golden Years," which he included on his *Station To Station* album after Elvis turned it down. It was easy enough to get the demo to Elvis as they shared a record label, RCA, and bizarrely Parker thought it might be a good idea for the two stars to collaborate. "There was talk between our offices that I should be introduced to Elvis and maybe start working with him in a production-writer capacity," said Bowie. "But it never came to pass. I would have loved working with him. God, I would have adored it. He did send me a note once, 'All the best, and have a great tour.' I still have that note."

The song came about when Bowie was trying in the recording studio to write something in the style of "On Broadway," a glitzy show tune that evoked New York, a real slice of nostalgia. Told his first attempt sounded too much like the old Brill Building song, he eventually came up with the disco doo-wop of "Golden Years," initially as more of a melodramatic supper-club ballad. It's simple to see why Bowie pitched the song to Elvis; it's remarkably easy to imagine Elvis's mid-Seventies house band working with one of Bowie's classic Philly-soul records. They would have given it lots of hi-hat, wah-wah guitar and piping horns, employing the kind of Vegas swing that would have allowed Elvis to glide over the top, singing "Come get up my baby … Come b-b-b-baby" with all the baritone playfulness he could muster, just like he did on "Teddy Bear" all those years ago.

Bowie was so keen for Elvis to record "Golden Years" that he even sang a little like him on the verses, pitching his voice as close to the King's as he could ("channelling the spirit"). I'm not sure how Elvis would have coped with the falsetto breaks, but he would have done wonders with the growling parts. I'm imagining it now, listening to Elvis attempting – successfully – to own the song in much the same way he owned "Proud Mary," "Burning Love" or "Suspicious Minds".

Bowie had studied Elvis's stage presence obsessively, stealing the bits he wanted, and folding everything into his own creation, Ziggy Stardust. Where Elvis was instinctive, and had arrived at his fame fully formed, Ziggy was a convoluted construct that took years to assemble. Bowie had worn eye shadow as a mod, knew that Elvis had worn it too, and so started using make-up in a way no pop star had ever done before – no male star, anyway. Some of the other glam rock groups may have worn cheek glitter before him, but Bowie did it with so much more panache. The journalist Nick Kent, wrote in *Oz* that in concert, Bowie was an "almost grotesque parody of early Elvis Presley complete with outrageously tasteless costume, butch hairstyle and calculated effeminate gestures." When Elvis launches into Little Richard's "Ready Teddy" on *The Ed Sullivan Show*, it's not only his dancing and the way his elasticated legs weave around each other that is so mesmerising, it's the way he looks, the way he holds a camera, and the magnetic pull he exerts on those watching him. It really didn't matter that Elvis was usually filmed from the waist up on American television, because people could still see his hair. With every shoulder shrug, every probing of his tongue, and every coy little smirk, Elvis seduced the audience. Bowie did the same, using his sculpted orange feather cut.

As he ended his songs, Bowie looked like Elvis, standing with his legs apart, crotch forward, before lifting his arms in an imploring way towards the audience, the hands slowly drifting ever higher until he looked like he'd been crucified. He even used to project images of Elvis on stage. TV Smith, who went on to form the Adverts, one of the most important, if short-lived, bands of punk's second wave, caught the Ziggy tour in the West Country. "It was just astounding. I'd never seen anything like that. I'd seen a couple of gigs already. But that gig really … so, no way were the Sex Pistols ground [year] zero, and you're not gonna tell me that they weren't informed by the [New York] Dolls and Iggy and the Small Faces as well …"

As well as Elvis.

I interviewed Bowie in the early Nineties in connection with some daft project of his, and he couldn't stop talking about Elvis. We were meant to be talking about wallpaper – Bowie had produced some for Laura Ashley (including a repeat print of his portrait of Lucian Freud), and appeared to be enjoying the ridiculous amount of attention it was generating – but all he wanted to talk about was the King's 1968 comeback, when he took diet pills for three months, and donned black leather for the greatest rock'n'roll comeback of all time.

"Elvis had the choreography, he had a way of looking at the world that was totally original, totally naive and totally available as a blueprint. Who wouldn't want to copy Elvis? Elvis had it all. It wasn't just the music that was interesting, it was everything else. And he had a lot of everything else."

By the time he became properly famous Bowie had tried a dozen different ways of looking at the world, of showing his face to the media, and by the early Seventies he had resigned himself to putting on the pout and the slapstick. Yet so many of his early guises had involved elements of Elvis, whether it was the way he stood, the way he smirked or the way he ran up to the last crescendo on a song. You can hear Bowie's Elvis on *Low* and *"Heroes,"* as well as on "Can You Hear Me" on *Young Americans* and parts of "Friday On My Mind" on *Pin-Ups*; his "Elvis voice" became something of a trope later on, too, and you can hear him delving down into his Elvis baritone on most of his post-*Never Let Me Down* albums, when Bowie was increasingly keen to reference his own past. For Bowie, Elvis was the consummate blueprint. He said himself that his debut album "seemed to have its roots all over the place, in rock and vaudeville and music hall. I didn't know if I was Max Miller or Elvis Presley." Bowie had been fascinated with Elvis ever since he saw one of his cousins dancing to "Hound

Dog": "I had never seen her get up and be moved so much by anything. It really impressed me, the power of the music. I started getting records immediately after that."

When quizzed in 1972 about the number of glitter-eyed young boys who were seen at T. Rex concerts dancing with each other in the aisles, Bowie responded, "What about Elvis Presley? If his image wasn't bi-sexual then I don't know what is. People talk about fag-rock but that's an unwieldy term at the best of times."

"[Elvis] was a major hero of mine," he said. "And I was probably stupid enough to believe that having the same birthday as him actually meant something. I came over [to New York] for a long weekend. I had a gig on the Thursday night at the Polytechnic in Middlesbrough so I dashed down to London that night, and got the plane early in the morning. I remember coming straight from the airport and walking into Madison Square Garden very late. I was wearing all my clobber from the Ziggy period and had great seats near the front. The whole place just turned to look at me and I felt like a right idiot. I had brilliant red hair, some huge padded space suit and those red boots with big black soles. I wished I'd gone for something quiet. I sat there and he looked at me – and if looks could kill! I just felt, Elvis is roasting me! He was well into his set – he was already doing 'Proud Mary.' I'm sure many of the audience thought Mary had arrived! I absolutely had to see him before anything happened to him. He was pretty good at the time. He was still in great shape and it wasn't long after the black leather show that was on television."

I've seen Bowie in concert dozens of times, and each time there was an Elvis element about his performance, a nuance, a trope, a tiny nod to the past. But the day I really understood just how much Bowie had taken from Elvis was the day I saw him play the Milton Keynes Bowl, on July 1st, 1983. Bowie didn't look like Elvis, didn't particularly sound like Elvis, and didn't move like Elvis; but the way he appeared, the way he *was*, the way he looked vacuous but intense in between songs, it was all so Elvis, and all so terribly cool. He stared at the crowd in an imperious yet oddly humble way, he locked his legs when he grabbed the microphone stand, and he hooded his eyelids when he was singing something especially heartfelt. Like many before him, he knew and understood the power of Elvis. Watching him from the side of the stage, I could see how he was reaching out to those in the crowd who were hundreds of yards away, and it worked. Completely. Grand gestures, captured on video, and transported to the back of the crowd, gestures that went all the way back to 1955.

Given how extraordinary, and how affecting Elvis's version of "Golden Years" would have been, it makes you wonder what he would have made of Bowie's "Fame." By the mid-Seventies Elvis was already imitating himself – in truth he was actually the first fake Elvis – and his interpretation of "Fame" would have been layered in meaning. I can hear it now, with James Burton churning away at the riff on his guitar, as drummer Ronnie Tutt grinds out the Vegas disco groove, oblivious to its implication.

Bowie performed the song on *Soul Train* in 1975, one of the few white artists to appear on the show, and one can only imagine what would have happened had it been Elvis instead. This could have been one of the most extraordinary moments in post-war pop culture, as bizarre and as potentially seismic as Frank Sinatra performing at Woodstock, or Mick Jagger guesting with the Sex Pistols. Picture Elvis taking to the stage, dressed in a black Rhinestone jumpsuit, surrounded by a trio of buxom black backing singers in floppy velour hats, and his ever-faithful band turning Bowie's funky treatise on success into a miscegenetic masterpiece. Bowie says he had to get drunk in order to perform on the programme; God knows what pre-mortem cocktail Elvis would have been on. I like to think he would have put as much effort into the performance as he did for his 1968 TV comeback, and shed enough weight to make a nation swoon again. David Bowie once joked that his 1974 album *David Live*, on the cover of which he looked anything but, should have been called *David Bowie Is Alive And Well And Living Only In Theory*. Towards the end of his life, Elvis was going the same way, but maybe the performance on *Soul Train* would have prolonged his desire to get back in shape, back on track, and get out once more into the world.

In fact, had Elvis lived, one wonders how he would have embraced disco, if indeed he would have chosen to go down that brightly under-lit path at all. He had enough of the redneck in him to publicly disparage disco and cast it aside, but he had built his reputation on appropriating black music, so why should the Seventies be any different to the Fifties? The Rolling Stones were about to "go disco," so why couldn't the King? Tom Parker appeared to have as much control over what Elvis did as ever. Not being remotely embarrassed about being expedient as to how he exploited his charge, the Colonel could have easily suggested to Elvis that it might be good for his career for him to record a disco album. Indeed, a series of disco albums, right through to the early Eighties, when Elvis might even have gone electro.

Just think for a moment. It's the autumn of 1978. Imagine Elvis on stage, having just finished his nightly performance of "Suspicious Minds," and wiping his face with a scarf before throwing it to some lucky housewife out front. Coloured lights swirl back and forth across the stage, and the spotlight falls on bass player Jerry Scheff as he starts to pump out the

Bill Wyman riff on "Miss You." The riff may not have been as incendiary as the twelve-bar fuzz guitar riff played by Willie Kizart on Jackie Brenston's "Rocket 88," released in 1951, and widely considered to be the first ever rock'n'roll record, but this is the first time that this crowd has heard Elvis attempt the song, and they burst into wild applause. This is Elvis in libidinous mode. He's lighter than he was a few years ago, and thinner around the gills; he's wearing black to disguise his paunch; and he's smiling lasciviously at various over-eager women in the audience. He still has the swivelling hips and the cocksure sneer he had as a boy, back in 1956, but these days every movement, every pelvic thrust, every facial tic, every wink is shrouded by the knowledge that he will be a sex object until the day he dies. This is a man who has spent his entire adult life as a sex symbol, which has given him the confidence of a hundred thousand men. Elvis could walk out on stage eating a cheeseburger and belching and women would still throw themselves at him.

Tonight, though, he's singing "Miss You," and he's enjoying it. He laughs, exultant, and launches into his familiar riff to the audience: "You know, when I started out, I was a little bitty guy, with a little bitty guitar. I had little bitty sideburns, and a little shaky leg. And then Ed Sullivan saw me and said, 'Hmmm.' Anyway, they put me on TV and filmed me from the waist up, and I'm ogling around with my eyes and my hair, trying to make the best of it all. Anyway, those of you who've never seen me before will realise tonight that I'm totally insane, and have been for a number of years ... They just haven't caught me right yet! Anyway, in 1956 I made my first movie ..."

His voice tails off as his microphone starts cutting out. He then begins to fool around, stealing microphones off his band, and ends up clutching four until he finds one he likes. As he throws the others away, his backing singers – all black – giggle at his horseplay. He looks over endearingly, and says, "You know what, tomorrow night I'm bringing in the Supremes. Maybe with Mahalia Jackson singing lead! Girls you gotta watch out now, I'm after you! I'm serious now. I know what you're up to now … Oh baby. Anyway, this next song has got nothing to do with that movie, it's got nothing to do with the Supremes matter of fact, as it's a great new record from the Rolling Stones, and I love it … What you say at the back? Now, I dig them, really. That boy Mick Jagger did a pretty good impression of me one time, but he's a good kid still, and I love this record, a good old rhythm and blues tune … He's a good ole' boy, even if he don't understand the American woman. He just thinks he can turn up and start loving. He don't understand that an American woman needs some loving, she needs to be taken care of, to be loved good and proper. But he writes a good record, and here is 'Miss You.'"

He almost talks his way through the verses, laughing and ad-libbing as he goes – "I've been holding out so long, I've been sleeping all alone, Lord I miss you … hey baby that's right, I miss you honey" – before putting all his effort into the bridge, the part of the song that begins, "Oh everybody waits so long …" and the room explodes. What a moment, what a shape shifter, one of the greatest entertainers of the century crooning his way through a piece of reductive disco that by rights shouldn't have worked for the Stones in the first place. But if they could get away with it, then why not Elvis? Hell, yes. This would have been like Tom Jones covering Prince's "Kiss," only before Prince, before Tom Jones, and before irony became a legitimate non-ironic cultural industry. Go on YouTube and you can see mash-ups of Elvis on-stage, cut to Lipps Inc's "Funky Town." It's funny, sure, but it works. Elvis would also go disco posthumously, in 2002, when Junkie XL remixed "A Little Less Conversation" and had a huge global hit in the process.

But then Elvis was never going to perform "Miss You," because Elvis was dead. He would never perform a Bowie song, either. The whole postmodern world would be lost to him on August 16th, 1977, when Elvis was suddenly enshrined as a man from the past.

That summer, Bowie, who had been living and recording in Berlin, had just finished recording *Lust For Life*, his third album with Iggy Pop. He first worked with Iggy and his band, the Stooges, when he produced their *Raw Power* album in 1973, and had been largely responsible for their second collaborative effort, *The Idiot*, released just a few months earlier. Both Bowie and Pop shared the same record label as Elvis, RCA, and as soon as he died, promoting a new album from "that guy who used to be in the Stooges" became a matter of diminished importance. When the *NME*, which had embraced punk with a fervour that shamed their rival *Melody Maker*, reviewed the album that September, they actually put Elvis on the cover.

Bruce Springsteen too was a big Elvis fan, and he took the news hard. Real hard, real Bruce Springsteen hard. He had bought tickets for the concert Presley was scheduled to play at Madison Square Garden that September, and when he heard the King had passed, started shouting at the futility of it all. According to one of his road managers, "He was really upset, just incredibly pissed off." However Springsteen used Elvis's death as a way to channel his creative forces. Two days later, he set off with guitarist Steve Van Zandt and photographer Eric Meola to try to capture Elvis's spirit in some publicity pictures. They flew to Salt Lake City, threw their bags in the back of a red 1965 Ford Galaxie 500XL, and drove off into the desert. As Meola eagerly snapped away, making the most of his moving target, Springsteen and Van Zandt chatted, discussing Presley's extraordinary ascent and even more extraordinary decline. Here was the classic example of the American Dream and how not to live it. Springsteen was disgusted by how the Memphis Mafia, his so-called friends, had allowed Elvis to become so diminished by drugs, without helping him. "All those guys, all his friends, abandoned him," said Van Zandt. The resulting photographs are among the best ever taken of Springsteen; he would never look more like a rock star, never look more like Elvis in his prime, in his pomp. During the troubled sessions that followed *Born To Run*, he even wrote a song as a tribute to his hero, "Fire." A studio take was recorded, but it wasn't officially released until 2010's box set, *The Promise*, although the Pointer Sisters had a huge hit with it in 1978.

"There have been a lot of tough guys," said Springsteen. "There have been pretenders. And there have been contenders. But there is only one King. He was as big as the whole country itself, as big as the whole dream. He just embodied the essence of it and he was in mortal combat with the thing. Nothing will ever take the place of that guy."

That guy.

Springsteen went on to describe seeing Elvis Presley on *The Ed Sullivan Show* in 1956 as his own "genesis moment," where the fusing of "a red hot rockabilly" with a suburban TV set gave birth to "the first modern twentieth-century man, creating fundamental outsider art that would be embraced by a mainstream popular culture."

That guy.

"Like so many Elvis fans, the moment I heard of his untimely death my entire history with Elvis seemed to flash by in my mind," said Max Weinberg, the drummer with the E-Street Band. "I was, unfortunately, returning home after attending the funeral of a beloved elderly relative. CBS-FM radio ... broke in with the news. Knowing of Elvis's health issues over the preceding few years I can say the event was not entirely surprising, but nonetheless, a total shock because Elvis had just always been such a presence in my life. His music, his movies, his importance, his outrageousness – just the very thought of Elvis informed my life, my friends' lives, and the lives of my colleagues in the E-Street Band. And, when you think he's probably the most impersonated individual in history, it's always been amazing to me that there was this man, Elvis Presley, who was the one and only actual Elvis!"

"When Elvis died, I was pretty much in a road daze, out there playing shows, night after night, lost in the never-ending one-night stands of gigs," recalled E-Street guitarist Nils Lofgren. "Man, it hit me hard. Another one bites the dust. So many God-given gifts in one man, gone. Sadly, I was a bit cynical about it at that point. The death of Jimi Hendrix was the first dream-killer for me. I couldn't believe someone that gifted could die so young ... I discovered Elvis through my first wave of musical heroes, the Beatles, Stones, Hendrix and all the rest. Elvis was the ultimate, trailblazing story of a human soul so joyfully possessed by such extraordinary gifts, that they dragged him through all prejudice and boundaries to a place where, lost in their sharing, he found himself connected and touching an entire planet with those very gifts he nurtured."

Isaac Tigrett, the co-founder of the Hard Rock Café and House of Blues chains, and a son of Tennessee, was sitting at home in England with his wife Maureen (who had previously been married to Ringo Starr), when he saw the news on TV.

"It stunned the core of our very being. We started playing 'Heartbreak Hotel' and wept."

"I can remember being shocked but I can't remember where I was, probably because I was drunk," recalls Tony Blair's former spin-doctor, Alastair Campbell. "I was busking at the time, as it was during my year out of university, travelling all over Europe on a motorbike. I think I was in Holland, a place called Utrecht. I can remember that for the next few days any bar you went into had Elvis on the juke box, and if he wasn't we put him on. It was a bad period for great singers dying. Jacques Brel is my top singer and he died a year later. Elvis challenges him from time to time but I love the legend. Brel plays to my dark side, Elvis to the desire to have a smile on the face. I cannot listen to the version of 'Are You Lonesome Tonight?' where he cracks up after delivering bogus lyrics without cracking up. I have heard it hundreds of times but it always feels the same. I later found out, having met him, that Bill Clinton has an identical laugh to Elvis."

For many fans the death of Elvis was also the end of a dream. Each of hundreds of thousands, perhaps millions, of girls around the world still thought that if she – Sheila, Jemima, Carly, Nicolle, Farrah, Shirley, Desiree, Delilah, Candy, whoever – had only been able to brush accidentally against Elvis in a bar, in a club, in a realtors, a soda-pop hop (ha, in their dreams!), a motorbike dealership, or, more likely, backstage at one of his concerts surrounded by his cronies, then he would be hers. How could he fail to be? They knew that all he had to do was look into their eyes, and he would belong to them. Many thought that the way to his heart was simply through sex, by making themselves available to him after a show, being introduced by a local promoter, a visiting celebrity, or the representative of a local charity. Others, however, held a torch for Elvis in the same way that many women still held a torch for Sinatra. There was always the scintilla of possibility that he could find in them what he had been searching for all his life – a home from home in someone else's arms. For women of his generation, this was a JFK moment and James Dean moment rolled into one. The dream really was over, and there was no way he was going to fall in love with them now. Without a living King, how on earth could there be a living Queen, how on earth could there be a living princess? With Elvis gone it meant there would be no white wedding, no wedding night garter belt, no bed-bound honeymoon. With Elvis gone, there would be no more kissing, and certainly no more fucking. So what was a sixteen-, twenty-five-, thirty-five-year-old virgin going to do now?

It was the thirty- and forty-year-olds who really suffered, though, especially the married ones, the ones who had inevitably settled for something less than Elvis, who heard the news on the radio and then looked across at their husbands, slumped in front of the television, drinking beer maybe, or eating a TV dinner, saying to no one in particular that Elvis hadn't been what he was for some time now and sure it's a mighty shame but he had gotten really fat so what the hell? These were women who had made a bargain with age, who had compromised by marrying below their weight, and who would now no longer be able to fantasise that their rhinestone knight might come and sweep them away.

No, it was really over.

In the early days of the internet, in the early Nineties, the web was awash with images of Elvis as a celestial being, as "The Sacred Heart Of Elvis," carrying a cross, or wearing an ornamental halo; there was even a cartoon that was turned into a T-shirt of Jesus, the carpenter's son, in his workshop, hitting his thumb instead of a nail, screaming "ELVIS H. PRESLEY!" Had the internet been around when Elvis died, the images of the King would probably have been mainly romantic, even if ironic – Elvis as Clark Gable in *Gone With The Wind*, Elvis as Woody Allen in *Annie Hall*, or Robert Redford in *The Way We Were*.

As well as appropriating black music, Elvis had initially made a name for himself by copying how black entertainers moved. "Elvis's reverse integration was so complete on stage he adopted the symbolic fornication blacks unashamedly brought to American entertainment," said Nelson George. "Elvis was sexy; not clean-cut, wholesome, white-bread, Hollywood sexy but sexy in the aggressive earthy manner associated with black males. In fact, as a young man Presley came closer than any other rock'n'roll star to capturing the swaggering sexuality projected by so many R&B vocalists."

Which made Elvis a challenge, a boy to be conquered, a man to be tamed, and tamed by the right woman. Who, on August 16th, finally knew that she would never get the chance. She was never going to bring him home to the saltbox house with the clapboard siding. Because Elvis wasn't there any more. Of course Elvis had already been tamed, by his manager, by the succession of soapy movies he made throughout the Sixties, but that only made the collective failure to win his heart even worse. Elvis was their Rudolph Valentino, their "Latin Lover." Half a century earlier, in 1926, an estimated 100,000 people lined the streets of Manhattan to pay their respects at Valentino's funeral. There were many reports, played up by the press, of public swooning and suicide attempts. A spokesman for the funeral home encouraged the frenzy by saying, "Never before have so many persons tried to see a body. Mr. Valentino's body is not being handled any differently than that of anyone else, excepting we are giving it special attention, and putting in an exceptionally great amount of time on it. The body arrived here at about two o'clock Monday afternoon, August 23rd, and we immediately began work on the embalming, keeping at it until the following morning, when it was placed on view until 1am."

The press had no need to exaggerate the emotion generated by Elvis's death, nor the shock felt by his legions of female fans as they digested the news. Their fantasy lover had finally gone

Raquel Welch, the actress, on the other hand, had long given up on Elvis. A former weather girl, she made her film debut with a bit part in the 1964 Elvis film *Roustabout*. She has seen Elvis in San Diego (her first rock concert ever) and his sexual aura had been a complete revelation to her. She wrote later about the impact: "I suddenly understood what sex is all about,' and 'what a sexy guy could be." The contrast with his demeanour on the set of *Roustabout* not so many years later was profound and shocking.

By then her idol had changed: "It seemed like he was more packaged." Not only was Welch dismayed with Elvis's change of wardrobe and his dyed hair held in place by spray but by the whole effect, "…it was a whitewashed, cleaned-up Elvis. They took all the sex out of him!"

Years later, in about 1972, Welch had a contract to perform at the Las Vegas Hilton, where Elvis was also playing. Presley was by then in full Las Vegas mode attired entirely in white with bellbottoms, a lot of jewellery and a high collar. The effect for her was now more like Liberace than reminiscent of the sex idol of her youth. They met up with Presley talking about his jewellery: "I went to his dressing room, and he was very sweet, very nice …But he didn't seem to be really happy in his eyes."

Welch was in rehearsal for another Vegas show when somebody came running into the room and said, "Elvis is dead!" "Everybody went numb," she remembered. "It was the end of an era."

The manner in which Elvis passed away scared some people, especially those whose social lives were arguably not too dissimilar. The Who's extraordinarily gifted, and even more extraordinarily headstrong drummer, Keith Moon, was among those shocked by the news. Moon was one of the true wild men of rock'n'roll, and his appetite for drink and drugs was legendary. He had become as notorious for his behaviour as for his proficiency on the drums, and was one of those rock stars for whom an early death would have been no surprise. Like Elvis, Moon had ballooned in weight due to his appalling diet and prodigious drug intake, and took scant interest in his health.

"Keith got very upset when Elvis died," said Moon's girlfriend, Annette Walter-Lax. "I think it woke his perverted thinking about death. He always knew he was going to die young. Often when I spoke to him, he would end it by saying, 'It doesn't matter because I'll be dead by then anyway.' So obviously he knew that he couldn't carry on living the way he was and survive."

Moon's immediate reaction to Elvis's death, apart from the worrying, was to drink a lot and take even more pills than usual. As if by Elvis's royal decree, Moon died from a drug overdose just a year later – again like Elvis, fat, addicted, scared, and more than aware that his best days were behind him.

One of the original bad girls of rock'n'roll, Ronnie Spector of the Ronettes, was also shaken by the news. On the day Elvis died, she was recording a new song – "It's A Heartache," later a huge hit for Bonnie Tyler – in Nashville with a lot of musicians who had worked with Elvis, but no one told them what had happened until after the session had finished. She saw the producer having something whispered in his ear, and then flee the studio booth. He walked back in a few minutes later, his eyes red and his breath smelling of whiskey. All he said was, "Let's finish this one up and get out of here." They did a few more takes and then went back to their hotel.

"That's when he told me Elvis had been found dead in his bathroom that morning," said Ronnie. When she asked the producer why he hadn't told her earlier, he replied that many of the musicians had known Elvis, and that as he had only one day booked in the studio, he couldn't afford to take a chance that some of them might not have been able to make it through the session.

Spector cried herself to sleep that night. "It's not that I was such a big fan of Elvis Presley or anything. It's just that his death got me thinking. Here was a guy who had everything – they called him the King of Rock'n'Roll! But he was so unhappy with his life that he finally destroyed himself. And after he died so suddenly, I couldn't help but wonder if I wasn't headed down the same road."

It wasn't just rock stars and rock critics who had been shocked into grief. In a fitting, if slightly ungainly tribute, a few hours after the official announcement, US President Jimmy Carter observed that "Elvis Presley's death deprives our country of a part of itself," and called it "a sad day for the Republic." The president already knew what a sorry state Elvis had been in prior to his death. Backstage after seeing him perform at the Atlanta Omni in 1973, Carter had been shocked by the sheen of sweat on Elvis's made-up face. A few weeks before his death, in a fit of pique seemingly fuelled by barbiturates, Elvis had called the White House to seek a Presidential pardon for a sheriff he knew who was in some sort of trouble. "He was totally stoned and didn't know what he was saying," said Carter. "I talked to him for a long time. I asked him what the sheriff's sentence was, and he said that he hadn't been tried in court yet. Well, I said, 'Elvis, I can't consider a pardon until after a trial and sentences and everything. I don't think he understood that." Elvis continued to call the White House to discuss the matter, but the president never spoke to him again.

Elvis's death affected millions and millions of ordinary lives. Women who swooned over Elvis as teenagers burst into tears, as did men who had idolised him for over twenty years.

"I will never forget the day he passed," one fan later recalled. "I was in a hotel room with my three children and husband …. The television was on and there was a newsbreak announcing that Elvis had been found dead in his Memphis home. My husband had gone out to get breakfast and when he came back I was crying horribly. He thought something might be wrong with the baby. It took me the longest time to stop crying. I, like millions of others, could not believe the King was gone … People were making jokes about his death, which I thought was unforgivable. Anyone who truly loved Elvis will understand my reaction, others will find it comical. To this day I have a hard time listening to certain songs or seeing certain footage without tearing up. I especially love to listen to him sing gospel music as it came straight from his heart."

British fan Bob Wilson was driving home and listening to the radio after watching Newport County's soccer fixture against Portsmouth: "… we were in a good mood getting into the car, but the laughter soon disappeared and a sense of amazement took over when we heard the news …. The reason we had been in such a good mood was that we had just watched what, to a relative neutral like myself at least, was a very funny football match which included perhaps the worst goalkeeping performance I have watched, by Portsmouth's Steve Middleton."

Steve Hollis, another British fan, was also on the road as he recollected later for the BBC. "I was returning from a night-fishing trip in my dad's car. It was around six in the morning when I turned the radio on to hear Elvis on Radio Luxembourg. The DJ was in tears as he re-stated the news that Elvis had died. As soon as I got home I woke my sister to tell her. We spent the rest of the day glued to the radio and television. All night vigils and movie shows followed ..."

Another British fan, Alan McMahon, told the BBC years later that on arrival at Heathrow airport "I was in the unusually long queue at immigration, when the pretty blonde in front suddenly burst out sobbing: 'He was all that mattered to me.' Young and newly single myself, I concluded that she had split up with her boyfriend, and to my surprise, found myself placing a reassuring arm around her shoulder and saying: 'I know just how you feel,' placing the necessary emphasis on 'just.' She looked up, smiled gratefully and managed a few words between sobs, which, it seemed to me, grew increasingly intimate as we approached the barrier.

"'Men just don't understand, do they? I don't mean you, you are so sweet,' she said. A few more minutes, and I would have seized her in my arms and kissed the tears off those limpid blue eyes. Then she said: '*Love Me Tender* is my favourite, I never tire of watching it, but my husband hates it. Ah, there he is ... What's your favourite? ... Why, what's wrong?'"

Even the skies were full of the news. Every internal US flight was interrupted by an announcement from the captain, a piece of theatre that had to be handled with the utmost delicacy. Airline pilots were used to imparting bad news – a delayed take-off, a delayed landing, a cancelled connection, an accident on-board – but it was rare that they had to act as anchormen. Today, every Pan Am, Airborne, Air Illinois, Air Midwest, Cascade Airways, Delta, United and Intermountain Airlines pilot was Walter Kronkite. A friend of mine was flying from New York to Fort Lauderdale when the pilot announced himself over the PA. After clearing his throat and apologising for interrupting the passengers, he slowly, very carefully told the flight that Elvis Presley had been found dead in Graceland. Initially there was disbelief, but when it dawned on them that this wasn't some kind of weird prank, they started huddling into family groups, quiet as church mice, whispering among themselves.

Adrian Wootton, the Chief Executive of Film London – the agency charged with developing the film and media industry in the capital – remembers exactly where he was on August 16th. As a fifteen-year-old he was on holiday at home in Lichfield, Staffordshire. The first thing he heard was a newsflash that night on the BBC, with just some very sketchy details. His first reaction was disbelief and shock followed very quickly by a sense of real sadness. "All three TV channels then started covering the story and I went to my room and scanned all the radio stations I could pick up," he said. "Just about every one I tuned into started playing Elvis songs. I don't think I slept much that night as I just alternated between stations, listening to the radio trying to glean, without much success, more information. Of course I kept playing my own Elvis records too, playing them on my headphones. The next day I bought a whole bunch of newspapers, as many as I could find. I still have some as my mum and dad kept them and gave them back to me many years later. It's amazing to think how little we knew about Elvis at the time, compared to contemporary rock stars, but also why for those of us who loved his incendiary, unique talent, it was so difficult to accept, to take in." When Wootton eventually met Sam Phillips – welcoming him to the UK for an appearance at the National Film Theatre in 2002 – he said it was "like listening to science fiction as I remembered being back in my room in the Midlands listening to the radio in terrible wonderment."

Perhaps the strongest emotion people felt was disbelief. Some later became distraught, numb, frozen, tearful, sentimental, even angry – but the immediate reaction for many was complete disbelief. How on Earth could this be? One young fan in Sydney fell to her knees and started to hyperventilate when she heard the news. As she had to go to school, she punched a two-hour cassette tape into her tape machine and started recording the news, to listen to when she got back.

Sonny West, one of the architects of *Elvis: What Happened?*, the show-and-tell biography that shed such a harsh light on Elvis's drug habits just prior to his death, was profoundly shaken by the news. Not only had he found it hard to handle the fall-out from the publication of the book he'd helped create – it may have made him famous, but he was vilified before anyone even knew what he looked like – but it had turned out to be more of a roadmap than a biography. In a neat PR move, the authors repeatedly claimed that they had only written the book to save Elvis from himself: on August 16th West discovered they had failed in their venture. When he found out, he burst into tears.

Coincidentally, that morning West had given an interview to Bob Greene, a columnist working for the *Chicago Sun-Times*. When Greene asked, "So it wouldn't shock you if one day you opened the newspaper and found that [Elvis] suddenly died?," West replied, "No, it would not."

Meanwhile, back in High Wycombe, our friend Sid disappeared. This became apparent to us mainly because he was suddenly no longer available to chauffeur us to and from gigs. For the next three or four weeks, whenever we wanted to see someone play in Aylesbury or London, we'd have to bully one of our other friends to take us, usually a boy called Allen, who drove a robust 1971 Triumph Herald, the last year they were produced. Allen took great exception to being asked to drive us around, so much so that he would occasionally take us somewhere, and then drive off in a huff, leaving us to find our own way home, usually by hitching. We also started taking the train up to Marylebone or Paddington, exploring the West End, and usually ending up in the Marquee. In those days it barely mattered who you saw, as long as it was a band of some description. We'd blithely turn up to see Eddie & The Hot Rods, Roogalator, Generation X, the New Hearts; even a second-division group was better than no group at all. We wasted several evenings trying to track down the Sex Pistols on their SPOTS tour – "SEX PISTOLS ON TOUR SECRETLY" – but always ended up in an empty north London pub, or back at the Nag's Head in High Wycombe. The Sex Pistols, like Sid, were nowhere to be seen.

This was the end of our gang anyway, as, in an echo of *American Graffiti*, we were all going our separate ways, some of us to college, and me to London, where in a few weeks I would be ensconced in a hall of residence in Battersea, walking to art school every day along the Kings Road. Never had I felt such a sensation of freedom, as I felt my past falling away like playing cards descending in slow motion.

I'm not sure I ever saw Sid again. For a while I went home at Christmas and holidays, and hung around with my old friends. But soon we were very different. Those who had left were wary of repeating old habits, and those who were left started to feel aggrieved. As for Sid, he just sort of disappeared. Perhaps he moved to Rickmansworth or Beaconsfield; in any case, we never saw him in the Nag's Head again. It was as though Elvis had killed Sid, too, almost as though Elvis's death had forced Sid to confront his so-called life, up sticks and move. Taking his van and his Elvis eight-tracks with him. I liked to think that he had made a pilgrimage to Memphis, worshipping at the shrine in Graceland, falling in love with a waitress in the process. But in reality he probably just moved to Slough to become a minicab driver.

CHAPTER FOUR
Punks Vs. Teds

*"The popularity of punk rock was, in effect, due to the fact
that it made ugliness beautiful"* – Malcolm McLaren

The Vortex, 203 Wardour Street, Soho, London, August 16th,
1977. Opened to some fanfare by Andy Czezowski just six
weeks earlier, the Vortex has become the most important
punk club in London. Czezowski has previously been the co-
owner of the infamous first punk club, the Roxy in Covent
Garden, before greedy landlords had forced him to move on.
By now he has already moved on from the Vortex in turn,
following an argument with his new business partner, but no
one has thought to tell the audience.

West Country punks the Adverts are playing tonight,
along with a third-rate band called the Outsiders, and the club
is heaving, with six hundred and fifty teenagers and twenty-
somethings dressed like horror-movie morticians jumping
up and down and hitting each other playfully. The pogo has
become the default punk dance, and so the audience randomly
leap into the air, each using the shoulders of the person in
front as a springboard, and seeming oblivious to whatever
music is being played. Which is usually reggae, anyway, when
the bands aren't on stage. A year ago, punk was still in its
infancy, still stylistically ambiguous and idiosyncratic, but
now the Vortex is full of identikit punks, who have signed
up to the craze without really knowing why. A year ago there
was something appealingly effeminate about punk, but by

the summer of 1977 it has become tribal, and the crowds you see at the Roxy, the Marquee, the 100 Club and all the other punk clubs now tend to resemble those at football matches. Violence isn't consequential; it is now habitual, almost a prerequisite. Spatial awareness is something that suddenly feels extremely old-fashioned.

Not for nothing has the media labelled 1977 the "summer of hate," as opposed to 1967's summer of love. By the summer of 1977, everyone is already trying to live up to an image that has largely been created by the media. Everyone has to look tough, and pretend to be working class. You need to look and sound like a rebel.

It's been a busy day for the punk fraternity. Up in Manchester, at the Electric Circus club, the city's most famous punk band, the Buzzcocks, have just signed with United Artists Records, signing the contract on the bar. "We signed to make records, not to be in debt to a record company," said singer Pete Shelley, naively. Chelsea and the Cortinas are playing Barbarella's in Birmingham, while in London the Jam are at the 100 Club, XTC at the Rochester Castle, the Boomtown Rats at the Nashville, and Penetration at the Marquee.

Back in the Vortex, as a reggae tune makes way for a particularly forthright Stooges record, several punks storm the stage and nearly succeed in toppling the eight-foot PA stacks. With punk, the cardinal sin is to look like you are posing, so you have to get involved one way or another, and if that involves jumping up and down and rushing up on stage, then so be it. There is also a lot of spitting, and so much steam is coming off the basement walls that walking into the Vortex tonight feels like walking into a giant kettle.

The place seems possessed, but then these days it always is; a week ago, during a Generation X gig, the audience had started throwing a large supermarket trolley around in an act of spontaneous punk theatre. No one had any idea where it had come from. After all, a big wire basket in a stainless steel frame with steel handlebars and hard rubber wheels was not standard issue at the Vortex, nor indeed any other punk club. There are no supermarket trolleys here tonight, but there's definitely a feeling of aggression in the air. There are also a lot of tomboys here, the kind of girls who are only interested in actions, not repercussions. And it's often the punk girls who act most violently. Punk girls have discovered that to get themselves noticed, they can't just act as decoration – they have to get involved.

Around a quarter to ten, halfway through the night, during another of the interminable twelve-inch reggae records that every punk DJ has to play, so few actual punk records being available as yet, a chirpy voice announces over the PA: "Just to let you know everyone, just heard that Elvis Presley is dead!" The announcer says it almost with glee, and as he does so, the whole club appears to cheer. The crowd starts jumping up and down, hollering, and clinking their beer glasses together, celebrating the death of what they obviously consider to be someone from the old school, the "old wave" incarnate. Never mind that this man had all but invented rock'n'roll, had once been the most libidinous, most licentious example of youthful rebellion, perhaps the defining figure of post-war pop culture; tonight, to this spittle-flecked throng, he is simply an historical figure who warrants vocal disdain.

"Ha, ha, Elvis is dead! Elvis is dead, Elvis is dead! The King is dead, long live the King!"

The cheering goes on for over five minutes. Jonathan Ross is here, ten years before he started to become famous as a chat show host, as is Marco Perroni, the chubby guitarist with Adam And The Ants. Both remember the cheering from the crowd, and both were quite shocked by it.

Malcolm McLaren, the Sex Pistols' manager, is at his Glitterbest management company offices a few hundred yards away in Denmark Street – London's Tin Pan Alley – when he is called with the news. "Makes you feel sad, doesn't it?" he says, showboating for the journalist, "Like your grandfather died ..." He smiles. "Yeah, it's just too bad it couldn't have been Mick Jagger."

This is especially ironic, as back in 1971, in one of his many previous attempts to draw attention to himself in the most contrary way possible – in this case deliberately rubbing up the Kings Road hippies he despised so much – McLaren had worn a powder-blue drape with black velvet trim, a gold waistcoat and slim-Jim tie, black shirt, black drainpipes, black crepes and black-and-blue striped nylon socks. Ever the opportunist, McLaren had dressed that way to publicise his then-new retail venture, Let It Rock, a shop designed to appeal to the bastions of the Ted revival as well as to annoy his joss-stick-sprouting neighbours. Like John Lydon, the Dickensian guttersnipe he later hired to be his mouthpiece in the Sex Pistols, McLaren was programmed for confrontation.

The journalist and broadcaster Danny Baker, soon to find fame and fortune as a youth TV presenter, is here at the Vortex tonight, and is more than incensed by the crowd's behaviour. Along with Mark Perry (who had set up the genre's first fanzine, *Sniffin' Glue*, with Baker, and founded the seminal punk band Alternative TV), Baker is in the process of joining the *New Musical Express*. The Vortex is his stomping ground, but the audience's behaviour starts to make him think that the mob-yob mentality associated with punk is already in danger of overshadowing it.

Baker is so angry that he suddenly leaps on stage, grabs the microphone and starts to harangue the crowd, calling them "Neanderthals," "drones" and "wankers" in the process. He tells the crowd that Elvis was the first punk, and that without him none of them would be here tonight. "I accused them all of being bandwagon jumping, knee-jerk shit-for-brains who had bought into a cookie-cutter cartoon nihilism the same way the *Daily Mirror* had ordered it," he later recalled.

Almost as soon as he starts speaking, he is hit by a bottle, arriving from the back of the crowd as if by rote. It hits him square on the cheek, and he is momentarily stunned, but as he starts shouting again he is pulled offstage by the lead singer of Sham 69, Jimmy Pursey, who knows that Baker's performance will only result in a trip to A&E. Backstage, Baker is bleeding and shaking. "Those idiot ponces! It's finished, this," he screams, meaning the punk movement. "Finished! Fuck the lot of them! Elvis Presley – what the fuck do they know about Elvis Presley other than what the papers tell them?"

As he looks up from his hands, which are by now covered in blood, he sees the radio DJ John Peel, who has tears streaming down his face. Peel can barely talk, he's so distressed by the announcement of Presley's death. He eventually thanks Baker for "getting up there," and then both leave the club, Baker to go home to play "That's All Right" and Peel to go off to Radio One to work.

John Peel adored punk, as it was primitive, anti-establishment, and – pointedly – new and young. He liked the basic warts-and-all quality of punk, the rough and ready aspect. He had championed both the Sex Pistols' "Anarchy In The UK" and "God Save The Queen" on his show, when it was almost impossible to hear them anywhere else. He became evangelical about the genre, and even after being physically threatened by the Sex Pistols' Sid Vicious at a gig in the West End he embraced each new release with an enthusiasm he hadn't enjoyed since his underground radio show back in the Sixties, *The Perfumed Garden*. Peel's show also fed the music press, and the editors of the *Melody Maker* and *Sounds* set great store by what he played on his late-night Radio One show.

Yet it had been Elvis who had turned Peel's head when he was a boy. The moment he heard "Heartbreak Hotel" on the BBC's *Two-Way Family Favourites* in 1956 (hosted by Jean Metcalfe and Cliff Michelmore, the show was conceived to reunite "our boys overseas" with their families at home, and listened to by sixteen million people), the sixteen-year-old Peel was smitten.

"It sounds idiotic to say it now," Peel remembered in 1998, "but it was a revelation, just like being transported to another planet. The only thing that came close was when I heard Little Richard a few weeks later. It was genuinely frightening.

"'Heartbreak Hotel' had the effect on me of a naked extra-terrestrial walking through the door and announcing that he/she was going to live with me for the rest of my life. As Elvis walked in, Frankie Laine and Johnnie Ray tiptoed out and nothing was ever the same again."

That day became firmly etched on his memory; he went into Liverpool and bought the record at Cranes, opposite Central Station.

In 1977, Tony Parsons was one of the *NME's* star writers, hired, along with Julie Burchill, who later (albeit briefly) became his wife, to interpret punk for the paper's readers. The *NME* was where Parsons made his name, interviewing everyone from the Sex Pistols to Iggy Pop, and the Buzzcocks to Johnny Thunders. Tony became synonymous with punk, although ironically his career has lasted a lot longer than most of the people he interviewed back then. Twenty-eight years later he wrote a *roman à clef* about his time at the paper, called *Stories We Could Tell*, and he set it in London on the night Elvis died. As the protagonist Terry rubbernecks in the basement of a nightclub called the Western World in Neal Street – the Roxy, as was – "five thousand miles away, behind the gates of a great house in Memphis, Tennessee, a forty-two-year-old man was taking his dying breath."

Parsons dramatises the Danny Baker story, setting it in an old-fashioned discothèque rather than a punk club. But the drama is just as intense.

"'Ladies and gentlemen, boys and girls,' the DJ said, uncertain of the tone he should adopt, and sounding both solemn and facetious. 'The King is dead.' No reaction on the dancefloor. 'That's right – we just heard that Elvis Presley died tonight.'"

And then the crowd begins to cheer ...

Like Baker, Parsons is a huge Elvis fan, and his portrait of the man was tender and respectful.

"Without Elvis, the Beatles would never have left Liverpool," he wrote, at the time of the novel's publication. "Without Elvis, Madonna would be a teacher in Detroit. Without Elvis, white music would have stayed timid, and black music would have stayed underground. He was an uneducated white boy from the Deep South, and yet he did something truly remarkable – he redrew the map of modern music.

"There are plenty of places in America where they have forgotten all about your Princess Diana. But everyone still remembers Elvis. Elvis is not remembered because he had a taste for junk food, high-collared jumpsuits and Vegas schmaltz. He is not remembered because he died at the age of forty-two on a toilet, the saddest man in the universe.

"Elvis is remembered, truly remembered, for what he did when he was that young man, the Memphis Flash ... Whatever our age, we have all grown up with Elvis in the background, and it is difficult to think of him as a human being. Sometimes Elvis seems to share more in common with a Disney character than one of the dead Beatles.

"But there was a real man behind all of these cartoons, and that is why so much of his music was infused with a rich, complex, vibrant humanity. And it's strange that the image of Elvis that persists is Elvis at the end of his troubled life, Elvis with one foot in a Graceland grave, because nobody has ever made music so full of life. He was loved because he was full of life."

In Parsons' book, Covent Garden – the old fruit and vegetable market, and the home of the Roxy – still looked like the surface of the moon, an old bombsite in search of a shopping mall. "I remember how old fashioned the world was back then," said Parsons. "There were Teds in the street, and dance music was still very much underground. The modern world – *Saturday Night Fever*, good restaurants and Mrs. Thatcher – were still around the corner."

London was sopping wet that summer's evening, as it had started raining in the afternoon and hadn't stopped. It just rained and rained and rained, and the heavens wept. Over twenty factories were affected, along with twenty shops, several schools and churches, a few railway stations and over a thousand homes, some of which were flooded to depths of nearly five feet. Over forty thousand home telephones were disconnected, as London turned into a third-world swamp. The weather matched the mood of the city. There really was a sense of shock and disbelief about Elvis dying. Suddenly we realised that the post-war rock'n'roll generation would get old and die – just like everybody else. "Elvis dying was the first intimation of mortality among people who thought you either died young or got to live forever," said Parsons. The idea of Elvis would last forever, but not the man.

Punks themselves had an equivocal relationship with Elvis, with many of them despising everything he stood for. In his lyrics for the Clash song "1977," Joe Strummer had recently written "No Elvis, Beatles or the Rolling Stones, in 1977," and this became one of punk's most abiding slogans. The Adverts, who had just released their macabre classic "(Looking Through) Gary Gilmore's Eyes," played a club called Tiffany's in Stockbridge, in Edinburgh, a week after Elvis died. A number of punks who had taken the Clash's words to heart turned up with photocopied portraits of Elvis pinned to their T-shirts, with his eyes torn out. For the punks in the audience that night, Elvis's death was like the gold statue of an old Eastern European city being toppled by the mob in the market square, its head kicked down the street, a small boy standing on its plinth, waving a pro-democracy flag for the benefit of the six o'clock news. In Elvis's case, though, it would have been a gold lamé statue.

The bouncers in Tiffany's, confused and disgusted by the punks in equal measure, reacted savagely to the T-shirts, beating up many of those whom they eventually let in.

At the time Elvis seemed to belong to the past. There was almost nothing about his life that appealed to a British teenager. Even though rock'n'roll was barely twenty years old, Elvis might as well have been Al Jolson. He was from another era, one that appeared to have little relevance in 1977. When Strummer dismissed Elvis, the Beatles and the Rolling Stones, he was referring to the old wave of institutionalised rock icons, the tsunami of nostalgia acts who were still parading around the world as though they were still in their prime. He did so at the behest of Clash manager Bernie Rhodes, who wanted the group to be more political and outspoken, and thus distance themselves from the outrageous but less overtly political Pistols. In reality, the Stones were the principal focus of Strummer's ire, as the Beatles had broken up, and Elvis was no longer topical. The Stones were prime targets as they were considered by many to be a hoary old rock cliché, dinosaurs from a different time and place. The Stones were still out there, treading the boards and trying to be relevant, while Elvis had long since given up anything approaching relevance. In a sense he really was living in a parallel universe – back then, that was what Las Vegas was actually like.

Almost as soon as he became famous, Elvis had been cocooned – first by the Army, then by the movies, and finally by Vegas. Each stage took him further away from his audience, even though it should have been the other way round. In the Army, he was largely invisible, posted abroad and available only through his records and the occasional film. In the movies he was available to anyone who could afford a cinema ticket, distant but ever-present. So being in Vegas, actually live, in the flesh, in front of a real-life audience, should have brought him closer to his fans. But in reality he was as far away as he ever was, as he ever had been, which served to remind everyone just how far he had strayed from the original blueprint, and prove once and for all that the old Elvis was gone for good.

For many, Vegas Elvis was already Dead Elvis.

Punk iconoclasts the Fall were playing at the Electric Circus in Manchester the night that Elvis died, and quickly wrote a song in Elvis's honour, "Your Heart Out." "He was a working-class hero to us, so it was a genuine tribute, but it was semi tongue-in-cheek," said the band's guitarist, Martin Bramah. "We weren't breaking our hearts over it. It was all very distant and removed – he was just an idol who died."

Not surprisingly, the Sex Pistols weren't overly perturbed by Elvis's death, either. "I remember it clearly because I wasn't sad," said their guitarist Steve Jones, who was in Wessex Studios performing some additional power chords for the band's forthcoming album *Never Mind The Bollocks Here's The Sex Pistols* when he heard the news. "I just thought I'd better get back and do those guitar overdubs."

John Lydon was rather less circumspect. "He came to represent everything we're trying to react against," he said. "I never wanted to become like Elvis. I don't want to become a fat, rich, sick, reclusive rock star. Elvis was dead before he died, and his gut was so big it cast a shadow over rock'n'roll in the last few years. Our music is what's important now."

Who could be more antipodal to punk than Elvis?

He was revered, though, still treated as a deity by his followers. When writer Nick Kent joined the *NME* from the underground press in the early Seventies, staffer Roy Carr gave him some salient advice: "Don't ever write anything bad about Elvis or you'll get your legs broken." A lot of people read the paper, including a lot of Elvis fans.

The day after Elvis's death, several hundred fans congregated in London's Trafalgar Square, holding homemade flags ("In Loving Memory," "Elvis R.I.P.") and dancing to the Elvis song "Let's Have A Party." There was a smattering of Teds in the crowd; you can still see them on YouTube, glum in the afternoon sun, and suddenly looking incongruous, as though dinosaurs had been found in London Zoo. At the time there were regular running clashes between punks and slightly older Teddy Boys on the Kings Road. The Teds saw the punks as unnecessary transgressors, and so punks started to see Teds as their cultural enemies. Teds represented orthodoxy, and had transmogrified into the kind of people –

mainly white, working-class men of a certain age – who were suspicious of anything outside their comfort zone, especially punks. The punks actually helped define the Teds for a new generation, as the Teds' antipathy towards the new breed of shorn-haired iconoclasts gave them a new purpose in life, at least initially. Almost acting as cultural policemen, they wanted to stamp out what they considered to be political or sociological degeneracy. Like punks, Teds were defined by their hair, pieces of tonsorial sculpture created by urine-coloured pomade and metal combs. Whether they were sporting an elaborate sausage-roll quiff or a lacquered wave, their hair announced they had arrived and were ready for business. I once saw a group of approximately attired Teddy Boys strolling through a park on the outskirts of London and, seeing that my friends and myself were dressed in similarly approximate punk clothes, they had hastily scribbled "Punks are wit" (sic) on the back of one of their leather jackets, in chalk, and in disgust.

During 1976 and early 1977, Elvis became something of a talismanic figure, with a number of punk's more illustrious figures adopting his style and flaunting his image on button badges and T-shirts. Elvis might have been an icon primed for desecration by a new generation of rebels, but for some of those rebels he was, at least in his earliest incarnation, still a hero.

Joe Strummer was photographed in his kitchen for the music paper *Sounds* in his west London flat just before Christmas 1976 wearing an Elvis T-shirt. At this stage in the Clash's career it was actually confrontational to wear anything associated with Elvis. It would have been so for any punk band, but for a group of their stature, this blatant appropriation of rock'n'roll imagery was positively antagonistic, like wearing a pair of crepe-soled brothel creepers. "We were almost Stalinist in the way that you had to shed all your friends, or everything that you'd known, or every way that you'd played before," said Strummer. "I'd like to think the Clash were revolutionaries, but we loved a bit of posing as well. Where's the hair gel? We can't start the revolution 'til someone finds the hair gel!"

Clothes became paramount: trousers had to be narrow, while haircuts needed to be short. Strummer regularly teased journalists about their sartorial shortcomings. When he was interviewed by Kris Needs, one of the many writers who had long based his look on Keith Richards circa 1971, Strummer disappeared under the pub table and stared at his flares. "What do you call those, then?" Fashion, like your musical tastes and your friends, needed to be exact. You were either on the bus, or off the bus. When the Clash were first interviewed by *Sniffin' Glue*, Strummer uttered his immortal phrase, "Like trousers, like brain."

For many people in the punk movement, the appetite for destroying rock'n'roll dinosaurs, from Elvis to Pink Floyd, was simply an easy way to show allegiance to the new gang. Before punk, Wire's Colin Newman had been a "total hippie," into Neil Young, Traffic and Stevie Wonder; so too had Poly Styrene of X-Ray Spex. Dismissing the past was the same as dyeing your hair: a ruse to get noticed. To be a true punk, you not only had to express a hatred of most of what had gone before – musically, at least – but to deny any virtuoso tendencies in yourself. "To be a musician went against the whole idea," said Chrissie Hynde of the Pretenders. "The minute anyone got serious about their musicality, they lost what was interesting about the punk scene." You were obliged to assume a confrontational attitude; the swastikas initially worn by Siouxsie Sioux weren't "badges of intolerance" but "symbols of provocation." It also helped if you had cast-iron working class credentials. Joe Strummer didn't, so he had to make them up, like so many rock stars in the past. Strummer was the son of a diplomat, yet to talk to him you'd think he'd been brought up in the docks. He was the world's greatest rock'n'roll front man, yet he was a worse mockney than Mick Jagger, and spoke as though he were trying to talk like someone of limited intelligence. John Lydon, a genuine working-class Londoner, always thought Strummer's voice was preposterous; he sounded as though he was underwater, as though all the stress of being a working-class rebel could be alleviated simply by adopting the voice of a barrow boy. Strummer's persona was one of the most indelible and most cherished in punk, but in some respects it was completely false. Strummer was a manic, pompadoured public-school troubadour with sloganeering Tourette's, a man who disguised his voice so much he was actually difficult to understand. He wrapped himself in an accent as thick as a pair of Seditionaries bondage strides – as he put it himself, "I sound like someone speaking Arabic through silt at the bottom of the Nile".

Strummer was half way to being Elvis already, on a journey that culminated when he appeared in Jim Jarmusch's 1989 movie *Mystery Train*. Using Elvis as its central motif, the film was a triptych of stories set in a dilapidated hotel in downtown Memphis, overseen by a night clerk played by Screamin' Jay Hawkins, and featuring a portrait of Elvis in every room. The first story centres on a teenage couple from Yokohama making a pilgrimage to Memphis, one of whom is obsessed with Elvis and believes in a mystical connection between Elvis, Madonna and the Statue of Liberty. The second story involves a widow visited by an apparition of Elvis, while in the final part Strummer plays a character actually called "Elvis," and holds up a liquor store.

Punk's disdain for old-fashioned rock'n'roll culture was riddled with contradictions. As Marcus Gray says in *Route 19 Revisited: The Clash And The Making Of London Calling*, "However he cut his hair and overhauled his wardrobe, Joe Strummer still performed like a hot-wired Eddie Cochran. Even by early 1977 he had started slicking his hair back on his nights off and regularly attending rock'n'roll revival shows … out of town. Johnny Rotten's microphone technique was pure Gene Vincent (via Ian Dury). And when Johnny left the Pistols, Malcolm McLaren would keep the rump of the band in the charts by having Sid Vicious gurn his way through a couple of Eddie Cochran songs."

As Gray also points out, in 1978 Strummer was asked by the American filmmaker Diego Cortez to provide a cover version of "Heartbreak Hotel" for a never-released film called *Grutzi Elvis* (*Hello, Elvis*), which took its inspiration from the "approximate synchronicity" of Elvis's death and the emergence of punk. He was also considering getting the Clash to record a whole album of covers, including Bobby Fuller's "I Fought The Law," Vince Taylor's "Brand New Cadillac," Johnny Burnette's "Train Kept A Rollin'" and Elvis's "Crawfish," from the 1958 movie *King Creole*.

While gearing up to record *London Calling*, the band as a whole started taking a lot more interest in Fifties rock'n'roll. They even considered calling their new album *The New Testament*, on which they would add some punk ballast to old rock'n'roll staples (*The Old Testament* obviously being Elvis's first album – duh!). The Clash stepped back from a full-blown homage, but still embraced traditional rock'n'roll by recording a stunning version of "Brand New Cadillac". The cover of *London Calling* was a deliberate homage to Elvis's first LP cover, and echoed its style and design in its typography and colour scheme. As many have pointed out, including historian and author Howard Sounes, on the original cover Elvis is seen holding his guitar aloft, heroically, setting out on a great new musical adventure; on the Clash's cover, bassist Paul Simonon is shown smashing his bass on the stage, dealing rock'n'roll a much-needed death blow.

"I'd chucked my basses around before and didn't have any respect for them in the first place," said Simonon. "The moment I got a new bass I'd get a hammer and start bashing it around, digging bits out. I saw it as a tool, that's all. We were playing the Palladium in New York and there was a lot of tension, it felt like we were playing London. Getting near the end of the show I was feeling that nothing was complete. I didn't feel satisfied. Possibly because the audience was restricted to sitting down and couldn't get up and dance, even though we always stressed that whenever we played the audience should stand up and be close to the front. It made me feel empty and out of frustration I pulled the bass off and bashed it around – because there's been no interaction with the audience, which is what we as a group thrived on. Pennie Smith took the photograph of that."

As Simonon was smashing his bass onto the stage, a girl leapt up from the audience and ran behind him, swiftly followed by a member of the US road crew. Before he could reach her, lead guitarist Mick Jones stepped in and whisked her to safety, leaving the stage with her as Topper Headon's drum kit exploded into the orchestra pit, having been disturbed by all the commotion. This all happened in the space of three minutes. "The whole thing felt like a scene from a movie," said Jones.

According to roadie Johnny Green, Simonon was simply showing off for Blondie's Debbie Harry, who happened to be in the audience that night.

The *London Calling* cover came about through Strummer's

fondness for the *NME* cartoons of Ray Lowry, himself an old rocker who used to place Elvis in increasingly unlikely situations in his comic strips. He struck up a relationship with the cartoonist, and even invited him on an American tour, as a kind of 2HB Boswell. One Lowry missive from the tour was an *NME* cartoon that featured a reproduction of Elvis's eponymous album, with THE CLASH replacing ELVIS PRESLEY in the chunky block type around the LP's left and bottom sides. "The Elvis tone of things was set by the band's own mutation into greasers, and a copy of the first Elvis album that I picked up for six dollars in Wax Trax in Chicago," said Lowry. His graphics and Pennie Smith's portrait of Simonon resulted in the final cover, the frustrated flipside of Elvis's exultant debut.

The album was promoted by full-page ads in the music papers featuring a photograph of Elvis in his gold lamé jacket holding a copy of the album. "Strummer came up with the press ads idea," said Lowry. "At the time, I thought we might get some trouble with that one, but – as far as I know – nothing ensued. Shows you how much the boy went along with the rock'n'roll thing, which at the time I thought might be pushing it a bit."

If you were ever lucky enough to see Strummer around town – and if you lived in London spotting famous punks became something of a spectator sport: "Look, there's Billy Idol ..." "There, coming out of the Gents – Hugh Cornwell ..." "The drummer in the Banshees just came up the stairs ..." – he always looked like a Teddy Boy on speed, with bad teeth and a bouffant quiff. The roadies and the hangers-on were the ones who dressed like generic punks – Mick Jones tended to channel Mott The Hoople or a member of a US heavy metal band, while Strummer was the angry Ted.

I saw Strummer once, in late 1977, in the upstairs bar of The Cambridge pub in Cambridge Circus, and he looked like the meanest Teddy Boy you could ever hope to cross. Of course, I was a naive seventeen-year-old who didn't know that Strummer was a public schoolboy desperately trying to talk like a docker, but nevertheless he still looked like one of Elvis's bodyguards. Even his hair was identikit Ted. The band were always worried about being able to escape the punk pigeonhole, and Strummer found the easiest exit through the door marked "1956," taking a step back before making another forward – both strides involving bright white leather brothel creepers.

Many people involved in punk were from respectable families, and had been brought up well and gone to good schools. All of which had to be disguised, as everyone needed street credibility in order to play.

"I know in America people think it ridiculous that one can fight to the death over articles of clothing, but in these islands it's a different story," said Joe Strummer. Teddy Boys were rock'n'rollers, so named after their Edwardian dress style, and punks came in and took the Teddy Boy jackets, which were lovely – long, fingertip-length with moleskin lapels – and ripped them and put safety pins in them.

Johnny Rotten was particularly good at decorating a jacket.

Rotten used to enjoy "quiffing" his hair up and dressing like a Teddy Boy. They were "the enemy. Therefore they interested me. So I'd go to the Teddy Boys' gigs. They'd know who I was, but they would think it was funny that this horrible king of punks was sitting there among them with a better quiff." Rotten's attempts to flout an already understood convention almost backfired when he was nearly beaten up by a punk tourist at the Roxy who didn't recognise him, for "looking like a Ted."

According to Strummer, "Teddy Boys didn't like punks because they thought it was disrespectful what they were doing to their clothes. Which I suppose it was. And for one summer in 1976 it was fairly dangerous to walk the streets of London dressed as a punk, especially on Saturday afternoons on the Kings Road, although you'd get involved with Teddy Boys on any day, really. It was their last stand, though, they were blown away by it all. They were the old thing and punk was the new and there was never going to be a real contest."

The Clash once did a show at the University of London with Shakin' Stevens. There were Teds everywhere, who didn't like the band one bit. "After our set we were in the dressing room and a bunch of them tried to get in and have a punch-up," said Paul Simonon. "Joe and I tore Coke cans in half so we had a jagged half in each hand. We said, 'Alright come on then,' and opened the door for them but when they came in and saw the cans they figured that we were going to do them so they backed out of the room again."

Joe Strummer was beaten up in the toilets at the Speakeasy club, a young Boy George was punched in the face for wearing brothel creepers, and punks of both sexes were regularly kicked or head-butted for daring to wear drape jackets. The Teds had no qualms about beating up punkettes, either. June Waller was on her way to the Roxy one night when four Teds flagged down the bus she was on. "Nobody helped me as I was a punk," she said, "not even the conductor. They ripped my drape (asking for it, I know! But then I didn't envisage bumping into them when I pulled it on), [and] I held onto to the bars of the bus for dear life. They battered me senseless and nicked my studded belt! I spat blood from my split lip at them, which did splatter everybody else on the bus. I kicked, yelled abuse and acted like a real head-case, which I probably was in those days. Who would have thought that four strapping Teds couldn't handle one little punkette!"

The war of attrition between the punks and the Teds became so pronounced that various people tried to build bridges between the two factions. Leee Black Childers, who at the time was managing Johnny Thunders & The Heartbreakers as well as the rockabilly band Levi & The Rockats, was beaten up by some punks at a Boomtown Rats gig just a month before Elvis died, having been mistaken for a Ted. So incensed was he that he announced a joint "Ted/punk" concert featuring the Heartbreakers and Shakin' Stevens at the Global Village in London's Charing Cross. However the gig was swiftly cancelled due to concerns that it would turn into a bloodbath.

The following year, with tensions still running high, and as a way to publicise their single "Eddie & Sheena," about a love affair between a Ted and a punk, Wayne County & The Electric Chairs did a few gigs with Levi & The Rockats. The vain hope was that if Teds and Punks started hanging out and watching bands together, they might realise they had more in common than they imagined.

DJ Jay Strongman saw a couple of dates on the tour. The one he remembers best was at the Music Machine in Camden. "Both bands were great but being a sartorial cross-dresser at the time (quiff hairdo and biker jacket with Gene Vincent t-shirt, bondage trousers and Seditionaries boots), I missed out on the benefits of non-violence the gig was supposed to be all about. Threatened in the gig by newbie punk thugs sporting Mohican haircuts as a 'fucking Ted,' almost mugged by skinhead half-wits outside the gig and having to do a runner from a gang of moronic bottle-wielding Teds for being a 'fucking punk' whilst waiting for a night bus, I began to appreciate the saying that 'the road to hell is paved with good intentions.'"

This attrition actually helped bind the many disparate strands of punk together.

As Strummer recalled, "To begin with, things were really friendly between the Pistols and the Clash and it only got unfriendly when Malcolm [McLaren] realised that by preventing them playing they'd become more famous and they didn't like it, especially when we were out there doing it. They probably thought we were stealing their thunder and animosity built up. But at this time punk rock was the best time, when you had to be in league with each other because there were so many enemies out there. We'd play art schools and the audience would throw wine bottles at us, trying to fracture our skulls. I can't over-emphasize how people were against punk. Not just Teddy Boys, it was incredibly vicious and dangerous. It was circle the wagons time."

The war of attrition between the punks and the Teds continued throughout 1978. On the first anniversary of Elvis's death, the Buzzcocks were playing at Torquay Town Hall, in Devon, an event the local Teds thought completely inappropriate. How dare they? How dare these skinny, funny-haired ingrates sully Elvis's "deathday"? The portly snaggle-toothed Neanderthals, in their over-dyed brothel creepers, Carnaby Street bootlace ties and mail order drapes, thought it was inflammatory that all the punks would be coming in that day on little country buses from the likes of Newton Abbot and Ipplepen and Marlden and Ottery St Mary. How damn rude! A year ago, the only band they got to see with any regularity was the Adverts, who were almost local, but now that punk had gone nationwide, dozens of groups were touring each month, eager to cash in, many coming down to Torbay, the "English Riviera." But this was too much – fancy partying on the King's deathday!? The Teds were so fired up that they spent most of the afternoon running after and beating up any punk they could find. Anyone with dyed hair or make-up was fair game, even the girls. The punks had come into town early to trawl the record shops, but there was a terrifying hour after they closed and before the town hall opened when they had to hide or take shelter in case they were caught. Bus shelters. Cinemas. Parks. Under pub awnings. Anywhere would do, anywhere they could find. They were in the city now, and even though Torquay was hardly London, it was still oppressive, still a town of dank dark alleys, dead-ends and pub brawls. In this respect Devon was a little like West Virginia, dead poor and rural, with the Teds acting as local white-trash vigilante groups, and with the punks going out of their way to treat their hero, Elvis, as the anti-Christ.

In London in 1977, Elvis tropes could be found everywhere. Besides being the principal DJ at the Roxy club, where he had pioneered the idea of playing reggae, Don Letts also ran a clothes stall called Acme Attractions in Antiquarius in the Kings Road, which was one of the very few places the new breed could buy their street and stage gear. Sex Pistol Sid Vicious had bought a gold lamé jacket from Letts, under the illusion that Elvis had owned it.

"I still laugh at that," said Letts. "He wanted the jacket, then he wasn't sure it fit him perfectly, so I mentioned that it had been owned by Elvis, purely on a wind-up, and he bought it, in more ways than one."

The jacket had actually belonged to Keith Moon, who had worn it in the film *Stardust*. After Sid bought it, the jacket went on to be worn by John Lydon and Viv Albertine from the all-girl punk band, the Slits.

Joe Strummer saw Vicious in the jacket a few days later, when the Pistols supported the 101'ers, the pub-rock group he soon left to join the Clash, at the Nashville Rooms in west London. Strummer was blown away not only by the Pistols themselves – "When I saw them I realised you couldn't compare the Pistols to any other group on the island, they were so far ahead" – but by the way they looked, and in particular by Vicious' jacket.

"Oi, where'd you get that jacket?" asked Strummer, expecting a mouthful.

"Oh, it's really good innit?" said Vicious. "I'll tell you where I got it, you know that stall ..."

A few years later, Malcolm McLaren even started calling Sid Vicious the "new Elvis": "A surrogate Elvis Presley of punk rock, Sid was everything everyone else was not. He never saw a red light, only green."

McLaren even had designs on filling Elvis's boots, quite literally. In 1979, while Vicious was awaiting trial for the murder of his girlfriend Nancy Spungen, McLaren was having various conversations with Las Vegas promoters about taking a residency there when he was acquitted. "Sid's trial was going to cost a fortune and with the Sex Pistols' account drained, I thought this was an excellent new adventure and money-maker," said McLaren.

The cultural intransigence of the Teds was one reason why John Lydon would wear a drape jacket in his early performances with the Sex Pistols, subverting something which was already so old-fashioned and established. In 1978, Richard Branson, the founder of Virgin Records, went on a trip to Jamaica, with the express purpose of signing some reggae acts for his label. He invited Don Letts along, as well as Lydon, who he knew had been at a loose end since leaving the Sex Pistols. Branson wanted to visit some of the sound systems in Trenchtown, which at the time was a fairly dangerous thing to do if you were a white tourist. Branson and Lydon knew they would be all right as soon as they stepped through immigration. As they walked outside to find a taxi, a group of Rastas started pointing at Lydon and shouting, "Hey! Johnny Rotten! God save the Queen!"

Lydon looks like a different person in the photographs taken on the island – calm and relaxed in some, and quietly apprehensive in others. A mixture of the climate, the ganja and being away from the British media completely put him at ease. Yet he still looks like an extraordinary character, not least because of the red pointed Robot brothel creepers he is wearing in every shot. At the time, Lydon was a genuine sartorial iconoclast, and his appropriation of the traditional Teddy Boy footwear not only diffused their power, but also amplified it.

The whole sartorial mess was cyclical, not that it was in anyone's interest to point this out at the time. Joe Strummer, for example, copied a lot of his on-stage "passionate" persona from Bruce Springsteen, a man who had in turn taken so much from Elvis in the first place. The Clash had to be seen to be going out of their way to disparage anyone who had been before them, and yet Strummer had already proved that he was a massive Springsteen fan. After seeing Springsteen at the Hammersmith Odeon in 1975, Strummer had immediately started incorporating his sweat and muscle into the 101'ers. "Bruce is great," he would say, "and if you don't agree with that, you're a pretentious Martian from Venus and you don't understand rock'n'roll. Bruce is the man, just like Elvis was the man."

Years after punk, in 1989 to be precise, Malcolm McLaren admitted to writer Jon Savage that Elvis had actually been an inspiration behind the Sex Pistols. "The irresponsible nature of it all was the key to it, and once people started becoming responsible … we prevented it becoming responsible for as long as we could hold out. You never wanted to be part of the New Wave, rock'n'roll liberal tradition, looking like you were doing good things. I never believed that was behind Eddie

Cochran, or Elvis Presley. Elvis Presley was a punk rocker, and so was Gene Vincent. So was Marilyn Monroe. So was anybody who was irresponsible and lived their lives in a way that you felt bigger, bolder and better than you could. They were punks, they were anti-establishment, and they were gods. Marilyn Monroe today is bigger than ever, and so is Sid Vicious. I don't see Johnny Rotten in the Lower East Side on a T-shirt. I see Sid Vicious all the bloody time. That's got to be the difference."

McLaren had started out, along with his girlfriend Vivienne Westwood, as the brains behind a series of shops at 430 Kings Road, starting with Let It Rock in 1971, which sold secondhand and new Teddy Boy clothes, designed by Westwood. Westwood and McLaren's clothes weren't meant to service the Teds; they were meant to act as ironic distortions of them. They deliberately plundered and misappropriated them for comic effect. The whole idea was almost like an installation, with their customers acting as walking billboards. This was less about the bruised lips and blue-black quiff of Elvis and all his lookalikes, and more about the youth culture symbolism of the clothes themselves. Which is why both McLaren and Westwood found it so easy to move their collections into greasy rocker-wear, sex-wear, and finally the transformative clothes that gave birth to punk. Although according to McLaren, who spent the first half of the Seventies dancing around in brothel creepers, and the second half parading around in leather drainpipes, "Punk was just a way to sell trousers."

The address was already infamous as the former site of Tommy Roberts' Pop Art fashion emporium Mr. Freedom. That had been bought by entrepreneur Trevor Myles, who turned it into Paradise Garage, a retro shop specialising in boiler suits and Hawaiian shirts, in which McLaren had a small shop-within-a-shop selling records and old Teddy Boy clothes. Myles sold out to McLaren, who promptly launched Let It Rock. This was an era when the hippy movement was still unfolding its flowery power and rock'n'roll in the traditional sense was temporarily off the airwaves. It was at that moment in 1971 that Let it Rock started selling its Fifties memorabilia and vinyl. Elvis was forging a recovery and fans from all over the UK were searching for pegged trousers and brothel creepers as a revival took hold. McLaren called the shop a "fraudulent haberdashers," as the drape coats that he designed were made up by an East End tailor, and the mohair jumpers and drainpipe trousers by a local seamstress.

"I used to drive Malcolm around in Vivienne Westwood's car to the tailors in London in the days of Let It Rock," remembers Sex Pistols' guitarist Steve Jones. "Malcolm was definitely the Brian Epstein of punk – without him it wouldn't have happened the way it did. My fondest memory of Malcolm, and I loved the guy, was his birthday gift to me when I turned 21 – he got me a hooker and some heroin."

McLaren would parade around the store dressed to the nines in Ted attire. He was nostalgic for the rebelliousness of the Fifties, looking back to a time when the demob suit, the snap-brimmed trilby and the insurance salesman's raincoat were cast aside for the loose-fitting vividly coloured jackets and zoot suits of the American jazz bands – a style that eventually resulted in "Ted."

According to McLaren, "It was black, we had a juke-box [playing classics by Gene Vincent, Elvis and Buddy Holly] and in the back room we devised a whole Willesden front room set, where the Teddy Boys would have been sitting watching TV with their old ladies. Brylcreem in the cocktail cabinet. Photographs of James Dean, Elvis Presley and Eddie Cochran, piles of old magazines."

A living Klapholz installation.

Like many of his peers, McLaren couldn't fail to be influenced by Elvis's generation. When he was in art school, McLaren had even tried to make a documentary about Billy Fury, whom he considered to be the only bona fide British rocker. It was the attitude of the music rather than the music itself that appealed to him, an attitude he tried to mirror in Let It Rock. Although he had little time for the Teds themselves, he loved their bad behaviour, and the shop became legendary for its clientele as well as its schmutter.

The staff would treat the customers abysmally – you were lucky if they ignored you.

"Very heavy it was," said McLaren once, talking like a Dickensian Yoda. "No one'd dare come in the place unless they were Teds. Mick Jagger stood outside the shop for half an hour once and never came in. Ringo Starr was the only one who dared to actually come in on a Saturday. But I had to do all the deliveries – I thought it was the customary thing for Kings Road shops to do until I realised everyone was too scared to come inside the shop."

Jagger actually did come in once. McLaren had commissioned a T-shirt saying, "You're gonna wake up one morning and know what side of the bed you've been lying on!," with a list of people who were deemed to be happening and a list of those who very much weren't happening. Jagger came in one day, saw the T-shirt and said, "Ooh, I'm on the wrong side!"

The Kings Road site was chosen as a gesture, as McLaren wanted to place a bomb in the middle of what he saw as the oh-so-smug post-Sixties vibe pervading Chelsea. Shepherd's Bush would have made more sense, but the Kings Road drew more attention.

"I remember when Iggy Pop and James Williamson used

to come in all the time [the Stooges were living in London then, recording *Raw Power* with David Bowie], asking for such-and-such a record," said McLaren. "I'd tell 'em to get out. I thought they were a couple of bleeding hippies then.

"It took the [New York] Dolls to really turn my head around, so to speak. I mean, one day – I'd never heard of them before – they all trouped into the shop in their high-heeled shoes and I was immediately impressed by the way they handled themselves. I mean, there were all these Teds hanging around thinking what the hell are these geezers doing here? But the Dolls didn't care at all. David [Johanssen] just went ahead and tried on a drape jacket while Johnny [Thunders] was over by the [AMI] jukebox looking for some Eddie Cochran records. I was really taken aback."

McLaren went on to briefly manage the band before setting his sights on what became the Sex Pistols.

Let It Rock was a mausoleum of high style, announcing itself through a window display containing a black T-shirt decorated with chain and chicken-bone lettering spelling out the name of the shop. "Teddy Boys for Ever! The Rock Era Is Our Business!" yelled the store's advertising brochure, readily exploiting the tribal nature of youth culture.

As Vivienne Westwood remembers it, "Malcolm was terribly, terribly intense about that shop, but then he got fed up with it, disillusioned with the Teddy Boys, number one, because although they were some expression of revolt against society, all they really wanted was free clothes and giveaways from the record companies. But number two, they were a cult, and cults want rules and all they ever wanted to know was that they were doing everything right. And he wasn't interested in that, so the shop got into something else."

Let It Rock became a magnet for anyone looking for something new as well as a focal point for the middle-aged ex-Ted whose insistence on authenticity was as strong as his memory. At the time there was also something of a renaissance in Fifties rock'n'roll, reflected in the success of groups like the American band Sha Na Na and the risibly derivative Showaddywaddy. The shop's success eventually caused McLaren to drift off to New York, leaving Westwood to run it; he had grown tired of the Teddy Boy revivalists stealing goods and threatening the customers as he revealed to *Vice* magazine:

"I did it [dressing up as a Ted] as an act of revolt against the hippies. I made myself a blue suit, copying the cover of an old Elvis Presley record, and I walked down the Kings Road to try and do something with my life. I wanted to be exploited but no cunt would even look at me! I was brought up in a family that worked in fashion and I had my art school hooligan imagination. The two came together and I set out to create anti-fashion."

In 1973 Let It Rock turned into Too Fast To Live, Too Young To Die, which it stayed for a year before turning into Sex a year later, and then Seditionaries in 1976. Since 1980 the shop has been called World's End; it still has its famous clock on the outside of the building, with a second hand that spins forever backwards.

During punk, traditional rock'n'roll Elvis tropes were everywhere. Richard Hell, lead singer of the New York proto-punk band the Voidoids – whose lifestyle manifesto involved post-modern nihilism – even adopted Elvis's trademark lip-curl.

At the time of his death, the King, the Teds' own personal deity, had recently been usurped and undermined in another, very particular way, too, by a nerdy-looking upstart called Elvis Costello. A former computer programmer called Declan MacManus who fancied himself as a singer-songwriter, he acquired his new name at the prompting of his manager at the newly formed Stiff Records, Jake Riviera. "How are we going to separate you from Johnny This and Johnny That?" asked Riviera, not unreasonably. Hence Elvis Costello, a combination of Elvis Presley's first name and the stage name of Declan's bandleader father.

Costello was an immediate hit with critics and public alike, and for a while in the early summer of 1977, whenever anyone in the music industry mentioned Elvis, you assumed they were referring to the young pretender. Punk's scarecrow singer-songwriter quickly became a televisual pop star, a conceptual bandleader who turned his short stories – lacerating tales of romantic frustration, political expediency, hapless social climbing and all the rest – into classic three-minute pop singles.

For a while the idea of Elvis Costello seemed incendiary, almost revolutionary. How dare he steal Elvis's name? How dare he try to marginalise the King? Because none of us knew that Costello was allowed to legitimately use this surname, we just thought he had stolen that too: what was that about, mixing a rock'n'roll hero with one half of a superannuated comedy duo? What's more, the fact that Costello's marketing revolved around an angry-young-man schtick made him appear far more aggressive than he actually was, almost as though he was using his appropriated Christian name as a weapon. When Presley died, Costello's song "(The Angels Wanna Wear My) Red Shoes," which had actually been written months before, looked as though it was simply rubbing salt into the wound. How on Earth could he write that about the King?

Compared to so many artists' names of 1976-7, Elvis Costello retrospectively looks like a moniker crafted for longevity but at the time it was a shrewd, calculated provocation, not any sort of musical homage. Costello was later to tell *Details* magazine his parents' views on rock'n'roll, that they, "didn't think it was very groovy, and I tend to agree with them. If you grew up with Charlie Parker, Bill Haley wasn't very hip." Or the Elvis Presley of 1977 for that matter. Yet as time has gone on Costello (always hard to pigeonhole) seems to have grown more interested in his namesake. He has performed Presley songs, even used a couple of the King's former backing musicians and admiringly referred to Peter Guralnick's two volume biography of Presley. But back in 1977 the lack of cultural relevance *was* the point.

For many of a certain age, Costello was the only Elvis that mattered. "It was the summer holidays, I was sixteen, and I was throwing shapes at a midweek dance in the local yacht club," said the journalist Neil McCormick, about that fateful August. "The DJ played 'Way Down' over and over and kept saying things like, 'The King is dead.' News travelled slower in those days. It didn't sink in until we were walking home, a gaggle of kids trailing along the sea wall on a dark night, singing 'Way Down,' chattering about the impossibility of death, still young enough to struggle with the notion that a great star like that, such a permanent fixture in all our lives, could just blink out of existence. I know there would have been an element of provocation in my own response. Elvis wasn't my king, he was the movie star who went to Vegas and got fat. I had fixed my flag to punk rock and thought the only Elvis that really mattered was Elvis Costello. But even in my teenage cynicism, I was shocked enough for the moment to be fixed in my mind forever. This is what I see when I think of the death of Elvis, not the great rock star on a toilet in Memphis, but a gang of Irish boys on a harbour wall, lamplights, night sky and the dark sea."

Just a few days after Elvis's death, Costello set out his own manifesto in the *NME*: "The only two things that matter to me, the only motivation points for me writing all these songs, are revenge and guilt. Those are the only emotions that I know about, that I know I can feel. Love? I dunno what it means, really and it doesn't exist in my songs."

Costello would later experiment with country, soul, rockabilly and even what was still pejoratively called "easy listening," but for the summer of 1977 he was punk's very own bard. Rockabilly briefly became fashionable in 1979, when the Zeitgeist's fairground pellet-gun alighted on the likes of Johnny Burnette, having moved on from New Wave, power pop and ska. In those days everything was fashionable for five minutes, so there was no reason not to alight on rock'n'roll music for a while. However rockabilly was only trendy for a few months, as most post-punks found it reductive and not a little naff. They just couldn't get the image of Bill Haley – a fat old man with a kiss curl and a big-band blazer – out of their minds.

Elvis Costello was not the first singer to call himself after the King. Ten years previously the Troggs, the British pop band from Andover, had done something similar. As their singer had the decidedly un-rock'n'roll name of Reginald Maurice Ball, their publicist Keith Altham decided to change it in 1966, just as they were starting out. You might think he would have started with the singer's Christian name, but instead Altham changed his surname to the unenviable pseudonym of Presley. The singer found out about his new name when he read a piece about the band in the *NME*, and promptly rang Altham to find out if he'd been dropped.

"All of a sudden [my management] told me to read this article in the paper and I couldn't find it," said Presley. "I phoned them back and I said I can't find it. They told me where and I went, What? You've changed my name to Presley! I said why couldn't you have gotten a less well-known name like Crosby or Sinatra? But, you do grasp it very quick. Everybody starts calling you Presley. You think, Oh, well. And then all of a sudden I have to use his name more than my original name. It grows on you."

The Troggs had half a dozen hits, including the proto-punk rock "Wild Thing," "With A Girl Like You" and the original version of "Love Is All Around," the song that was covered in 1994 by Wet Wet Wet and used in the film *Four Weddings And A Funeral*. They soon faded into obscurity, though, and their reputation became entwined with a bootleg tape of them rehearsing in the late Sixties. A studio engineer had secretly kept the tape rolling while the band were airing musical differences between takes, an hilarious recording which became popular with bands on tour, and was parodied in a scene in Rob Reiner's 1984 comedy *This Is Spinal Tap*. "The Troggs' Tapes," as the bootlegged session became known, begins on an optimistic note, with one member explaining that: "This is a fucking number one. It fucking is. This is a number fucking one, and if this bastard don't go, I fucking retire. I fucking do. Bollocks. But it fucking well won't be unless we spend a little bit of fucking thought and imagination to fucking make it a fucking number one. You've got to sprinkle a little bit of fucking fairy dust over the bastard."

Later, Presley can be heard offering some advice to Ronnie Bond, the band's drummer. "You can say that," Bond responds, "all fucking night. Just shut your fucking mouth for five minutes. Don't keep fucking ranting down that fucking microphone. Fuck me, Reg. Just fuck off and let me keep going fucking through it. I know it ain't fucking right. I can fucking hear it ain't right you fuck. Fuck me. When I fucking hear it in my fucking head, that that's what I've gotta fucking do, then I'll do it. You big pranny."

Ironically the song in question, never released, was entitled "Tranquility." And while the deliberate obfuscation with Reg's surname worked with most people – especially gullible journalists, who would often ask if he was related to Elvis – it didn't work on Paul McCartney, who would always refer to him as "Reg Trogg."

In some ways Elvis's death served to validate punk, as though the movement's collective disdain for all that had come before had been somehow officially recognised. How could anyone argue that rock music had not become bloated and remote, when the man who had practically invented it was found fat and dead on his toilet, in the confines of his secluded mansion, behind enormous electric gates?

In the US, Elvis had nothing to do with punk, and there was no association, pro or con. The New York scene – Richard Hell and the Voidoids, the Ramones, the Heartbreakers, Television, Talking Heads et al – was an expression of the art underground, the downtown crowd, and was less ribald, less political and a lot less tribal. Bands like the Ramones and Blondie were glorified garage bands, just like the Standells, the Stooges and the MC5 before them. US punk was not so much a revolution as simply the continuation of a narrative arc (the Jonathan Richman album that was so revered by the punk fraternity, *The Modern Lovers* – which contained the two-chord classic "Roadrunner" – had actually been recorded in 1972 even though it wasn't released until 1976).

The US punk bands were so different from each other. Take Blondie, whose tongue was firmly in its collective cheek. Even their name was a giveaway – a band called Blondie fronted by a girl who obviously wasn't. Debbie Harry may have been a sex kitten, but she was certainly no bimbo, and she set about exploiting her sexuality before anyone else

111

got a chance. From the beginnings of the group, Harry was always toying with the ambiguity of pop iconography and the implications of sexual role-playing. The endless Monroe comparisons were taken with liberal pinches of salt by both Harry and her boyfriend, band member Chris Stein. The irony was eclipsed when Blondie went on to become one of the most commercially viable pop bands of the late Seventies – the supreme global wet dream. They were also one of the first groups to successfully fuse disco and punk.

Tom Verlaine's Television on the other hand were a fetishist's delight. They were at the apex of the hip New York downtown scene as punk broke, and their 1977 debut album, *Marquee Moon*, was a splendid lurch away from the Neanderthal hubba-hubba-1-2-3-4 of bands like the Ramones and the Heartbreakers. Duelling guitars ("Marquee Moon" itself was over ten minutes long), desperate vocals, and proper outsider status (they were photographed by Robert Mapplethorpe, hung with Patti Smith), Television were pounced upon by any old hippie who couldn't quite cope with the likes of the Sex Pistols and the Damned. If you had spent the early parts of your adolescence trying to build a carapace of cool, there was no way you were suddenly going to pretend to like the oiks who bounced up and down to Eddie and the Hot Rods, so Television were the perfect respite, looking like new wave, sounding like old wave.

Music, said W.H. Auden, "can be made anywhere, is invisible, and does not smell." This was Talking Heads when they started out. They came from New York but could have come from any state; they were deliberately contrary, and decidedly anti "rock." Looking back now, it's difficult to imagine just how shocking Talking Heads were in 1976 and 1977, when they began supporting the likes of the Ramones. Even if the

Ramones were the perfect example of hard-core cartoon punk, they still looked like rockers, as many new bands did at the time: they wore denim jeans, leather jackets and skanky old T-shirts, and gave the impression of never being comfortable anywhere other than the subway, the street, or on stage. Talking Heads looked like architecture students, with button-down shirts, skinny ties and square haircuts. At the dawn of punk, this was almost revolutionary – it was certainly confrontational – as by staring at them for the first time you really had no idea what they were or what they did.

Punk drew a line under everything that had gone before. It promised a new life for all involved, as long as they relinquished their past. In retrospect, of course, it's easy to see the relationship between punk and so much that had come before, including everything from the pub rock scene to the old festival circuit. If you look at the sensibility of record labels such as Stiff and Chiswick, the through-line from amphetamine-fuelled guttersnipes to denim-clad country rockers is immediately apparent; in 1977, however, it helped if you turned a blind eye to the past and carried on with the future.

For punk to work it needed to keep its guard up all the time, as the construct was too brittle for anyone to drop their game face. Consequently it helped if you could pretend to be aggressive, wear confrontational clothes and respond with a sneer whenever you were asked anything. Your attitude needed to be manufactured with care, as to admit weakness or any kind of fallibility could be detrimental to your style. And punk was about nothing if not style. While it was all very well to say that punk was a blank canvas, the epitome of fresh beginnings, it soon developed very particular tropes of its own, ones based entirely on fashion.

With punk, as with every youth cult before it, you were either in or out. Five years previously, Roxy Music and David Bowie had been the very definition of cool, but although many of the original London punks had been instrumental in the club scene that evolved around glam rock, Bowie and Roxy Music, while still considered cooler than any of their peers, had to be momentarily banished as the punk cognoscenti drew their own line in the sand (using the heel of a winkle-picker or a bright red brothel creeper). The primary targets for their ire were the hippies, or at least the last vestiges of the Sixties counter-culture. Long hair, flares, beards, Pink Floyd: the punks hated them all.

And as for Elvis Presley, well, he may as well have been from another planet. Punks could hate aliens just as much as they could hate hippies.

In the summer of 1977 I joined the foundation course at Chelsea School of Art, which was housed in an old primary school building in Bagleys Lane, just off the New Kings Road. Every morning I would walk there from my room at the Ralph West Halls of Residence in Albert Bridge Road, opposite Battersea Park, positively skipping down the Kings Road. My excitement at having moved to London was compounded by all the sartorial and counter-cultural activity around me, as at that time Chelsea seemed to be the most exciting place on earth. It appeared to me that the most important commodity was the notion of "cool"; the more you had, the cooler you were. What trousers you wore suddenly became oh-so important, as did the records you listened to at night at the Halls of Residence. It wasn't enough for you to have bought the trendy imported reggae album of the moment – you needed to have bought it a week before it was reviewed in the *NME*. Although it's often supposed that style culture only began to blossom in the Eighties, the whole thing started with punk, as this is when we all started reinventing ourselves. Sartorial elegance suddenly became the easiest way to make your way in the world, and like many of my peers, I started changing my look at the drop of a wide-band trilby. One minute we were Lower East Side punks in plastic leather jackets and baseball boots – for my first six weeks in London I dressed like Johnny Ramone – the next we were Soho secret agents, stalking moodily around West Wonderland in cheap raincoats and floppy fringes. I spent the first three months of 1978 wearing little but army fatigues and ostentatiously carrying Kraftwerk albums whenever I walked into the cafeteria at Ralph West.

In hindsight I was tragically conformist, as dressing like a punk was what everyone was doing at the time. What you simply didn't do was dress like a Ted. When I left Chelsea I started a design course at St. Martin's School of Art in the Charing Cross Road, in the heart of the West End, which made us all think we were at the very apex of the modern urban experience. And while we all thought we were tremendously cool, the two people who drew the most attention were two boys called Alan and Pete, who were both on the painting course. Alan turned up on induction day wearing a full-length leather trenchcoat, leather trousers, jackboots, a huge black fringe, and what could only be described as a "Hitler" moustache. The first time we saw him we all took bets on how long it would be before he was beaten up. Just two weeks later he turned up for college having been beaten senseless the night before.

He wasn't the most confrontational student, however. That was Pete, who insisted on coming to class every day dressed as Elvis. Pete would turn up wearing a stripy matelot top, a Lewis leather jacket, proper imported starched and riveted Levi 501s (with a two-inch turn-up), navy blue brothel creepers, and the most extraordinary blue-black Mr Whippy quiff, which was sculpted into position using Black & White hair pomade (this, along with a thin steel comb and a seemingly auto-replenishing packet of Camel cigarettes, appeared to be the only thing Pete actually owned). No one could understand it. It was all very well coming to class looking like a hippie, or a "straight," or any variation of punk, but to turn up looking like Elvis, complete with curled lip and deliberately nonchalant attitude? Well, what was all that about? Seriously, where was the cultural traction in looking like a Fifties throwback?

Yet Pete drew more attention than any other boy in the school.

On closer inspection, he was actually quite normal. Apart from having a newly acquired fondness for rockabilly – everything in those days was newly acquired – he was much like the rest of us. He just enjoyed looking like Elvis. And as he did this extremely well, consequently he looked cooler than all of us, not that we would ever admit it, of course.

Honestly, why would anyone want to look like Elvis Presley?

Nineteen-seventy-seven was also when I bought my first Elvis album. At the time I was desperately trying to keep up to speed with the vast number of pre-1976 records that the *NME* said had been formative influences on punk, and was trawling Virgin, Our Price, Rough Trade and all the charity shops I could find in London looking for albums by the MC5, Big Star and the New York Dolls as well as some of the more esoteric Velvet Underground stuff. This of course was in addition to the huge number of new singles and albums that were demanding our attention – I remember August and September that year being a mad rush to keep up with new records from Iggy Pop, Talking Heads, Blondie, Richard Hell,

Ian Dury, Split Enz, XTC, Elvis Costello, Television, ATV, Wire, Throbbing Gristle and the Ramones – in addition to the "old wave" records we put on when everyone else had gone to bed: John Martyn, Steely Dan, Joni Mitchell and Mr. Halfway House himself ("There's old wave, there's new wave. And there's …"), David Bowie.

Most people of my age already had pretty eclectic record collections, usually comprising of the following elements: records we had enjoyed as a child, records we had stolen from our parents, records we had bought during the first flush of glam, disco, long-hair rock, and a quickly assembled arsenal of punk. So in a way we were preconditioned to follow our own idiosyncratic paths, filling our collections with esoterica. In my case, I leapt back into the past, accumulating old soul singles from the Sixties, as well as a lot of classic post-Beatles easy-listening pop (Sandie Shaw, Dionne Warwick, Jackie Trent, Tom Jones, Frankie Vaughan). I also bought my first Elvis album, *Elvis' Golden Records Volume 3,* a 1963 pell-mell greatest hits collection that contained a lot of post-Army singles, namely "It's Now Or Never," "Stuck On You," "Are You Lonesome Tonight," "Surrender," "Little Sister" and "(Marie's The Name) His Latest Flame." I got it in the basement of Cheapo Cheapo in Rupert Street in Soho, and probably cost paid less than £3. It had a blue sleeve, covered with a gold disc and Elvis's face superimposed over the label, and looked as though it had taken about ten minutes to design. Oddly, when I bought it, I felt almost decadent.

In those days, an evening was usually spent at a gig, watching any number of punk bands in the West End before catching a bus back to Battersea, where we would sit around in someone's room – often mine – listening to whatever was currently taking our fancy. I remember the look on people's faces when, having just played the latest trendy imported single (no doubt bought at great cost from Rough Trade, Rock On or Kensington Market), I would slip on Elvis's "Little Sister" and watch people nod with approval as the swampy rockabilly guitar rolled into its groove, and then look up in horror when the vocals came in.

In 1977, Elvis was as divisive as icons came.

CHAPTER FIVE

Elvis Is In The House

"I'm sitting in the back of a Cadillac with my sunglasses on and my feet propped up saying, 'I'm a movie star, I'm a som'bitch...'"
– Elvis Presley

Elvis was not born the kind of person to have a perfect life, and didn't feel the urge to pursue one once he became famous.

He had nothing to measure himself against, only his own experiences. According to Elvis, his life was good enough; who cared that he didn't have the artistic freedom he wanted? He didn't exactly crave it, and didn't really know what he would have done with it anyway.

"When I was a boy," as he put it in the only formal speech of his life, "I was the hero in comic books and movies. I grew up believing in a dream. Now, I've lived it out. That's all a man can ask for." For many, Elvis epitomises what middle class white Americans feel they deserve: success, money, and a mansion in Memphis.

The Elvis Presley story is a twentieth-century fairy story, albeit one that ends in drug addiction, obesity and premature death. His story involves everything from a mother fixation, voyeurism and group sex to – tragically – acute substance abuse, spectacular dietary problems and incontinence.

According to the well-worn myth, Sam Phillips, a 31-year-old producer at Sun Studios in Memphis, Tennessee, repeatedly expressed the thought during the early 1950s that:

"If I could find a white boy who could sing like a nigger, I'd make a million dollars."

Whether Phillips used those precise words remains highly controversial – he and others claimed that he would never have used the "n" word – but several witnesses insist the general tenor is true. One day in the summer of 1953, he opened the studio door to find an eighteen-year-old truck driver from Crown Electric appliances called Elvis Presley, who had turned up to cut a record as a gift for his mother. Here was the answer to Phillips' unspoken prayer. Elvis asked Phillips if he could record one of the double-sided acetates that they sold for $3.98 and then set about recording two songs, "My Happiness" and "That's When Your Heartaches Begin." Phillips said the boy's voice wasn't bad and asked for his name and phone number, just in case.

A year later, on July 5th, 1954, Phillips finally called Elvis in for a recording session, putting him in the studio with Scotty Moore on guitar and Bill Black on bass. Nothing gelled until they started fooling around with Arthur Crudup's blues song "That's All Right," speeding it up, giving it a new rockabilly beat and a country-tinged guitar riff. According to Phillips, "Ninety-five percent of the people I had been working with were black, most of them of course no-name people. Elvis fit right in. He was born and raised in poverty. He was around people that had very little in the way of worldly goods."

Working with a bunch of hillbilly musicians who really didn't know any better, Elvis managed to fuse black styles with country music and come up with something that even sorcery couldn't have imagined. When he recorded "That's All Right," "Blue Moon Of Kentucky," "Good Rockin' Tonight" and "Mystery Train" – every one a classic of its kind – rock'n'roll was truly born. As critic Paul Du Noyer wrote, "It took entire generations of people to bring about this moment

– migrant populations, black and white, all rural and poor, converging on the crucible of Memphis in the Mississippi Delta with their respective centuries of folk history. Add the novel ingredient of radio waves crossing the tracks that separated those populations and, suddenly, something like Elvis was conceivable. But in the last analysis, it was still about something inexplicable – not sociology, but magic."

"We played simple instruments and the equipment was simple," Carl Perkins later recalled. "The Sun sound was just hillbillies playing the best they could with what they had."

When Phillips heard Elvis and the boys crashing through their souped-up version of "That's All Right," he had the same visceral feeling he'd had when he first heard Howlin' Wolf. He felt there was something special here, something fresh, even though the song was not original and the musical arrangement was ragged. He didn't know what it was, but it was something he liked.

Suddenly, rock'n'roll was here to stay.

Elvis's first appearances at Sun are among the most fetishised moments of his life. "If I was going to make a movie about Elvis, the whole film would be about the day he walked into Sun Studios," Quentin Tarantino said once. "Everything you need to know about Elvis happened that day – that's what you want to see, that's what you want to know. He walked in there wanting to make his mark on the world. It's all there!"

When Elvis first auditioned for Sam Phillips in 1953, the office manager, Marion Keisker, accused Presley of basing his entire vocal sound on Dean Martin. Although it's assumed this was swiftly knocked out of him, you only have to study how his career developed to see that this influence didn't entirely go away. In 1955 Martin had a huge hit with "Memories Are Made Of This." With a loping, easy swing that appealed to young and old alike, it was a huge hit. Compare it to Elvis's "Don't Be Cruel" a year later and you see how easy Elvis found it to appropriate Dino's style and mix it with a bit more of an R&B feel. The thing is, Elvis only needed to "invent" rock'n'roll once, and thereafter he could simply repeat the exercise. Not that Elvis was a one-trick pony, far from it: the rockabilly sound of "That's All Right" (with the impossible-to-copy "Sun echo") is a genre away from the muddier, easier rocking beat of something like "Don't Be Cruel," as are the Wham-Bam-Thank-You-Ma'am! gymnastics of "Heartbreak Hotel" and the knee-jerk chugalug of "I Got Stung." In just a few years Elvis created a road map for rock'n'roll, creating forms and rhythms that will be around for as long as people continue to make music. Phillips knew that "white youngsters" enjoyed R&B, "but there was something in many of those youngsters that resisted buying this music. The Southern ones especially felt a resistance they probably didn't quite understand. They liked the music, but they weren't sure whether they ought to like it or not. So I got to thinking how many records you could sell if you could find white performers who could play and sing in this same exciting, alive way."

Black performers wanted the white audience too, and everyone from Chuck Berry and Fats Domino to Ruth Brown and Ike Turner had been desperate for their records to cross over, but it would take a white man making black rockabilly to bring "rock'n'roll" to the masses.

Lux Interior, the front man of the goth rockabilly band the Cramps, used to tell an alternative, and rather more entertaining, version of the rise of Elvis. He claimed to have heard it one drunken night from Knox Phillips, the son of Sam Phillips: "Yeah, we were told that Elvis wasn't discovered as such at all! He was just some freaky looking kid always making a nuisance of himself around Sun Studios and nobody wanted to know him. Like, here's this guy who dyed his eyebrows and dressed in black pimp clothes – and this was the Fifties in the South, you've got to remember – and Sam Phillips and all the session guys thought he was some disgusting little faggot!"

According to this version, Elvis did have one piece of luck, in the shape of his mother, who had a terrible weight problem. Her doctor prescribed her an enormous supply of diet pills that just happened to be Benzedrine, which was at the time one of the most potent forms of speed.

"And all those Sun guys just lived on speed, man. So, when Phillips found out that Elvis could get bottles of these things, he let him hang around. So, like, here was Elvis every week bringing huge bottles of these pills to the guys at Sun until, as he was the studio's main source of supply for speed, Phillips was more or less obliged to let him cut a record.

"So like, rock'n'roll was born simply because Elvis Presley was Sun Records' number one speed dealer."

Regardless, even Phillips was amazed at the public's reaction to his boy: "Elvis went from high school boy to hit entertainer so fast it was hard for any of us to realise the change had come."

Rock'n'roll had arrived, yet another metaphor for teenage sex. What no one would admit for years to come was the fact that, like "jazz," "rock'n'roll" was just another way to say "fuck." And fucking appeared to be here to stay too.

When Elvis Presley first came to the attention of middle-class white America, seemingly fully formed, in 1956, he was the devil incarnate. Here was a Southern white boy who danced and sang like a black man. He dressed in a flashy fashion too, primarily in black and pink. Elvis hated denim, because denim was what you wore when you went to work, especially if you were driving a truck. "If you're going to be a star, you should look like one," he said. His unblushing narcissism launched the peacock revolution in men's fashion, simply by drawing attention to himself.

Although Chuck Berry had already had a major hit with "Maybellene" in 1955, his music was still considered to be "race" – black, marginal. Elvis was however to name-check as influences black musicians Arthur "Big Boy" Crudup, Fats Domino, Ivory Joe Hunter and B. B. King. A journalist during Presley's first New York interview commented that Elvis cited blues singers who "obviously meant a lot to him," saying Elvis was trying to "carry on their music."

In another interview, a few months later, Elvis said, "The coloured folks been singing it and playing it just like I'm doin' now, man, for more years than I know. They played it like that in their shanties and in their juke joints and nobody paid it no mind 'til I goosed it up. I got it from them. Down in Tupelo, Mississippi, I used to hear old Arthur Crudup bang his box the way I do now and I said if I ever got to a place I could feel all old Arthur felt, I'd be a music man like nobody ever saw."

Rock'n'roll in its formative state had been going a good few years before Elvis appeared on the scene. Not only did he focus people's minds on the music, however, and not only did he fuse the worlds of countrybilly and R&B, but he soon became the biggest symbol of Fifties teenage revolt, bigger even than James Dean, and thus the most enduring icon of the pre-Beatles era.

Bill Haley and Ike Turner were already trying to combine white and black music before Elvis came along, but Haley was too fat and old for the masses, and Turner too black. Elvis was the only one who could make it work, and his seamless fusion actually created a successful new genre.

On top of all that, Elvis looked like nobody else on earth.

Look at photographs taken at punk gigs in 1976 and you'll see a lot of short-haired men on stage, and a lot of long-haired men in the audience, demanding they vacate it. Look at pictures of Elvis performing in 1955 and 1956, and the majority of the audience are men with generic crew-cuts, the style every young boy was encouraged to take by his ex-serviceman father. If it was good enough for them in the war, it was good enough for their offspring in peace.

But not Elvis. No, Elvis was determined to stand out from the crowd with as much panache as possible.

He was threatening because he was so flagrantly dirty, owning, among other things, the world's sexiest haircut. His hair was Presley's trademark, his strength, and an accessory that only added to his animal sexuality. In *Elvis World*, their 1987 homage to the King, Jane and Michael Stern describe his crowning glory: "Like the man to whose scalp it is attached, the hair breaks loose onstage. Appearing first as a unitary loaf of high-rise melted vinyl etched with grooves along the side, it detonates at the strike of the first chord."

"Without preamble, the three-piece band cuts loose," wrote *Time* magazine on May 15th, 1956. "In the spotlight, the lanky singer flails furious rhythms on his guitar, every now and then breaking a string. In a pivoting stance, his hips swing sensuously from side to side and his entire body takes on a frantic quiver, as if he had swallowed a jackhammer."

It was around this time that RCA commissioned a 26-year-old freelance photographer called Alfred Wertheimer to take a set of publicity pictures of Elvis. These turned out to be some of the most iconic photos ever taken of him – Wertheimer shot 3800 frames – and include the famous photograph of Elvis French kissing a mysterious Kim Novak-style blonde in a black dress on a stairwell, backstage at the Mosque Theatre in Richmond, Virginia. Many have compared the picture to another classic image, captured eleven years earlier for *Life* by Alfred Eisenstaedt, of a sailor and a nurse spontaneously embracing on V-J Day in Times Square. When asked why he decided to follow Elvis when he was still unknown, Wertheimer replied that Elvis "permitted closeness, and he made girls cry."

"Here I was with somebody who I didn't know was going to become famous," said Wertheimer. "But I did know two things: I knew that he was not shy – I mean, Elvis was shy in the sense that he was introverted, but he was not shy to the camera… and he made the girls cry."

Years later, the blonde came forward and announced herself as Barbara Gray. Her detailed description of her courtship by Elvis includes one telling exchange…

Elvis: "Would you like something to drink, a beer maybe?"

Barbara (confused, as they were in a coffee shop): "No."

Elvis: "That's good, 'cause I don't let my women drink."

Barbara: "I'm not your woman."

Elvis: "Do you smoke?"

Barbara: "No" (she lied).

Elvis: "Good. I don't like my women to smoke, either."

Barbara: "I told you I'm not your woman… If I want to smoke and have a beer, I'll do it."

She was a brave woman to play hard to get. Elvis's world was awash with women who would literally throw themselves at him, swept away by his eyes, his lips, his hips and his hair.

So good-looking was he that he was often beaten up. The writer Larry McMurty remembers the sloe-eyed country boy getting stomped by a gang of oil field roughnecks outside a Wichita Falls roadhouse in the mid-Fifties. What they hated most about him was his hair.

These days Alfred Wertheimer lives in a brownstone on

New York's Upper West Side, surrounded by the detritus of a lifetime living with Elvis. Or at least, living with meta-Elvis. On the first floor of his house, his kitchen is full of Elvis dolls, cut-outs, posters, framed prints, mugs, scrolls, and boxes and boxes of recordings of TV shows, films and radio interviews. Wertheimer also keeps a record of all his own interviews, and he recorded ours using an iPhone 5 as well as an old-fashioned cassette recorder. "I record everything," he told me. "I'm a hoarder, a big, big hoarder."

When Elvis died, Wertheimer hadn't looked at his Elvis pictures for two decades; since then barely a day has gone by when he hasn't had a request for one."

"I was on the phone talking to the picture editor of *Time* magazine. I hadn't heard anybody interested in an Elvis Presley photograph for nineteen years, and suddenly they want the pictures. They called me and said, 'Come up right away, bring all your photographs with you.' I asked, 'What's happening?' And they said that Elvis Presley had died."

Wertheimer was working for a pharmaceutical company, doing pack shots and photographs for commercials, and hadn't thought about Elvis for a very long time. "My work was bread and butter kind of things. So, I went down to *Time* at the Rockefeller Center and they said, 'We're gonna make you an offer you can't refuse.' And I liked that, I thought that was something I could cope with."

Time wanted an exclusive on everything he had, buying up his collection and preventing him from going to *Newsweek* or any other magazines. Wertheimer hadn't seen Elvis for nearly two decades, but he was shocked by how much his death affected him.

"I was sad, truly sad. Everyone was sad – the scene in Memphis was unprecedented. But I consider myself a realist. Elvis certainly helped bring it on himself. He was falling apart at the age of forty-two. At one point he was on drugs, and the story was, 'Look, if you don't get me those drugs, I'm going to have to buy a drugstore and I'll be able to get anything I want.' At that point, he had the wherewithal to be able to buy a drugstore. At the beginning of 1956, he was essentially a middling person – economically – and at the end of '56 he was a rich man, he was a millionaire. It's no wonder he changed."

Wertheimer went along to the CBS TV studio in Manhattan, where Elvis was hanging around waiting to appear on *Stage Show*, hosted by big band leaders the Dorsey Brothers. He was ushered backstage and introduced to the young singer, who was taking a break from rehearsals after travelling all the way from Memphis to New York.

When Wertheimer first met Elvis, the singer seemed more interested in his fingers. "He doesn't look up. He's not very sociable, and he's looking at his finger, and he pays as little attention to me as necessary, to be somewhat sociable. He's more focused on the man who's sitting next to him on his left hand side – turns out he's a ring salesman. The ring salesman had just delivered a diamond encrusted gold ring in the shape of a horseshoe, and that was his new good luck ring. That's what kept him preoccupied."

Wertheimer warmed to the singer immediately.

"I liked him, but didn't fully understand what he was doing. I was a nerd, mostly listening to Mozart, Vivaldi, Beethoven. I was of the classical bent, I was also into early jazz..."

He bonded with Elvis because they were both young and not especially conversant with their respective roles. As a result, Wertheimer ended up with some of the most candid photographs ever taken of a major celebrity, photos that over the last fifty years have become almost as famous as Elvis himself. If Edward Hopper had taken photographs of Elvis Presley, they would have looked like this.

"I had a relationship with Elvis because he wasn't famous!" says Wertheimer. "His first gold record was a month after I met him. People ask me, ultimately, what was it about Elvis that made him so unusual? Well, besides his voice, which I thought was very fine, he permitted closeness. By that I mean he didn't permit just photographing from a distance, he permitted photographing like this, that close – three feet away. And when you do that, you're starting to get texture, you're starting to be able to use a wide-angle lens for portraits rather than a telephoto. And when you use a wide angle, you get in there. It's like you make yourself vulnerable and they become vulnerable, and you feed off each other's personality. I was with him everywhere, in the bathroom, at his house, when he fell asleep, when he woke up...

"I went on a train with him from New York to Memphis one day, as I thought it would round out the stuff I'd done for RCA in Manhattan. So I decided to take it on myself to go down there. So now I've got this 27-hour train journey ahead of me. I was an amateur shrink – everyone thinks they can figure out someone else's personality – well, I thought I could.

"So, I'm watching Elvis very carefully, and the boredom just gets to him. He finally picks up this panda bear – four foot at least, and he puts it on his left hip. Colonel Tom has fallen asleep, and Scotty Moore and DJ Fontana are sitting there. Elvis would never tell you what he was doing or what he was about to do, so you had to be on your toes. He begins to walk down the centre aisle of this public train, and there are people who are not part of our entourage looking at this grown man with a big doll on his left hip. When he gets to the other end of the car, what does he do? He doesn't put the panda down, as I thought he would, but there were at least three or four seats empty, what he does he manipulates a paper cup at the water fountain, and somehow squeezes this triangular flat cup, pushes the button, gets the water out of the container, and without spilling it, which was an amazing feat, drinks from the cup, throws it away, and turns around, sort of catching my eye; he's got a wry grin – I knew he was up to something, but I didn't know what – and he proceeds to walk back down from where he came, makes a sharp left turn, and he looks these two young ladies in the face, who were maybe sixteen- or seventeen-year-olds, and he says, 'Are you coming to my concert tonight?' in Elvis talk. And they pop back, and they say, 'Well, who are you?' And he says 'I'm Elvis Presley.' And they say, 'How do we know that?' and he says, 'You see this photographer pointing at me?' (I'm now standing on seat cushions that I have been taught never to stand on, because it's just not the right thing to do, but when I have a camera in my hand I feel that everything is fair game in order to get the right height). 'Do you think that that photographer would be taking my picture if I wasn't Elvis Presley?' All of that made a lot of sense to the two girls, and that was as much as I could get out of that little episode, so I decide to go back to the Colonel and relax while he chatted up the girls. He then comes back and falls asleep with the panda on his side of the car. But that's what he did, he never explained anything."

As Wertheimer made me another cup of builders' tea, I asked him if his subject was actually switched on, as so many people had accused Elvis of being dim.

"Elvis was a lot brighter than the people who said he was a hick and a dummy," he said. "He was very polite, always, 'Yes ma'am, no ma'am', but that was more of a Southern tradition. He played to his own tune. He wore clothes that were a little bit more distinguished than other people's clothes. He had these thin belts that had the buckle going way over the side, although his suits were made of the same fabric as Colonel Tom Parker's, who was rather conservative. Elvis didn't write his songs, but he did make the selections. He was basically a quiet person. When he wasn't on stage he was almost introverted. Only when he was on stage did all this come out, and his attitude was, 'Well, I'm paid to be an entertainer. If I just stand there like a dummy, I'm not entertaining anybody. Entertainers have to be outgoing.'"

Was he surprised that his photographs have endured, and that they have become some of the most iconic portraits of the twentieth century?

"I'm flattered to death that they are. I tried to do things in a classical way that will stand up for a hundred, two hundred, three hundred years. I hope that people hundreds of years from now would get an idea of what that personality's about. My formula was very simple: you get people doing things that are more important in their life than having their picture taken. That's assuming that they don't faff around and don't know what they're doing with their equipment. As long as they're competent you're going to get good pictures.

"You would never get this access these days, with anyone, but he didn't know any better and neither did I. He was staying in the Waldorf Hotel, and I just wandered into the bathroom. That's where I learned about his boil and his bad skin. I learned he was using Vaseline hair tonic; he had quite a few pimples on his back; he used an electric shaver; and he liked to use a little ladies' mirror to check the back of his hair. But whatever he did, whether it was combing his hair or shaving, or brushing his teeth, he was laser focused on what he was doing. If he was singing, he would be involved heavily in that. Same with shaving.

"With Elvis, when you're talking about closeness, you can't get much closer than I did.

"Elvis was good looking in an outer sense. His face was classically Greek, from a profile point of view. I think he was

131

wise enough to realise that he was going to become famous, and if he didn't co-operate with photographers, who were really the agents of the future, as they were the ones who were going to lock down the imagery of what he looked like. So that in order for them to realise who he was or how he did things, he would need people like myself who didn't expect anything from him. He couldn't get it from his manager, Colonel Tom, as he was a status-quo kind of guy: he wanted an Elvis with the high collars, like something out of the French Revolution, headshots-only for covers.

"After a few days with him, I found out he made the girls cry, and that was a revelation. I said, 'I think I've got a winner,' but no one else was absolutely sure they had a winner, even RCA wasn't sure, because when I asked to shoot colour they said, 'No, we're not going to pay for it. If you want to shoot colour, then you pay for it.' And I did, I shot about six rolls of colour, and I'm glad I did, not that's it's so good."

While many continue to endure plastic surgery in order to look like Elvis, no one has ever been able to properly reproduce his thatch. Although ironically, while Elvis's haircut is considered to be one of the most influential pop icons of the twentieth century, it was actually copied from Tony Curtis. Presley wore Royal Crown hair products during high school to make his blondish locks appear darker, but it wasn't until he saw Curtis in the 1949 film, *City Across The River*, that the fledgling singer adopted the greased duck-tail. Dyed blue-black, covered in grease, with truck-driver sideburns trailing his cheeks, Elvis finally had his five inches of buttered yak wool.

Famously, when he appeared for the third time on *The Ed Sullivan Show* on January 6th, 1957, Elvis was shot only from the waist up, because his wild, erotic dancing had caused such an uproar all across the US. In reality it made hardly any difference, because libidinous teenage girls could still see Presley's hair. Elvis kept his hair dyed black all through his career – using everything from Clairol Black Velvet to L'Oreal Excellence Blue-Black – originally to carve himself an image, then because he thought it photographed better on film (it did), and then finally because he started to go grey. When Elvis died, the hair beneath his blue-black dye was almost completely white.

"Elvis started every performance with every single hair in place," said Wertheimer. "He looked immaculate, but as he got into it the hair started to hang down, the sweat began pouring down his face, he'd wiggle and jiggle and shake and get down on one knee, and before you knew it, everybody in the audience was caught up in it and opening up to each other, especially the girls, crying and hanging on to one another."

While Elvis had already appeared on national television six times beforehand, before this outing it was his appearance on *The Milton Berle Show* on June 5th, 1956, that triggered the first real controversy of his career. As he sang his latest hit "Hound Dog" (on the UK release of which, British radio DJ Steve Race wrote in the *Melody Maker*, "I fear for this country. It ought to have the good taste to reject music so decadent"), he started using his pelvis in ways that had never been seen on TV before, only in the privacy of the bedroom, or maybe in the private bathrooms attached to TV executives' office suites. He was slammed by critics all over the US for "animalism," "vulgarity" and "appalling lack of musicality." The papers warned that more exposure to Elvis would cause widespread juvenile delinquency, and even the Catholic Church got involved, telling its members to "beware" the singer. After Berle's show, Ed Sullivan, whose own TV show was even more popular, declared that he would never book Elvis, while Steve Allen, host of *The Tonight Show*, was put under pressure from his network, NBC, to cancel a forthcoming Elvis performance. Fearing for his job, Allen neutered Elvis by dressing him in formal clothes and getting him to sing his single to a basset hound. Huge ratings ensued.

Naturally, Ed Sullivan then reversed his decision by announcing that he had signed "Elvis the Pelvis" to a then-unprecedented $50,000, three-show contract. For the first two shows Elvis was filmed from afar, but for the third and final show, he was only filmed from the waist up, even when singing a gospel tune. Towards the end of the show, Sullivan put an arm around Elvis and congratulated him on being "a real decent, fine boy."

It is difficult from a distance of over half a century to imagine just how different Elvis was at the time, and just how the previous generation thought him a messenger from the anti-Christ. He was lowly, he was libidinous, and he seemed to have the nation's youth completely in his thrall.

In 1956 the American men's magazine *Gentry* commissioned a pen portrait of Elvis from Feliks Topolski, the writer-editor-publisher of a little-known British magazine called *Topolski's Chronicle*. His verdict was typical, an opinion that soon became almost generic: "My generation's puberty was rather private," he wrote, sniffily, sounding not unlike John Betjeman. "We would steal our parents' books, thus learning the theory long before they thought it the right time to give us their progressive enlightenment. Nowadays, as in antiquity, Sex seems to be becoming an open and foremost preoccupation of the adolescent – in fact, it is developing its public rituals. The chosen god-symbol, supplied periodically from amongst the 'Stars,' serves as the approved fixation-object for awakening desires. And, since his sanctification is performed by the supremely august Business of Entertainment, the young virgins are free, even encouraged, to sublimate their urges in the public rites of adoration.

"But, however mystically chosen, why Elvis Presley? Because, I think, he possesses very happily the godlike value of all-embracing popularity: he is vulgar, yet stylish in the 'zoot' manner – hence he appeals both to the sophisticated and the simple. And his manhood is above suspicion..."

Above suspicion.

Since becoming famous, Elvis had been steered by "Colonel" Tom Parker, the entertainment impresario who had worked in the circus before moving into talent management. Parker is always portrayed as a Svengali figure who forced Elvis to make tacky movies and record hokey country ballads, but Elvis was as responsible for his own destiny as the "Colonel". Many forget that when Parker first saw Elvis in 1954, he was as blown away by his talent and charisma as anyone else.

Elvis became a brand almost as soon as he became a star. Not long after Presley started appearing on television, Parker signed a merchandising deal with Beverly Hills movie merchandiser Hank Saperstein for nearly $40,000. With eighty different ranges, from charm bracelets to record players, Presley merchandise had brought in $22 million by the end of 1956. Parker, who took 25 percent of the profits, was finding many inventive new ways to make money from his artist. He even came up with the idea to produce "I Hate Elvis" badges to cater for those who wanted nothing to do with the new star. And Elvis even lent his name to Southern Maid doughnuts, not that he knew it.

In April 1956, Parker made his first mistake with Elvis's career, booking him into a four-week Las Vegas engagement.

The older, more reserved audiences hated the young upstart, hated the way he looked, the way he danced, and – saliently – his music. Much was made in the press about the suggestion that whenever he wore tight trousers on stage, Elvis had a piece of rubber pipe down the inside of the crotch. After a cool reception during his first few shows, Parker cut Elvis's appearance down to two weeks.

This wouldn't be the first time Elvis had tried to enhance his equipment. David Houston, an early friend of Elvis who travelled with him during his first few years of touring, said that he would take the cardboard cylinder out of a toilet roll and put a string on the end of it. Then he'd tie the string around his waist. The other end, with the cardboard roller, would hang down inside his trousers so that when he got onstage and reared back with his guitar in his hand, it would look as though he had "one helluva thing there inside his pants."

Above all else, Elvis was cool, a boy who broke the mould. If you speak to anyone who was young at the time, they'll tell you that for them Elvis was like some kind of secular divine intervention. "My heroes are still the same heroes I had back then, back in the Fifties," says the photographer David Bailey. "In photography I loved Richard Avedon and Irving Penn, although I was never that blown away by music. I did like the blues and jazz, but I never really got into rock'n'roll. I remember liking Elvis and people laughing at me and calling me camp, but I thought Elvis was cool. I had a fight with Catherine Deneuve once just after we got married about the fact that I liked Clint Eastwood and Elvis, which she felt was too camp for words. I liked photographers like Helmut Newton, Jean Lucief and William Klein. But I loved Elvis. Elvis didn't give a fuck, which was the one thing about him that appealed to me most ... For me there was a link from the so-called Swinging Sixties right back to the dawn of rock'n'roll in America."

If Elvis had arrived in the Fifties fully formed, by 1977 he was formless. Having spent the Sixties sleepwalking through dozens of dreadful B-movies, he had since 1969 either been out on the road, or in residence in Las Vegas. During his movie career, Elvis didn't so much act as simply inhabit his films. The way he tried to wring some dignity from his film appearances was to frown, which he felt lent him the air of someone good enough to act. "I've made a study of poor Jimmy Dean," Elvis said, just prior to shooting *Love Me Tender*. "I've made a study of myself, and I know why girls, at least the young 'uns, go for us. We're sullen, we're broodin', we're something of a menace. I don't understand it exactly, but that's what the girls like in men. I don't know anything about Hollywood, but I know you can't be sexy if you smile. You can't be a rebel if you grin."

He didn't frown when he was onstage, but by then he didn't need to pretend anymore.

By 1977, his records had become almost incidental. Throughout the late Sixties and early Seventies, when the album became the coin of the realm, Elvis continued to be a singles artist. With only a few exceptions, he appeared happy to let his manager and record company schedule and package his albums, rather than pay them the kind of attention everyone else was giving theirs. Even though Elvis had had a greater impact on post-war pop culture than almost any performer other than the Beatles, it seemed that one transformative experience was going to be enough for him. For the first three years of his career Elvis was a cultural harbinger like nothing before, but as soon as he entered the Army (and thereby transformed a $105,000-a-month rock'n'roll idol into an $83.20-a-month GI), he became so risk-averse that culturally he seemed to implode. From that day on, Elvis was fascinating as a phenomenon rather than for anything he actually produced. His records, films and TV appearances became so pedestrian that he ceased to be of much interest artistically. He would always make the occasional great record, but these seemed almost accidental; that he recorded so many songs made it likely that at least some would bear comparison to his earlier work. Both Elvis and his manager were conservative beings at heart, and although Elvis occasionally tried to rebel, his bleatings were just that: if Elvis had been remotely curious about walking out of his comfort zone, he would have done it.

As the great Elvis expert Mick Farren once put it, "Presley had racked up so much affection in the Fifties that it was even hard to blame him for his dire output. More often than not the blame was laid at the door of Colonel Tom Parker. It may not have been logical, but even when he did his worst, it was hard to believe that it was Presley's fault."

In the spring of 1969, the hotelier Kirk Kerkorian was preparing to open his gargantuan, $60 million International Hotel in Las Vegas. With nearly 1600 rooms on thirty floors, it was going to be the largest resort hotel in the world, let alone Nevada. The International's swimming pool was the second-largest man-made body of water in the whole state (the largest being a reservoir). Kerkorian wanted Elvis to make his live comeback by opening the hotel's showroom, but Parker refused. "Absolutely not," he said. "It's much too risky. Let somebody else stick his neck out."

So it was left to Barbra Streisand to stick her neck out by opening the showroom on July 2nd that year, surrounded by scaffolding and without sets, singers, dancers, flashy lighting or even an opening act. Elvis went to see her perform soon afterwards, and thought she "sucked." Taking the temperature of the room, he did his homework and made sure he was far more prepared when he opened there himself a few weeks later. When he did, he was a massive success. He hadn't performed properly for over a decade, and backed by a thirty-piece orchestra, a six-piece rock band, and an eight-voice chorus, he tore through "Hound Dog," "Rip It Up," "Heartbreak Hotel" and all his early hits. He even had the bejewelled thirty-something ladies screaming through their gloved hands, reliving their youth, or, most probably, reliving a youth they never had. Here was America's most recent past, all before them, live and sexy.

Elvis's decision to turn his back on the movies and return to live performance is often interpreted as expressing his frustration with the kind of films he was forced to make, and his genuine desire to get back in front of a live audience. To some extent, however, the move was financially motivated; his income from the movies had been dwindling for some time. Tom Diskin, a spokesman for the Colonel, went public about this in 1968. While he declined to give an exact figure, he said the decrease was sufficient to cause Elvis "and his manager" to consider personal appearances.

"For the time that goes into it," Diskin said, "it's more profitable for him to appear in public. It takes Elvis fifteen weeks time to make a movie, on the average. If he appears for ten weeks, one concert a week, at $100,000 each he can do much better. In personal appearances these days $100,000 a concert is not an unrealistic figure."

Maybe Vegas could work? Vegas was a world away from the traditional nightclub milieu of stale lingerie and unfulfilled ambitions; out here in the desert you could wallow in an atmosphere of possibility. The Vegas world was a world of dreams and finely calibrated means of redemption – here, the American dream was only a roll of the dice away, and the winner could be you! The winner could be Elvis!

When Elvis opened at the International, the Colonel invited many of the New York rock writers to fly to Vegas in Elvis's plane – the first privately owned DC-9. The reviews were predictably positive. "Despite the flashiness, despite the fact that most of the male customers had awful James Bond fixations and most all the women seemed to dress out of the Fredericks of Hollywood catalogue," wrote Mike Jahn in the *New York Times*, "Elvis Presley made Las Vegas an incredible experience."

That August, London's *Evening Standard* sent a reporter to Vegas. Ray Connolly returned from the desert with something more than a review– a bona fide interview. It was classic Elvis, a mixture of bluff humility and smalltown stoicism.

As Connolly knew, getting through to Elvis was practically impossible. The "Colonel" micro-managed every aspect of Elvis's life, and paid close attention to anything that involved his client meeting the public or the press. Especially the press. Security guards with guns and walkie-talkies shadowed the singer both night and day, and Connolly found it tough convincing Parker that he deserved some face time with Elvis.

"He is sprawling on a red Spanish sofa in the sitting-room of his back-stage suite," wrote Connolly. "He's wearing the black karate-style suit designed for his season at the hotel, and his hair, dyed pitch-black as always, is swept back off his face in the style he created fourteen years ago."

Elvis was bluff about the hotel as well as about everything else. He often gave the impression that what he did was a bit of a chore, a chore that was usually at the behest of the "Colonel." "We didn't decide to come back here for the money, I'll tell you that … The time is just right. The money – I have no idea at all about that. I just don't want to know. You can stuff it."

Elvis went on to say that he'd completed all the contractual agreements he made when he came out of the Army, and that he was now looking for more serious film roles (he would say this a lot), and that he wanted to stretch himself. "I wouldn't be honest with you if I said I wasn't ashamed of some of the movies and the songs I've had to sing in them. … How can you enjoy it when you have to sing songs to the guy you've just punched up?"

The interview lasted just twenty minutes, long enough for the journalist to be overawed by the man in his presence, and short enough for him not to ask anything of any great value. Still, a coup was a coup.

The first International concerts were a success. Elvis couldn't have been more appealing on stage, and his fans found him as sexy as ever. Flick-haired women in ironed denim bellbottoms and flowery woollen tank tops tried to grab his microphone ("Don't pull my cord, lady," Elvis would say, smirking), stripped in front of the stage, and even threw their underwear at him. These women were quite unlike the women who came out to the desert to simply accompany their husbands. They had come for one thing and one thing only: to see Elvis. The men were different, as they were here for the weekend, for a vacation, for a convention, for the gambling, or perhaps some casual sex tourism. Vegas in the Seventies was as gaudy as it had been in the Fifties, especially at night, when the wilderness receded and the neon seemed to glow just a little bit brighter. After a good dinner – who would refuse the free brandy or the crème de menthe? – you would saunter down the Strip and see famous names like Frank Sinatra, Buddy Hackett, Ann-Margret and Shirley MacLaine emblazoned in gold and red on electric signs four stories high. You could wander into the chandeliered International or the blue-hued Tropicana, experience the gold and white togas of Caesars Palace or the deep red plush of the MGM, or you could amble downtown and visit Glitter Gulch, the Four Queens, the Golden Nugget, Binion's Horseshoe or the Mint.

Or you could go to see Elvis. Which is what every woman wanted to do. Or at least, some still wanted to go to see Sinatra, but mainly they wanted Elvis. In some respects he had become the human embodiment of the town. And even though Vegas would eventually start regenerating itself, there were some aspects of the town, like Elvis, that would forever be synonymous with the Vegas of old.

In some respects Elvis was no different from Sinatra (one man known exclusively by his Christian name, the other solely by his surname), as both had been the subject of mass adulation, had created a new kind of celebrity, inventing a new form of entertainment in the process. And while both ultimately turned out to be fiercely conservative – politically, socially, sexually, culturally – Sinatra was probably the more adventurous with his music. Elvis may have been the embodiment of rock'n'roll and a genuine force for change, but almost as soon as he discovered his form, he stuck to it. Elvis's records didn't really ever change, and while the Beatles defined the Sixties by continually moving their music forward, Elvis was stuck in a groove (if the Beatles had been as unadventurous as Elvis, all their albums would have sounded like *Please Please Me*). Sinatra at least experimented with his arrangers and his material. Elvis wouldn't have been caught anywhere near a bossa nova album, not a real one – he may have recorded "Bossa Nova Baby," but that was just pop fluff.

Elvis never sought out great material as much as he should have, and while he often chose which songs to cover, he was limited in his ambitions. One of the tragedies of Elvis was his lack of inquisitiveness, and the conservative nature of his musical choices. Despite his lifelong pattern of discontent, there is no profound spiritual autobiography in his work.

Having a song covered by Elvis was a career-defining moment for any songwriter, nonetheless. Bob Dylan once said that his proudest achievement was having "Tomorrow Is A Long Time" sung by Elvis in 1966, and that it was "the one record I treasure the most." When Elvis covered "The Fair's Moving On" by the British songwriters Doug Flett and Guy Fletcher, their first royalty statement arrived in the form of an "Elvis cheque"; they treasured it so much they considered getting it framed, before financial imperatives meant they had to cash it (and reluctantly relinquish it). Elvis recorded Simon and Garfunkel's "Bridge Over Troubled Water" in Nashville on June 5th, 1970, releasing it on the 1970 album *That's The Way It Is*, and immediately made it part of his set. Paul Simon showed up at one of these shows, and, after seeing Elvis's version of the song, he was said to have said, "That's it, we might as well all give up now." Presley carried on including the song in his set list most notably in his last live appearance on June 26th, 1977 in Indianapolis.

At the time of his death, Elvis's stock had recently begun to rise in the UK, where his single "Way Down" was enjoying some success, with the critics and public alike. Although the British music press didn't exactly welcome every new Elvis record with open arms, the hope that he might experience some sort of new epiphany having long since evaporated, each release was at least greeted with a modicum of curiosity. Recorded at Graceland, at Elvis's last session eight months before he died, "Way Down" was a kind of reprise of his "Burning Love" hit, featuring Elvis's TCB band and J.D. Sumner's basement bass voice. While its status was of course subsequently enhanced by being Elvis's last hit, it's still a great record, and one that only Elvis could have made.

It is axiomatic that when you ask someone what their secret is, they'll tell you that there isn't one. In Elvis's case, this was true. Almost everything he did musically was innate. If you'd stopped him and tapped him on the shoulder as he was about to walk through the proscenium to the stage, and asked him how he did what he did, he would have looked at you, respectfully, with the appraising gaze of a jeweller, but without breaking into the bubble of your personal space, and replied: "Ma'am, sir, I just do what I do." In that respect, Elvis believed he was blessed. He would continually ask himself: why on earth (our earth, this earth) had God decided to give him this talent, if he wasn't? Although Elvis always expected a brass brand of a welcome whenever he walked into a room or a hotel, or onto a plane or a stage, he usually went out of his way to be humble with the public.

He knew however that only he could do what he did. After all, when he first went into Sun Studios and was asked who he sang like, he said he didn't sing like "nobody"; he sang like Elvis Presley, and by God he knew it.

Elvis may have been accessorised to good effect by Sam Phillips in the early days, he may have been encouraged to wander into more pedestrian material in his middle years by the Colonel, and he may have become the most generic Las Vegas entertainer of them all; and, of course, he appeared to do all of this willingly. Yet Elvis was always unmistakably Elvis. The voice (that phenomenal instrument), the intonation, the slightly melodramatic presentation of the material – when you heard an Elvis record on the radio it couldn't have been by anyone else. You didn't have to crouch down a little, and say to the person with you, "Is that the new Bill Haley/Bobby Darin/Beatles/Stones/Who/David Bowie record...?" As with Sinatra before him and Bob Dylan after, when you heard an Elvis record, you knew you'd heard an Elvis record. With every entertainer who came in his wake, you felt they were peddling fantasy, whereas with Elvis his style was innate, instinctive, natural. With Elvis you felt he *had* to do what he did, whereas with most of the singers he inspired, you somehow felt it was a little too much for show. Elvis didn't look as though he could do much else, while many of those who came after him looked like they could do plenty.

There was a reliability about Elvis that appealed to his audience as much as it appealed to Elvis himself. He wasn't a jazz performer, didn't veer off his chosen course, had no interest in riffing, or improvisation, or anything like that. Everything he did – over and above his "secret," his thing, his "Elvisness" – was just theatre. Elvis's map of reality wasn't especially large, but it never changed. There was nothing monastic about his devotion to his training, and there was little time spent refining his technique: he was Elvis, and almost immediately we knew that just as much as he did.

What many loved about Elvis was the casual way in which he allowed people to enjoy themselves in a totally new manner. There was a sense, quite early on, that what Elvis was doing wasn't the result of some clever masterplan, some expedient trick of the light. It's conceivable that many Elvis fans didn't know why they liked him, and didn't think that Elvis knew why he liked what he did either. His fans didn't think he'd "planned ahead." The crux of the matter was that whatever he did clicked with their expectations. Elvis's lackadaisical, seemingly random dreams chimed with those of his fans, so what was the problem?

If you study Elvis's records from the late Sixties onwards, after he was finally done with the movies, they are all strikingly similar – maudlin, melodramatic, as if everything in life was something of a fait accompli. You can almost hear him shrugging his shoulders, giving up, feeling blue for you, on stage, on record, where everyone can see and hear. There would be the occasional tacky rocker, a schmaltzy R&B number that allowed him to swing his hips again and "rock out" a little, but the bulk of his material was sad and fatalistic.

Elvis never understood the album. As pop began to expand in the mid-Sixties, and concept albums became commonplace, Elvis stuck to the time-honoured formula of an album as a portmanteau collection of singles, bits and pieces and not much else. His albums were all filler, no killer. Elvis was never going to be interested in making anything like *Sgt Pepper* or *Wish You Were Here*, and neither was he interested in producing a modern echo of *Songs For Swinging Lovers*, the Frank Sinatra LP credited with being the first concept album. Elvis could be an exemplary interpreter of popular song. When he chose the right one, he'd find it relatively easy to turn it into a classic, or turn in a version that made people say he "owned it." But, absurdly, he couldn't knit together a dozen of them, had no interest in running alongside Simon & Garfunkel or Todd Rundgren, or even keeping up with Fleetwood Mac or Neil Diamond, a man who probably wouldn't have had a career were it not for Elvis. He was such an influential figure that he could have commanded the very best songwriters in the world to pitch him songs.

Would Bob Dylan have turned down an opportunity to write an entire album for Elvis? Would Jimmy Webb? Would Lennon and McCartney? When they started recording *Let It Be*, they would break into old rock'n'roll classics in between their new songs, bashing away at "Stand By Me," "Blue Suede

Shoes," "Words Of Love" and "Save The Last Dance For Me." Imagine if they had formed a relationship with Elvis... imagine him singing some of the more spartan material Lennon wrote for the *Plastic Ono Band* LP, such as "Working Class Hero." Imagine Elvis hearing a demo of "Let It Be" and deciding that he had to record it before anyone else, including the man who wrote it.

But of course Elvis was never going to hear the demo, because he never socialised, never travelled, and kept himself to himself, living out Groundhog Day at Graceland. Elvis wasn't going to a cocktail party, Elvis wasn't hanging out at the wrap party for *Taxi Driver*, wasn't going to the Oscars, wasn't going to appear on *The Tonight Show*, wasn't going anywhere outside Memphis, not if he could help it. "I like to keep myself to myself," he told a photographer at the Hilton. "I don't mind nobody and nobody don't mind me. You can take some pictures, but don't take too many, you know what I mean?"

Paul McCartney was forever in awe of Elvis's early records, and would often hanker after their sound. "To hear 'Heartbreak Hotel,'" he told *Uncut* magazine, "was a magical moment, the beginning of an era ... Of course it's an amazing song. Lyrically, for starters, it was a real shock. You have to remember that, in the mid-Fifties, pop lyrics were mostly fodder ... Then you had Elvis singing, 'Where broken-hearted lovers do cry away their gloom.' I remember thinking how odd it was to hear the word 'dwell' in a song ... It was those little touches that made it different from anything I'd heard before. Elvis is a truly great vocalist ... His phrasing, his use of echo, it's all so beautiful. It's the way he sings it, too. As if he's singing it from the depths of Hell ... Musically it's perfect, too. The double-bass and the walk-in piano create this incredibly haunting atmosphere. It's so full of mystery, and it's never lost that for me."

Describing "Heartbreak Hotel" as Elvis's most alarming performance, McCartney went on to say that when he hears it, he always gets this image in his head: Elvis is driving his Lincoln down the interstate on a clear night in Tennessee. The stars are twinkling, the air is balmy, and he and Bill Black and Scotty Moore are on their way back from a show, with Black's double bass strapped to the car roof. After Black died, in fact, Linda McCartney got hold of that very instrument, of which Paul remains the proud owner to this day.

Elvis didn't just ignore the present; he ignored the past, too. Sinatra was still making classic records in the late Sixties and early Seventies, still finding great ballads, torch songs and chest-beating anthems amid the more contemporary material he was offered, and there's no reason why Elvis couldn't have been the man instead to have recorded the original versions of "My Way," "You Don't Send Me Flowers" or "New York New York." Apart from his gospel albums, so few of Elvis's albums were cohesive musical works. 1971's *Elvis Country (I'm 10,000 Years Old)* was probably the most successful – an album made up of Western swing, bluegrass, honky tonk and rockabilly. Elvis missed so many opportunities to build on all the astonishing work he did in the mid-Fifties. To judge from his musical output in the late Sixties and early Seventies it's almost as though he had deliberately dropped out of the race, uninterested in consuming the music of his peers, let alone competing with it.

He would be influential, but rarely in the way he wanted to be. When the Beatles recorded *Sgt Pepper*, they chose to stay at home rather than tour, explaining that they actually got the idea from the King. "We had this idea that we'd make a record, and the record would go on tour for us," said Paul McCartney. "That came from a story we'd heard about Elvis's

Cadillac going on tour. We thought that was an amazing idea: he doesn't go on tour, he just sends his Cadillac out. Fantastic!"

This was actually a true story. It was announced in 1967 that instead of Elvis appearing in person, his gold Cadillac would be coming to tour Australia and New Zealand. Four round wheels instead of one long cock. Tom Parker was keen to point out that the car would be raising money for various charities, and would be filled with a thousand dollars' worth of toys to give away to needy children. The car arrived in Sydney in January 1968, and was immediately brought to a press conference at the Sydney Trocadero. The car was never idle, and thousands of Elvis fans and car fanatics saw the car during its trip, as it made almost fifty separate appearances. For many, seeing the car was almost as good as seeing Elvis in the flesh. "I cannot understand why I did not take both the super eight camera and the hand held camera," said one obsessive, Don Hudson from Melbourne. "It is the biggest regret that I have had over all these years."

Traffic stopped whenever the Elvismobile appeared, and mobs would surround the car. It even started touring the US. Colonel Parker had managed to talk RCA into buying the car for $24,000 and sending it on tour. So the Cadillac opened shopping centres and was repeatedly wheeled out to be admired in the parking lots of movie theatres to encourage people to see the latest Elvis film. The tour was a great success. In Houston, 40,000 people came to take a look and take home a free "Elvis Presley's Gold Car" postcard. In Atlanta, the car was the guest of honour at a dinner for 250 local dignitaries.

Painted with gold lacquer, diamond dust and fish scales, which gave it a turquoise tint, it had a bar with an ice-maker and a fridge, as well as a custom-made lounge, television and phone. In the back there was an electric shoe polisher, a record player and two eight-track cartridge machines. It was like something out of *Thunderbirds* or *The Jetsons*, with a gold curtain separating the front and back seats, and a fur-lined floor. The headlight rims, door handles, exterior mirrors and hubcap bullets were all plated with 24-carat gold.

With Elvis living in cloistered seclusion in Graceland, his car could make all the personal appearances he wanted it to.

CHAPTER SIX

What Happens In Vegas …

"I came out here, to Vegas, and I made me some neon promises, to be good to myself, to my audiences, my fans, and my women"
– Elvis Presley

While Elvis was never invisible, his inner world always remained terra incognita. Elvis hardly ever agreed to interviews, and those he did tended to be anodyne, casually monosyllabic and ultimately opaque.

Take the transcript of his press conference on June 9th, 1972, at Madison Square Garden. He adopts the guise of a humble entertainer, one whose reluctance to offer an opinion, or deviate from his script, makes him appear stoically bland. It's remarkable how respectful he is of his audience, forever grateful for his success and unblemished by the slightest hint of weariness or haughtiness. Elvis's soundbites here are little different from the ones he gave seventeen years earlier, when he was just starting out in the business, and could hardly look at a TV camera without blushing. He is flanked by the Colonel and by his father, both of whom give the impression that they're holding on tightly to invisible string, attached to every part of Elvis's mind and body. His behaviour also suggests that his aggressive attitude on stage was the result of a genuine transformative act. For his fans, the fact that he was so normal in the flesh made his stage persona even more extraordinary.

Dressed in a pale blue suit with black trim on the lapels, he smiles throughout the conference. Watching today on

YouTube it's easy to be mesmerised by his good looks – his way of being both bashful and arrogant at the same time makes him come across as supremely confident, as well as highlighting his handsomeness – but if you only read the transcript, Elvis seems utterly ordinary.

Elvis: Would you like me to sit down? ... First of all, I plead innocent of all charges! Okay ...

Q: I love you Elvis!

Elvis: Thank you dear, I love you too. Thank you. Okay.

Q: Elvis, what took you so long to play New York City?

Elvis: I think ... I think it was a matter of not getting the building, the proper building. We had to wait our turn in order to get the building.

Q: You couldn't get a building in all these years?

Elvis: Couldn't get a good building in fifteen years! No, all kidding aside, we had to wait our turn to get into the Garden, you know?

Q: What do you think of performing here live?

Elvis: Oh I like it you know, I enjoy it ... I just hope we put on a good show for everybody.

Q: Mr. Presley, why do you think you've outlasted every other entertainer from the Fifties, and for that matter the Sixties as well?

Elvis: I take vitamin E! No, I was only kidding. I just ... embarrassed myself, man. I don't know dear. I just enjoy the business. I like what I'm doing.

Q: I hear from a lot of press reports that you really are a shy, humble, wonderful human being. Would you agree with that?

Elvis: Oh I don't know what makes them think that, I got, you know, this gold belt and ...

Q: Elvis, you seem to have less grease in your hair these days.

Elvis: No, I stopped using that greasy kids' stuff just like everybody else did, man.

Q: You used to be bitterly criticised so much for your long hair and gyrations and you seem so modest now.

Elvis: Man, I was tame compared to what they do now! Are you kidding? I didn't do anything but just jiggle, you know?

Q: Give us a jiggle! No, how do you feel about entertainers today? How do you feel about the way they perform?

Elvis: Oh, I don't know. I really can't criticise anybody in the entertainment field. I think there's room for everybody and I hate to criticise another performer, you know?

Q: Are you satisfied with your image?

Elvis: Well, the image is one thing and the human being is another, you know, so ...

Q: How close does it come? How close does the image come to the man?

Elvis: It's very hard to live up to an image, I'll put it that way.

Q: Do you think that your audience, or fans vary to any great extent?

Elvis: It's according to what you're talking about, I don't know. No, I don't know, I'd like to think so.

Q: What I mean is, what kind of audiences do you attract now?

Elvis: Well, I've found that in the audiences we have, it's mixed. It's older people, younger people and the very young and all types of people you know, which is good.

Q: Do you have any new projects? What are you up to now Elvis?

Elvis: I just had a movie of the last tour that I did. It's the first live concert that we ever filmed, so that's my next project that's coming out.

Q: Elvis, what finally made you come out of seclusion and decide to make personal appearances again?

Elvis: I just missed it. I missed the closeness of an audience, of a live audience. So just as soon as I got out of the movie contracts, I started to do live concerts again.

Q: Will you be continuing to do more live work in the future?

Elvis: I think so. There's so many places I haven't been yet. Like I've never played New York. I've never been to Britain either.

Q: Would you like to go there then?

Elvis: I'd like to, yes sir. I'd like to very much. I'd like to go to Europe, I'd like to go to Japan and all those places. I've never been out of the country except in the service.

Q: Mr. Presley, as you've mentioned your time in the service, what is your opinion of war protesters and would you today refuse to be drafted?

Elvis: Honey, I'd just sooner keep my own personal views about that to myself cause I'm just an entertainer and I'd rather not say.

Q: Do you think other entertainers should refuse to be drafted?

Elvis: No, I can't even say that!

Q: Elvis, they filmed your Boston concert last year so why aren't they allowed to film here?

Elvis: Are you allowed to what dear?

Q: Why did they film your Boston concert but they aren't allowed to film here?

Elvis: I don't know, that's a good question! Why is that Colonel?

Colonel Parker: I didn't hear. What's the question?

Elvis: She said why did they film the show in Boston but they couldn't film it here?

Colonel Parker: If they filmed it here, I don't want them spreading it around!

Elvis: There you go!

Q: Elvis, do you think you'll ever totally change your style?

Elvis: I just don't feel that it's time yet, you know? Maybe I will someday but not right now.

Q: Elvis, have you ever considered pursuing a political career?

Elvis: No sir. I don't have any other aspirations in politics or anything of that nature.

Q: Would you ever consider doing a more demanding movie role then?

Elvis: Yeah. I'd like to do something in the way of a movie script if I can find the right kind of property. In fact, we're looking for it now. You're talking about a non-singing type thing? Yeah, I'd like to do that.

Q: Elvis, you seem to have shied away from rock'n'roll music in recent times. Do you have a reason for this?

Elvis: It's very difficult to find that type of song. It's hard to find good material nowadays for anybody, for all of us, you know.

Q: But you don't seem to record any rock'n'roll songs at all now.

Elvis: It's very hard to find any good hard rock songs. If I could find them I would do them.

Q: Elvis, who do you find sexy in the world of show business?

Elvis: I don't know. There's a lot of people that I like ... I got out of that one didn't I?

Q: There are a lot of stars today joining politics. Are you campaigning or ...?

Elvis: No sir I'm not. I'm not involved in that at all, I'm just an entertainer.

Q: Elvis, what do you miss most about your past fifteen years making movies and so forth?

Elvis: I don't really miss that much about it. I enjoy it just as much now, if not more than I did then. I would like to think that we've improved ourselves over the past fifteen years.

Q: How about musicals?

Elvis: That's what I mean. I mean musically and vocally and everything. I'd like to think that I've improved over the past fifteen years.

Q: Do you ever feel like taking time off to relax and probably try your luck at escaping the autograph hunters for a while?

Elvis: No, I've got used to it. I would kind of miss it if it didn't happen. If nobody saw me or nobody recognised me or whatever and ask for an autograph … it's part of the business and I accept it. I think I would miss it.

Q: Elvis, do you know if they'll be recording concerts here?

Elvis: It's possible you know, it's possible. I don't know! They have RCA Victor officials here, so I don't know.

Q: Elvis.

Elvis: Yes sir?

Q: What is your favourite recording that you've ever done?

Elvis: "It's Now Or Never." You know "O Sole Mio"?

Q: Which one was the biggest selling?

Elvis: That one. "O Sole Mio" was the largest selling and the next one to it was "Don't Be Cruel." I think, then "Hound Dog" and "Heartbreak Hotel" or whatever!

Q: Elvis, what time did you arrive in New York?

Elvis: I came in last night very late and had to go to bed, cause we're having a rehearsal now and I have to go back to the rehearsal after this press conference … unless you've got something better in mind?

Q: Is your wife with you?

Elvis: No she's not.

Q: You mentioned earlier, Elvis, the shortage of recording material. There's just been a suit filed in Nashville, Tennessee by Nashville songwriters for major recording companies saying that they're not given a fair chance. In your estimation and in your knowledge, are the songwriters, the independent songwriters given a fair chance with major recording companies?

Elvis: I don't think so. I think there's so many companies that everybody becomes independent. Once they have one hit record and they form their own companies and there's so many. And also the people who write them are starting to record their own songs and that's why I said it's more difficult to get good material.

Q: From independent songwriters?

Elvis: Yes.

Q: You don't have any publishing houses yourself, do you?

Elvis: Yes, I'm a publishing firm but I'll take songs from anywhere or from any writer if they're good. It doesn't have to be in my company, it could be just completely an unknown person or anybody who writes a song. If they can get it to me and if it's good, I'll do it.

Q: To your knowledge though, have recording companies favoured the songwriters that work for the subsidiary publishing houses they may own? Do they favour these songwriters?

Elvis: Probably so. Probably so, and being honest I would have to say, yeah.

Q: Mr. Presley, what is your opinion on the suit filed by the Nashville songwriters committee and do you have any say on the matter?

Elvis: Honey, I'm really not aware of this particular suit that you're talking about so I can't answer you accurately, you know? I don't even know the details about it. I went to Hawaii to get a tan for ... New York, yeah! So I'm not aware of it, really.

Q: If a songwriter isn't in publishing then, do you agree that their material should not be used by major record companies?

Elvis: I don't think so. If they're not heard and if they've got good material and they're good songwriters, I think they should be heard.

Q: Elvis, can you give us a few lines of your latest record so that we know what to expect when your next single comes out?

Elvis: I really can't sitting down! No, I can't do that. I'd just sooner save it for the show.

Q: Elvis, where did you get that gold belt from?

Elvis: The belt is an award from the International [Hotel] for the attendance record. It's like a trophy but I wear it just to show off.

Q: Elvis, do you talk to your father?

Elvis: Do I talk to my father? I have to, he handles all my personal affairs.

Q: Can we ask your father a question or two then?

Elvis: Sure.

Q: The other Mr. Presley, at what point did you realise that your son was indeed becoming a very, very famous person?

Vernon Presley: Well, it's kind of hard to say. You know, it all happened so fast it's hard to keep up with it, you know? It just boomed overnight, and there it was! So I'd say maybe 1956, after the first television show.

Elvis: I tried to tell him sooner but he wouldn't listen!

Q: Do you have any regrets?

Vernon Presley: No, I have no regrets of it. In fact, I have enjoyed it, really.

Elvis: All kidding aside, it happened very fast to all of us. My mother, and my father and all of us. You know, everything happened overnight and so we had to adjust to a lot of things really quickly. A lot of good things.

Q: Mr. Presley, do you think that in that time, Elvis has changed in any way at all?

Vernon Presley: No, not really. I can't tell any changes.

Elvis: I sweat more!

Q: Elvis, what kind of songs do you enjoy doing most? Would you prefer to do say, rock or ballads? In other words would you favour a contemporary ballad such as "Bridge Over Troubled Water" or an oldie such as "Hound Dog"?

Elvis: It's a conscious thing, you know? I like to mix 'em up. In other words, I like to do a song like "Bridge Over Troubled Water" or "American Trilogy" or something, then mix it up and do some rock'n'roll, do some of the hard rock stuff.

Q: Are you tired of the old stuff?

Elvis: No. I'm not in the least bit ashamed of "Hound Dog" or "Heartbreak Hotel" or whatever.

Q: Elvis, do you see yourself retiring at all?

Elvis: No, not really. I've got too much energy. I don't think so. Not as long as I can.

Q: How about doing a world tour then?

Elvis: I think they're planning one now, they're talking about this one now.

Q: Elvis, are there any new groups that you like particularly?

Elvis: I can't ...there's a lot of 'em. I can't think of any off hand.

Colonel Parker: I'd like to live up to my reputation of being a nice guy. This is it folks!

Elvis: I've got to go back to rehearsals folks. Thank you very much.

Elvis had a fairly prosaic vocabulary, but occasionally would favour something so surreal it could only have come from his mouth. According to Tony Barrow, the Beatles' former press officer, he used a particularly curious turn of phrase when he welcomed the Beatles to the US: "If there's nothing but catfish in the market not many come to buy. If there are several kinds of fish it draws a bigger crowd, and that's good for show business." When the Beatles first met Elvis, at his Bel Air home on Perugia Way in 1965, they were bored. The meeting predictably turned into a contest to see who had the biggest entourage. Elvis was overly self-conscious, short on conversation, and, according to John Lennon, stoned. "Long live the King," Lennon quipped as they were leaving the house three hours later. "It was more fun meeting Engelbert Humperdinck. I can't decide who's more full of shit, me or Elvis Presley." One of the many paradoxes about Elvis was the fact that he would never display the kind of behaviour associated with his music. He was polite and deferential, saying "Yes, sir" and "No, Ma'am" and standing up when older people entered the room. He wasn't angry, and didn't embody the defiant, disaffected, liberated attitudes of some of his contemporaries.

Around the same time that Elvis met the Beatles, future James Bond star Roger Moore was introduced to Elvis backstage at the Moulin Rouge club in Hollywood. Elvis was ridiculously nervous and insisted on calling Moore "Sir" throughout their conversation, and acted as though he was in awe of the actor.

"Him! In awe of *me!*" said Moore.

In the early days Elvis would never assume that people knew who he was; later, when he knew damn well that they did, he could be just as respectful, and not always as a disguise.

Initially, he didn't even set out to shock. "The very first appearance after I started to record, I was on a show in Memphis where I started doin' that [gyrating his hips]," he said in an early interview published in the book *Elvis: Word for Word*. "I was on a show as an extra added single ... a big jamboree in an outdoor theatre ... uh ... outdoor auditorium. And, uh, and I came out on stage and, uh, uh, I was scared stiff. My first big appearance in front of an audience. And I came out and I was doin' a fast-type tune, uh, one of my first records, and everybody was hollerin' and I didn't know what they was hollerin' at. Ever'body was screamin' and ever'thing, and, uh, I came off stage and my manager told me they was hollerin' because I was wigglin'. Well, I went back for an encore and I, I, I kinda did a little more. And the more I did, the wilder they went."

It's easy to wonder sometimes whether Elvis knew what he had unleashed all those years ago, what exactly he had stumbled upon or invented. Did 1956 actually mean anything to him? What he certainly knew was that he had become famous very, very quickly, that a lot of young people loved his records and bought pretty much anything he made. But did he know what it was about him that was so special? Judging from the way he allowed his career to be so mismanaged by Tom Parker it's not hard to imagine that he perhaps didn't know as much as everyone assumed. Even if he did, he obviously didn't care enough to do anything about it.

Elvis could afford to be nonchalant about the whole thing, as success had stuck to him like a fever. How different his life was from the one inhabited by Carl Perkins, who had just as much right to be called the King of rock'n'roll, and whose song "Blue Suede Shoes" was as influential as anything by Elvis or Chuck Berry. But then Carl Perkins didn't look like Elvis, and was in 1955, at the age of 23, already losing his hair. What's more, just as "Blue Suede Shoes" was climbing the charts, a car crash put Perkins out of action for six months. Twelve days after the accident, as Perkins lay recuperating in the hospital, he saw Elvis on *The Milton Berle Show* announce to the nation that "Blue Suede Shoes" would be his next single. "Elvis had the looks on me," Perkins told an interviewer years later. "The girls were going for him for more reasons than music. Elvis was hitting them with sideburns, flashy clothes, and no ring on that finger. I had three kids. There was no way of keeping Elvis from being the man in that music."

There seemed to be no way to stop him squandering it, either.

The *New Yorker* critic Pauline Kael once observed that Elvis's joyless Vegas stardom had given him the look of a mutant. To judge from some of the other things she said about Elvis she was being kind, but then the King in his later years was certainly starting to morph into a different kind of entertainer. Had he lived, it's quite possible that he would have become even more surreal, even more gothic, even more of a self-parody. After all, Elvis understood irony, and he understood it from the very beginning. It wasn't Big Mama Thornton's version of "Hound Dog" that he decided to copy for his own version back in the day, but Freddie Bell & The Bellboys' slapstick cover, the kind of record that wouldn't have offended anyone.

But would irony keep him alive? Would irony really keep him from himself?

Elvis was bored almost the minute he got to Vegas. He wanted to be at home, didn't like being out in the desert, and didn't care for the claustrophobic nature of the International. He performed two shows a night – at 8pm and midnight for a month at a time. Band members said he'd usually get to bed about 3am but sometimes the group would stay up all night.

"On average of about once a week, Elvis would come to our dressing room and say, 'Hey guys, would you come up to the penthouse tonight – I'd love for you to come up and just hang out with me,'" recalled back-up singer Terry Blackwood. "Of course when Elvis invites you, you can't say no. So we would all go up to the penthouse. He wanted to go up there and sing."

An Elvis concert quickly became a ceremonial event, repeated every night, twice a night, with only minor variations. He might be in good voice, he might just mumble, but whatever was on offer was good enough for those out front. No one knew he had already tired of what he was doing, as most assumed that after a decade of pissing away his talent in his awful adolescent movies, he was ready to get back where he belonged, live and in front of people. Sure, he needed a bit of pageantry these days, but wasn't that a good thing?

By 1970 Elvis was already starting to ape some of the more traditional Vegas performers, such as Sammy Davis Jr. Sammy's place of identity was the road. He flew across the country, free as a bird, with his Gucci and Louis Vuitton luggage, his Tiffany jewellery, his custom-made suits and bench-made shoes, like a gentrified vaudevillian, unable to slow down, and certainly unable to stop. This tiny giant was forever in motion. And he took a sweet-shop of accoutrements with him: a pair of six-shooters, a cape, a sword, half a dozen tape recorders, three record players, four transistor radios, cases of Scotch, cartons and cartons of cigarettes, a set of barbells that no one ever saw him use, a silver shoehorn, a trumpet, a brace of tambourines, a four-season wardrobe, trunks and trunks of gaudy jewellery and, obviously, a box containing an assortment of glass eyes.

On the road, Mr. Peripatetic was answerable to no one (as long as he stayed away from the South, and the potential embarrassment of being refused entry to restaurants and hotels). When it came to "haters" in the audience, Davis had a tactic which he outlined in his autobiography of 1965 *Yes I Can*. If he spotted one he would inject extra energy and life into his performance in order to "get those guys" to "neutralize them and make them acknowledge" him. In a very brave and canny way Davis transformed actual racial prejudice into a means of raising his game and a source of inspiration in his performance. And he partied, too. "He was on the road fifty weeks a year," said one of his entourage. "He was fucking everything he could get his hands on."

That became the blueprint for Elvis's new touring life, and long-term residencies in Las Vegas.

Sammy was also a big Elvis fan. When Elvis opened there in 1969, Davis was right down in front – front row centre. Right in the middle of the show Elvis specifically singled out Sammy, walked down to the edge of the stage, took off one of his big rings and just handed it to him. "Here, have my ring," he said. Elvis was a big Sammy fan, too. Sammy was thrilled, because he too was obsessed with jewellery – jewellery, clothes, money and fucking.

When Elvis started performing in Vegas, the idea felt somehow appropriate. The desert paradise was still considered by many to be the apotheosis of the American Dream, a hallowed place that could bestow riches on its citizens. There was still a sense that the town was lucky, that if you needed a short cut to fame and fortune, then Nevada was where you went, to the go-to town in the sun. Entertainers had been first drawn there because the hoteliers needed bait for the amateur gambler, and the money was too good to turn down. You went to see Sinatra because you'd just dropped $300 on the blackjack tables, and frankly you needed cheering up.

By the time Elvis got there, Vegas already had a strong history of success, much of it built around Frank Sinatra. The Sinatra/Vegas axis traditionally takes in the Rat Pack – the singer's hard-drinking gang, co-starring Peter Lawford, Dean Martin, Sammy Davis Jr., Joey Bishop and Shirley MacLaine – along with a lot of high jinks, a lot of horsing around and lots of lame gags about boozing. But Sinatra also performed hundreds of concerts there on his own, in casinos as varied as the Sands, Caesars Palace and the Golden Nugget. Vegas grew during the Fifties and Sixties as a destination resort while also representing the surface smarts of American post-war prosperity, during a period when Europe was in the doldrums, and Britain in particular was experiencing the fall-out from the break-up of its empire. Vegas was sexy. Vegas was the future. And Vegas had Sinatra. Here was a man in a tux holding a microphone and a glass of bourbon. And nothing else. His show didn't have pyrotechnics, or dancing girls, or lavish, expensive stage sets. There were no spinning orbs, no back-projection, no banks of neon, and no hoary old stage theatrics. There was a singer and some songs, and an orchestra that could blow your bow-ties off. "We're gonna take this here building and move it three feet that way ... now!" he said one night with Count Basie's orchestra behind him. "Hold onto your handbags!"

According to Bill Miller, Sinatra's pianist, "Everything changed when Frank signed with the Sands. His career was on an upswing; he was confident, and it showed in his performances. Sometimes he would rehearse the same night another act would close. We would start around 2.30am, after they cleared the Copa Room, and Frank would rehearse the entire show with the band. That way he could choose the line-up of the songs for the show; we would rehearse until he was completely satisfied. When it came to the music, Frank was a perfectionist. Those were great days to be a musician and working in Vegas."

Here was a man in his natural habitat, treating the stage as though it were his living room or his terrace, taking a small trip between songs to visit the wet bar, and chew the fat with his band. "Morning folks, it sure is early," Sinatra said during one monologue, between "The Moon Was Yellow (And The Night Was Young)" and "You Make Me Feel So Young." "I don't know how you people can stay up till eight or nine in the morning in this town, I just don't understand it at all. We welcome you to the Sands, and hope that you're having a nice evening. Salut ... Jeez, I fell off the wagon with a boom-bang last night. I woke up this morning, my hair hurt." Then, two thirds of the way through the set, the temperature would be dialled down a notch, and Frank would go all gooey, but only in the way that a man's man can. "You know if you've seen us perform before, if you've seen me perform before, that we try to inject a little touch of this kind of song. It's what we call the saloon song, and I have a great reverence towards the saloon song ... I guess I've been singing them in more saloons than any other singer I've ever known in my life. And I've had torches so high I've burned down buildings. Yeah, get that bum outta here! This is a song that you wouldn't consider a sad song, normally I mean, because of the way you hear it done – it's usually done in jazz or Stork Club style ... But when you hear it this way it really does have a different kind of taste ..." And then he starts singing "Just One Of Those Things," and his brooding baritone bends sentences to suit his path, and it just breaks your heart.

Sinatra's ease with his audience, and the way he would ad lib seemingly without thought – muttering "Yeah baby" every couple of minutes, like a proto Austin Powers – appeared to be effortless. Even when he was being harsh, and telling off-colour stories or berating his friends, he was genuinely funny. In a good-natured response to a request from the crowd one night, he said, "Shhhh. When I want you to speak I'll turn the lights on you. No, I don't mean that facetiously, I mean it abruptly."

This monologue from one of his Caesars Palace shows

is typical: "Thank you ladies and gentlemen, and I'd like to say an official good evening to you and welcome you to the palace of the Caesars," he begins. "Where there are now thirteen – me! There were twelve before but we chased them out because they couldn't swing ... And I'd like to talk about Caesars Palace for a minute because it's one of the finest hotels on this side of the street. I don't know about the other side of the street, I rarely cross that, because it's suicide to cross over there. They got some fine saloons in here, they got a lot of action and they got a couple of good restaurants. And then when we close here they're gonna renovate the joint. No they're not, they wouldn't do that ..."

Sinatra always offered unique pleasures. Just when he appeared to be merely filling space, he would rescue everything with a perfectly timed key change or some weird lateral alteration to the melody. Even towards the end of his career, when his voice had lost its edge, its character, its indelible ghostly character carried the songs. You can hear Sinatra walking through songs the way Michael Caine walks through films – not somnambulantly, but as though nothing really could be more natural. Sometimes he couldn't hit the notes too good, but it was still Sinatra. On any given night, even though it was way past midnight, and even though most of the boozed-up audience had no doubt hoovered up a liquid smorgasbord of casino-supplied martinis, highballs, vodka gimlets, and God-knows-what-else, and had probably blown half a week's salary on the tables on their way to the show; even though, at the time, Nevada could still be considered as one of the ungodliest places on Earth, these people weren't simply at a concert, weren't nonchalantly applauding some after-dinner supperclub hack, they were at church, their own church, and had come for an audience with their own personal deity.

Elvis's relationship with his audience could not have been more different. Elvis was all about spectacle. In 1969, as you landed at the airport you could see the giant neon billboard for the show in twenty-foot letters of solid light: "Elvis In Person." Here he was, after a decade in the dark, illuminated for all to see. It may have seemed absurd, or even surreal, but as everything made sense in Vegas, so did the thought of seeing Elvis alive again.

The room itself – the Showroom Internationale – was enormous, and looked a lot like a barn covered in drapes. It was the opposite of intimate. Up on stage, looking like a wrestler in his blue karate jumpsuit, Elvis would rampage through his greatest hits, often at breakneck speed, racing his band to the end of the medleys. And what a band it was: a six-piece group from Memphis and behind them a 25-piece orchestra. To his right were the Sweet Inspirations, the soul group that served as his warm-up act, while behind them was Elvis's own back-up group, the Imperials, all dressed in fuck-me slingbacks and ridiculously smart blazers. Recently his backing singers had started to look like clip-joint girls, in their satin boob-tubes, feather boas and high heels, their silver lamé shorts reflected in the tessellated surface of the huge revolving mirror-ball, suspended from the ceiling. Above the band, above the two thousand paying customers and right near the mirror-ball were a pair of twenty-foot papier-mâché statues of Marie Antoinette and Louis XIV.

When the first fusillade had finished, Elvis would welcome the audience to the showroom. Then the band would start up again, as Elvis motored through another medley of his hits, sounding not unlike an Elvis Presley tribute act. Ten minutes or so later, the song would end abruptly, and the audience would be shocked into applause. After a pause to catch his breath, Elvis would mumble something inaudible, and then amble over to the side of the stage to get a drink. In stark contrast to Sinatra, it would never be whiskey. Later in the show, having turned in a couple of faultless performances of his famous ballads, he'd stand in the centre of the stage, and deliver one of his own monologues ...

"Like to tell you a little about myself ... I started out when I was in high school ... made a record and when the record came out a lot of people liked it ... there was a lot of controversy at that time about my moving around on stage so I went up to New York ... did *The Ed Sullivan Show*, and they just shot me from the waist up ... I was livin' it up pretty good there for a while and then I got drafted, and shafted and everything else ... When I got out I did a few more movies, and I got into a rut, you know there's this big rut just the other side of Hollywood Boulevard. They'll let me do my thing here for a while and then they'll put me away for another nine years ..."

The atmosphere in the dressing room later would reflect how Elvis felt about the show. If he thought it had gone well, the Memphis Mafia, who accompanied him everywhere, would agree with him. If he thought it had gone badly, they would concur in kind. All his buddies would be there, glancing at each other across the room, and trying to pick up Elvis's mood. If he laughed, so would they. If he got mad and denounced one of his band, the backstage crowd would steam in and agree.

Elvis was the biggest game in town, and he was under intense scrutiny. He didn't want to leave anything to chance, and for the first few weeks every show was a rehearsal of some sort. Even though Elvis was the biggest entertainer in the world, performing in Vegas was a big deal. Playing Vegas meant you'd reached the top. Playing Vegas meant you were playing the Big Room, the biggest rooms in the country. For a solo performer – one who wasn't going to end up in a sports arena or squeeze himself into a football stadium – this was the apex. Once you'd played one of the hotels' Big Rooms, the only way was down, or out. And once you'd conquered the Big Room, the only challenge left was to conquer it again and again and again. "A lot of names who meant only to settle into their act ended by hardening into it instead, but they were so big that nobody seemed to notice, or care," wrote Michael Herr, about the headline acts in Vegas. In the Nineties and Noughties, the stars who played Vegas were to learn that reinvention was the way to keep sane, and the way to encourage all your fans to keep coming back; but this wasn't a preset when Elvis turned up in the sand, as he was trying to reinvigorate a show he hadn't actually owned for over a decade.

Elvis soon conquered his own Big Room, by rehearsing his show so often that he could build the jigsaw again and again each night, dialling it up, dialling it down, using his talents to produce a show that was so full of emotion that you felt he had condensed his fifteen-plus-year career into a ninety-minute edit. In Vegas, Elvis discovered that he was extremely good at melodrama, and actually developed the acting skills that had eluded him for over a decade. He was a much better actor on stage in Vegas than he had been in any of his films, as he learned to manipulate his audiences and bend them to his will. Unfortunately, after a few months, Elvis found it so easy to work the crowd that he started first to be bored, and then to repeat himself. The audience would applaud no matter what he did, and laugh at his jokes regardless of how funny they were, and well up whenever he pretended to. By the forces of nature, and his ridiculous fame, Elvis could do with the audience what he liked, which makes you wonder just how far he could have pushed them.

Supposing Elvis had tried to keep all the madness and mundanity at bay by delving deeper and deeper into his act, and worked out a way to bring to the fore whatever had first attracted his millions of fans in the first place. Could, might Elvis have been able to reduce Elvis to his very essence, just as Julia Child or Alice Waters might reduce a sauce?

Picture an alternate universe in which Elvis grew ever darker, in his temperament, his choice of material and his stage antics. Imagine him prowling a rather more lurid, red-velvet world, in which an alter ego, an uber-Elvis, could thrive. Say this one was devilish, and fed the more extreme sexual side of his nature. What if Elvis had decided to exploit the very thing that many felt was responsible for his fame in the first place? What if Elvis had decided to maximise his cock?

As the Dark Star, Elvis could have draped himself in black velvet capes, and carried a black cane with a silver skull as its handle (like Screamin' Jay Hawkins, who'd brandish a pole topped with a rubber human head). Lucifer Elvis would still have had Elvis's self-deprecating sense of humour, but on stage that humour would be darker, more targeted, more scripted, and aimed specifically at the women in the audience. Who needed men in this environment? Who needed men to screw things up? It wasn't just the little girls who understood, it was every woman under the age of fifty.

Shows by the new dark Elvis would have been proper gothic theatre, with crucifixes and coffins everywhere. Instead of a zombie, Elvis would have had a beautiful young girl with a cemetery stare in his coffin, a girl who had been killed – so the story would go, when he told it every night – on his motorcycle. They had just got married, his bride and he, and speeding away on their honeymoon had crashed just before arriving at the Heartbreak Hotel. He would spend twenty minutes pining for her in song, before the coffin was taken away on a trolley and replaced by a neon tombstone inscribed with her name, "Lady."

Behind him on stage would be two large red neon signs, one promising "Non-stop Erotic Cabaret," the other advertising, "Legs, breasts and thighs, $3.95 all you can eat!"

Having been pursued by melodrama all his life, Elvis would finally embrace it, filling his stage show with lashings of sex and death. Especially sex. Even the security guards would look like the zombie mafia. Either that, or deranged lab assistants. The highlight of the first half of the evening, the gothic part, would always be a song that Elvis had found in a version by the psychobilly band the Cramps, and claimed as his own: "When I die don't bury me at all, Just nail my bones up on the wall, Beneath my bones let these words be seen, This is the bloody gears of a boppin' machine."

All this gothic stuff would play into the hands of those who believed the rumours, rife during the early Seventies, that Elvis loved to visit mortuaries in the dead of night. Once there, supposedly, he'd look at the dead bodies, and even join in private embalming sessions.

Elvis's song choices would be far more specific, too. Gone were all the maudlin ballads and puppy-dog songs; in their place were long, drawn-out versions of all those libidinous "grinding" rock songs to which Elvis could swing along, metaphorically fucking every woman in the audience. The slow part of "Hound Dog" would now last over twenty minutes, and serve as the finale of the show, twenty minutes of ridiculous, loping foreplay in which Elvis would stand and grind in front of the women like some hen-night stripper.

In essence, this new dark version of Elvis would be a sex act. Posters would declare his show to be X-rated, and women be encouraged to come in packs – unlike those few men who ventured inside who would find themselves mocked and effectively cuckolded. If a husband dared to come with his wife, she would be the centre of attention for a while, and the King might even French kiss her.

In this parallel world, Elvis would turn the godforsaken precinct of the Hilton's ballroom into a womb. Or, perhaps more accurately, a vagina. In which Elvis stood tall and erect, having entered to the sound of "Also Sprach Zarathustra," as he did every night without fail. There was a silly satanic side to Elvis now, at least on stage; when he would introduce a tune with the words, "This is a song the Lord taught me," he'd find the eye of a woman in the audience, wink, and roll his tongue out at her.

This was the devil's work he was doing, and had nothing to do with the Lord at all. Some of his performances would be so energetic, it was as though he were channelling electricity, and he still sang as though he had itchy underwear and hot shoes. "Thank you," he'd say, drinking in the applause, "you bring a lump to my billfold."

He would revel in the naughtiness of his new show. When he sang "Polk Salad Annie" he would crack up when he said "Polk"; when he sang the line, "they'd go down by the truck patch," he'd make it "Fuck patch," and watch the women gasp. At the end of the song, he'd say, "Well, that woke me up anyway!" He would scour the front row tables looking for someone to strike up a rapport with, or flirt with for a while. "I hope that's bubble gum, dear," he might say to one, or, "Honey, be careful with that pina colada you got there. Is that a chilli dog? Could you eat a whole one?" Occasionally he could get coarse – an anecdote might begin with, "I was talking to some pussy last night ..." – but the crowd didn't mind. By now this was what they had come to expect ...

Sometimes Elvis would just ramble, not that the crowd seemed to care: "I feel that if you can't control sex – the physical impulse for sex – then you can't control anything in your life. You cannot let your body – its desires – rule you. It cannot master your mind, your heart. If you allow it, then all is lost", carrying on, "I am the deciding factor and I rule. The day comes that I can't, then I'm dead. There is more to life than flexing muscle and I intend to follow a code of honour in my life – that's important ..." and so on.

Elvis now served up soft-focus sleaze in a mock-depraved atmosphere. He would wander the audience and touch the women, his women, and it became such a part of his show that the girls, his girls, his lovely perfumed girls, would squeal and holler if he didn't come down from the stage to touch them. If he hadn't come down among them by the intermission, they would start screaming, demanding he come amongst them, so to speak.

Everything about Elvis's auditorium smelled of sex. The leatherette. The fake leopard-skin. There were candles everywhere, all the cushions were in reality pink and fluffy pillows, and the cocktail list contained such concoctions as "Slow Comfortable Screwdriver," "Hot Pearl Snatch" and "Hot Pearl Of Woman Need." This was an ornate bordello, but one that treated its guests as stars. Women weren't simply playthings here; they were Elvis's celestial goddesses, and would be treated accordingly.

Elvis had started commissioning songs to suit his new guise, too, overwrought Latino ballads with titles such as "What's Inside A Woman" and "Till I Come Inside," which would send the women out front into fits. The seats were often soiled afterwards, just as they had been when Elvis first played movie theatres in the mid-Fifties. "He's so dirty," one woman would explain, in fake outrage. "I know, it's great," said another, smiling. "I think I caught him looking at me during one of the early songs, and I could swear he knew what I was wearing underneath. I truly blushed, if you know what I mean. I had to go to the bathroom right after! I felt real dirty but there was no one to see, and I'm not so sure it happened anyway, it was just a fleeting glance. And he's looking at someone else right now, so I'm not going to pay it any mind."

The slump-shouldered waitresses in the room were largely fallen pompom girls and former cheerleaders who had fucked themselves into a job where the tips were always bigger than the wage. At least that was the idea. The thing was, serving drinks to giggly menopausal women was never going to make them rich, so they had to fuck their line managers again to get out into the casino pits. The waitresses were dressed as though they'd just come from the Playboy Club, with high heels and fishnet tights segueing into strapless, low-cut sequined swimsuits with white powder-puff tails. Many still wore the super-heavy eyeliner and super-high teased hair. The difference with these girls was that they had little devil's tails poking out of their powder-puffs, and horns instead of sparkly bunny ears.

The root of the Elvis magic lay in his well-honed showbiz instinct for knowing exactly which lip-curls, pelvis-thrusts and yelps would whip a hall full of slightly tipsy housewives into a frenzy, and his girls didn't expect anything less. Or want anything less. They were there to be manipulated and would have been very unhappy if they hadn't been. The waitresses would shuttle back and forth between the bar and the tables, encouraging the women to have another gin sling but all any of them wanted to do was stare at the stage. They'd had enough free drinks in Vegas not to worry where the next glass was coming from, even if they occasionally had to pay for it themselves. Everything in Vegas was on tap, including Elvis. Tonight there was a table of black women towards the back of the room, and a table of sullen journalists, and an Indian couple, who didn't look like they really knew what was going on, but practically everyone else in the room looked the same – white women of a certain age with big hair and shiny red lipstick. Two of them were in wheelchairs, clutching their handbags tightly on their laps.

Cynics would say that Vegas had started to resemble the final hours of the Roman Empire, as everywhere you looked, some prominent entertainer was degrading him- or herself in public. But no one watching Elvis felt degraded; tonight, like every night, every button was being expertly pushed …

Elvis always had a voodoo sensuality etched on his face, but recently he had started to play up to the look, even including "I Put A Spell On You" in his stage set. For this number he often flung rubber snakes around the auditorium, although he hadn't done this for a while, as the phallic nature of the toys proved too much even for him. He enjoyed teasing the crowd, and was pleased with the way he had developed this new stage persona, but even he drew the line at throwing glorified dildos around the place.

When all the raunch and the touching had stopped, after he had finished his penultimate song, the "Burning Love" soundalike "Sunglasses After Dark," Elvis's final song of the night was always the same. Kneeling on the floor, with his microphone in one hand and his cane in another, he'd sing "Love Me Tender," accompanied only by a saxophone, being played low, way offstage.

He would stroll back and forth across the stage, accepting the applause as if he were a Roman emperor, acknowledging the crowd's enthusiasm by feigning surprise, like the faux-humility of a fashion designer at the end of a catwalk show. He would walk back and forth, back and forth, bowing, and mock scraping. Aah, my subjects!

And the women loved it, and loved him for it. They sat there in the dark, smiling lasciviously in the soft pink glow of the little lamps on their tables ... In here it was warm and musky: out there in the night, in the desert and sagebrush, it was cold and heartless.

Women had always loved Elvis, but they loved this new dark Elvis more than ever. He loved them, too. He even considered recording a live album at the venue, *Elvis On Main Street*, its cover an homage to the Rolling Stones, full of photos of Elvis's "girls," pictures taken by a roving photographer, who charged $25 a pop.

Tonight Elvis walked down from the stage and started to thread between the tables, saying his hellos and kissing hands and giving all the girls his genial smile. As he walked, he joked into his microphone, referring to himself in the third person. When Elvis had taken to the stage at the Russwood Stadium in Memphis in July 1956, he had been preceded by over two hours of novelty variety acts. When he took centre stage, he announced to the 14,000-strong crowd, "I'm gonna show you what the real Elvis is like tonight." Tonight he had a similar line, although the real Elvis tonight was a much more laid back one, if slightly ragged around the edges.

When one of the women complimented him on his jumpsuit, he said his collar was so big it even had its own hangar, next to the one he kept his jet in. Everyone laughed. Elvis moved on, stopping to comment on a woman's hair.

"You sure look lovely ma'am. I'd love to mess with that hair of yours. Would you like me to mess with you, honey?"

Even in this light, you could see her blushing. So Elvis leaned over and kissed her on the cheek, his low-plunging V-neck revealing a smooth, tanned chest. His heavy red belt and studs caught the lights, and then he was off again, trying to outwit the beam.

The women stroked his hair, draped their fingernails down his collar, and stayed a little too long when they went in for a kiss, even if they were just brushing his cheek. Some would whisper room numbers in his ear, while others would slip keys or notes into his hand. Often a husband would put a restraining arm around his wife's waist as she started to make a fool of herself. When Elvis was in the room, a husband would always know exactly how attractive his wife was in comparison to all the other women there, and a protective arm would often pull an over-excited spouse away from the object of her lust – not out of jealousy, but out of love. As they were pulled away the women would paw Elvis one last time, banking a memory.

Five minutes later he would be back on stage, introducing his next song, a version of Billy Swan's "I Can Help," in which he would thrust his groin upwards whenever he sang the word "help." Each time, there were hollers from the crowd.

After the song finished, his voice would drop to a whisper as he began to thank the crowd for coming, looking as sincere as he could. Which wasn't much.

"I came out here, to Vegas, and I made me some neon promises, to be good to myself, to my audiences, my fans, and my women. But I must say there is a lot of temptation here tonight, and there are some mighty pretty ladies here tonight. I'm getting hot and hard just thinking about you girls …" – a massive roar along with embarrassed squeals from the crowd – "but I want to leave you with a song I hope to be singing to one of you later…"

There were two thousand people, mainly women, here tonight, like every night, and the Hilton's baroque ballroom, with its red-velvet booths, midnight-blue wallpaper and crystal chandeliers – some of which had diamante stilettos dangling from them – was alive with lust. As he sang his song, he indulged in his usual "kiss-fest", heading under the stage to deliver kisses to the eager women below to the accompaniment of groans, giggling and astonished gasps of breath. The women were rapt, and you could almost hear them panting.

Who knew Elvis could be such a slut? He hadn't yet resorted to strolling onstage wearing nothing but a pendulous cock, but the temptation was certainly there. As he left the stage, he pulled a pair of red panties out of one of his hip pockets, and wiped his mouth with them. Then he winked at an imaginary girl in the front row, licked the panties so that even those in the back of the ballroom could see, leered once more at the imaginary girl, and then put the panties back where they'd come from.

Then he was off, as the band played a loping version of "The Stripper" by David Rose as he sprang backstage.

As the house lights came up, and the crowd began to pour back into the lobby, one woman's voice sang out as the band suddenly stopped: "Oh my good God. I know it's wrong and I know I'm a married woman, but you know what Cissy, I'd stay in Vegas one more night if I could just get down on my knees and suck some of that Elvis cock. That boy could fuck the living daylights out of me for a week and I wouldn't come up for air, not even if Bobby was knocking on the bedroom door ... I swear I gotta go and clean up as I'm as wet down there as my whirlpool bath."

As the women left, there behind them, hanging from the top of the atrium, was an enormous Velvet Elvis, a black

179

velvet flag the size of a racquetball court. The Elvis depicted was not the skinny one with the slicked-back hair where he's holding an unplugged guitar. And it wasn't the flabby one, when he momentarily looked as though he was about to die. The Velvet Elvis in the Hilton showed the present Elvis, with a touch of blue in his hair, a collar that suggested one of his black magic jumpsuits, and lips that quivered if you stared at them long enough.

The women would carry on talking, ignoring the giant lips as they went back to their rooms to freshen up.

CHAPTER SEVEN

Are You Lonesome Tonight?

"He didn't want to be reminded that he wasn't Elvis Presley any more" – Tom Jones

Elvis's last concert took place at the Market Square Arena in Indianapolis, on June 26th, 1977, in front of a crowd of 18,000. As with every night of his ten-day final tour, Elvis wore his "Aztec" jumpsuit, embroidered with a Mexican-inspired sundial motif. This was sacramental glamour. Bill Belew, the costume designer responsible for many of Elvis's best-known outfits – the jumpsuits, the capes, the boxing-style belts – had been working on a new stage outfit for the last few months.

Elvis and the Colonel had discussed finally going to Europe, perhaps as soon as the spring of 1978, and they knew they would need a new look. Belew had gone as far as he could with the jewels and the embroidery work, and was working on a new idea involving lasers: "We designed all the wires and everything so that when he walked onstage in the jewelled cape there would be a remote control he would press and eight lasers would shoot out from different points all over the suit. That's what we were working on." Belew showed the designs to Elvis on August 14th, and they were thinking of trying it out on the new tour, which was due to start on August 17th. On the day of Elvis's death, Belew and the electricians were planning to spend the afternoon testing it.

Preposterous as they were, Elvis's jumpsuits and capes were enormously influential in a theatrical sense. They were copied shamelessly by many entertainers, not least the US daredevil, Evel Knievel, who also borrowed Elvis's sideburns and swagger. Throughout his career, Knievel was so renowned for his leather jumpsuits as to be almost unrecognisable without them. When he started wearing them, he had a penchant for aggressive, carnival colours, but though he experimented with many designs over the years, he eventually became totally identified with the star-spangled Stars & Stripes leather jumpsuit, complete with cape and boots. Jumping over rows and rows of cars on his motorbike, he looked like a cross between a traffic cop and Captain America. This particular jumpsuit peeled open with a rabbit's foot to give a v-shaped glimpse of the man-pelt beneath. The reason for all this, Knievel would say, was because he saw how Liberace had become not just a performer, but the epitome of what a showman should be. So each new stunt, each new TV jump, each new public appearance required another jumpsuit, each one more extravagant than the last. So synonymous with the jumpsuit was he that he was even lampooned in the TV cartoon *South Park*:

Lady: "Oh, love the Elvis costume, Chef."

Chef: "Elvis? I'm Evel Knievel. Why the hell would I dress up like Elvis?"

Lady: "Well why the hell would you dress up as Evel Knievel?"

As far as Elvis was concerned, no new stage outfit could disguise the fact that he was overweight, obviously tired, and lacklustre on stage. There were also increasing rumours about his drug abuse.

"The last year of his life was rough," wrote Priscilla Presley, who divorced him after six long years of marriage in 1973. "I knew that. I knew he was having all sorts of heartache. He wasn't happy. As a result, he abused his body. It was that abuse that killed him. Elvis thought he was indestructible. We thought the same thing. After all, he was worshipped by a world of fans who treated him like a God. He was misunderstood by those around him, especially at the end. We underestimated his emotional pain. And he lacked the means to fully express that pain."

How right she was.

Elvis was worried about his future. In 1975 he had missed out on the possibility of starring opposite Barbra Streisand in her remake of *A Star Is Born*, yet another career miscalculation of the kind that had kept him in a state of stasis since he emerged from the Army in 1960 – famous but neutered. The decision was made by Parker, who was always scared when Elvis wanted to veer outside his comfort zone, but Elvis went along with it. Streisand and her producers met with Elvis on several occasions to discuss the film, which intrigued Elvis as he thought it could revive his film career. Yet not only did Parker insist that Elvis have top billing – even though he hadn't had an acting role since 1969 – but he also demanded a huge advance. In essence he deliberately priced Elvis out of the picture, as he didn't want him to do it – he didn't want Elvis portrayed as a man having anything resembling a show business career in decline.

There were many other film offers like this, all turned down. *Halloween* director John Carpenter – who later helmed the 1979 *Elvis* biopic starring Kurt Russell – even wrote a script for Elvis in the early Seventies, called *Blood River*. "I wanted Elvis and John Wayne to make a movie together," he said. "I thought that would be so fun and cool." Elvis had also been discussed as a possible choice for the Joe Buck character in John Schlesinger's *Midnight Cowboy,* the role eventually played by Jon Voight. Elvis's MGM agent said that all they needed to do was "clean up the script, and get rid of some of the smut," as well as ask Elvis to record Fred Neil's "Everybody's Talkin'" instead of Harry Nilsson.

Elvis's sense of isolation must have been overwhelming. He lived in Elvis World where nothing and nobody was allowed to gain entry unless they were in thrall to the cause. In the Elvis World bubble there were no duets, no co-stars or joint headliners on stage, on record or on film. There were no collaborations, no charity records, no guest stars in his live show – there was nothing but Elvis.

The King had long been talked about as a possible singer for one of the James Bond films; his arch baritone would have worked perfectly with many of the John Barry-penned theme songs of the period. Just imagine what Elvis could have done with "Thunderball," "From Russia With Love" or "We Have All The Time In The World"; just imagine how he could have livened up "Diamonds Are Forever" or "Mr. Kiss Kiss Bang Bang." Barry's music shimmered with class and significance, immediately transporting you to a retro-future world of girls, guns and inflammable clothing. It positively swaggered with purpose. Back in the Sixties, when Barry was in his pomp, his themes epitomised glamour when glamour wasn't yet a career option, evoking a sophisticated world full of mystery, travel and sex. He did everything on a grand scale, making music both delirious and maudlin, great orchestral sweeps that made you feel as though you were gliding through space, careering down a ravine, or driving at speed along an Italian motorway.

All of which would have been very Elvis. Just imagine him singing the counter-melody over the top of any Barry instrumental from the time – "Vendetta" or "The Ipcress File" for instance – and it's easy to see how Elvis could have successfully reinvented himself in a heartbeat. Barry's music gleamed with menace, and in the Sixties and early Seventies, a time before irony had been exhausted as a cultural trope, a period before self-referential art, when prefixes like ultra-, neo-, cyber, uber-, super-, demi- and mega- were not yet necessary, Barry's soundtracks encapsulated pop's ability to transform popular culture by mere association.

Which could have done wonders for Elvis.

The Bond films were, like some Elvis films – especially the Hawaiian ones – simply travelogues, showing an out-of-reach Pan-Am jet-set world full of exponential fun and danger. But whereas Bond was always pushing the envelope – Bond creator Ian Fleming was obsessed with self-improvement – everything about Elvis's films was reductive, especially the songs.

The thought of Elvis as Bond is not original; many people have enjoyed the idea of Elvis doing a Bond movie. Go on YouTube and you can see a marvellous mash-up of Elvis's "Surrender" and various John Barry flourishes accompanying a *Skyfall* trailer, as well as a video of Elvis as Bond, using "The Edge Of Reality," a single he released in 1968, as its theme song. Then of course there's the 2003 Paul Oakenfold remix of "The James Bond Theme," onto which he grafted some instrumentation from "A Little Less Conversation." However, the Bond films scored by John Barry would have suited Elvis's baritone the most; his slightly arch, occasionally camp voice would have benefited enormously from Barry's swirling, maudlin strings, and the staccato flourishes of glockenspiel and vibraphone. How satisfying it would have been to hear a theremin or a cimbalom on an Elvis record, singing something in a minor key, buttressed by a Chinese wall of sound. To compound this, Bond's self-deprecation, and the ironic nature of his lifestyle in the films would have helped humanise Elvis, and no doubt brought him a whole new audience. A younger audience …

Elvis himself loved Bond, not least because he was a gadget freak, and took great delight in trying to secure – or in some cases, even manufacture – the boys' toys he saw in the films. He loved to collect fake guns from movie sets, and he loved walkie-talkies and attaché cases too – to keep his toy guns in. He owned one of the world's earliest mobile phones, having seen Sean Connery use a car phone in *From Russia With Love* in 1963. The device was retained in a carrying case the size of a suitcase complete with his name etched on the front in black letters on a gold label. He loved nothing better than going for a ride in his limo, and then making a call in front of his passengers. This was living!

The last film Elvis ever saw was a Bond movie – *The Spy Who Loved Me*, late at night on August 10th at a special viewing at the General Cinema in Whitehaven, Tennessee. He particularly liked the tickertape watch and the KGB music-box radio, both of which he jokingly said he wanted delivered by the time he was back from the new tour.

John Barry also wrote the theme for *The Persuaders*, the 1971 Bond-on-TV irony-fest starring Tony Curtis and Roger Moore as two international playboys-cum-crimefighters. For many men of a certain generation, the title sequence was a formative experience right up there with their first cigarette or first kiss. Curtis. Moore. An Aston Martin DBS. A Ferrari Dino. Girls. What more could a boy want? A decade before *Miami Vice* or *Moonlighting*, this was a show that had a gun in its pocket and a tongue in its cheek. Barry's haunting theme remains attached to the period like the broken zip on a pair of purple slacks, and was one of the least ironic parts of the whole equation. The irony in *The Persuaders* was ripe, and

Elvis would have been interesting in the Tony Curtis role, perhaps the perfect foil for Moore's snooty proto-Bond.

Elvis may not have been a great actor, but he knew exactly what was expected of him, which is sometimes just as important, especially in a Bond movie. Just before Daniel Craig's first Bond film, *Casino Royale*, I asked John Barry what he thought of the latest 007. "I hope Daniel Craig will be all right," he said. "He's a very good actor, probably one of the best. But that's never been a necessity for Bond. This could be the death of him! It's a fine line, that Bondian thing. Sean [Connery] made it work better than anybody else. I hope he doesn't take it too seriously."

Elvis wouldn't have taken it seriously at all – wouldn't have been able to – which is why he could have been perfect.

By 1977, Elvis's concerts were far from perfect. In fact they had become tragic-comic spectacles, and the photographs that were making the papers made him look like a carnival freak. Elton John and writing partner Bernie Taupin went to see him perform in Washington just a few months before he died. According to Taupin, "It was absolutely pitiful. He was so drugged, he could hardly sing – he just stood there, handing out scarves. Then we were taken backstage to see him. There was this dressing room, full of the Memphis Mafia, with Elvis in the middle of them on a stool, wrapped in towels. He looked awful, he was sweating, with the dye from his hair running down his face. And all these guys in suits around him in a huddle. I don't think he even knew who we were."

As they walked away, Elton said, sadly, almost to himself, "He's not long for this world."

Harvey Kubernik described a similar Elvis in *Melody Maker* in 1976: "The show began with 'C.C. Rider,' and the screaming never stopped. He still gets 'em hot. But his movements are now so restricted that at times the concert is sluggish and pathetic. He dropped the microphone a couple of times and, even if it's a gimmick, forgetting the words to songs is a poor gesture to a sympathetic audience."

Even if Elvis no longer drove his female admirers into screaming paroxysms of delight, his concerts were always full. Still using some of the moves he appeared to copy from Edmond O'Brien in *The Girl Can't Help It*, which predated Presley's performance in *Jailhouse Rock* by a year, Elvis could still milk his crowd like a prize fighter. At an appearance in Hollywood in Florida in February, one fan was asked whether a paunchy 42-year-old Elvis could still be sexy. "It doesn't matter," she said. "He's Elvis."

Of course you could say that one reason Elvis was so reluctant to expand his talents was his fans. The closed-circuit relationship of star and fan has no need for the outside world, so even if the outside world is looking for artistic expansion, the co-dependent relationship of idol and worshippers may not. Why struggle to find a new formula when the old one keeps on giving?

"I think Elvis is genuinely amazed by some of his fans," said a member of his entourage. "I've seen looks in his eyes that say, 'Man, you're weird.' I mean, how could he take it all seriously after all these years?"

Millions loved the grandiosity of his music in the Seventies, and in some respects there was a poetic truth to his bloat. "As he swelled, so did his music," wrote one Elvis fan. "When, finally, his shows had become as grandiloquent as grand opera and his voice as mighty as a primo tenor's, he truly looked the part, as formidable as Pavarotti or Caruso."

At the time, Elvis liked to entertain after his concerts, and to receive any rock luminaries, or indeed any new pretender, anyone stepping up to flex their muscles and try to steal his crown.

Led Zeppelin's Robert Plant was particularly impressed by him. "The first Elvis song I heard was 'Hound Dog,'" he told *Rolling Stone*. "I wasn't equipped with any of the knowledge I have now, about the Big Mama Thornton version or where all that swing was coming from. I just heard this voice, and it was absolutely, totally in its own place. The voice was confident, insinuating and taking no prisoners. He had those great whoops and diving moments, those sustains that swoop down to the note like a bird of prey. I took all that in. You can hear that all over Led Zeppelin.

"When I met Elvis with Zeppelin, after one of his concerts in the early Seventies, I sized him up. He wasn't quite as tall as me. But he had a singer's build. He had a good chest — that resonator. And he was driven. 'Anyway You Want Me' is one of the most moving vocal performances I've ever heard. There is no touching 'Jailhouse Rock' and the stuff recorded at the King Creole sessions. I can study the Sun sessions as a middle-aged guy looking back at a bloke's career and go, 'Wow, what a great way to start.' But I liked the modernity of the RCA stuff. 'I Need Your Love Tonight' and 'A Big Hunk O' Love' were so powerful — those sessions sounded like the greatest place to be on the planet."

When they met, Jimmy Page joked with Elvis that the band never soundchecked, but that if they did, Plant would insist on singing Elvis songs. Elvis thought that was incredibly funny and asked Plant which ones.

"I told him I liked the ones with all the moods, like that great country song 'Love Me' – 'Treat me like a fool/Treat me mean and cruel/But love me.' So when we were leaving, after a most illuminating and funny ninety minutes with the guy, I was walking down the corridor. He swung around the door frame, looking quite pleased with himself, and started singing that song: 'Treat me like a fool ...' I turned around and did Elvis right back at him. We stood there, singing to each other."

Elvis obviously had a lot of female visitors backstage, many of whom were simply groupies, and while he liked to share the love, he also liked to appear choosy. This is where he differed from his rock'n'roll peers, Jerry Lee Lewis and Chuck Berry, both of whom were far more eager to embrace their fans. Once, when the Rolling Stones were hanging out in Lewis's Winnebago after a gig, three scantily dressed young girls popped their heads round the door.

"Hey Jerry," said one, in a deliberately sexy Southern drawl. "You smell nice. What's that you got on?"

To which the Killer answered, "I got a hard-on. But I didn't know you could smell it."

Although Elvis would joke about women with his buddies – he was caught on camera in the back of a car with some of the Memphis Mafia, saying he had missed an altercation the previous day as he had been "buried in a beaver" – he hated appearing trashy in the press.

"I don't read movie mags," he told one audience. "That stuff is junk. If they don't know something about me, they make it up. I know they have a job to do – they have to write something – but if I had done one tenth of what they say, my karate instructor would not allow me to wear that belt. I would not be who I am – I would not walk out on this stage. I could not face my daughter, or my father."

Few people turned down the opportunity to meet Elvis. Like Sinatra, the idea of Elvis was bigger than the man himself, and most interested parties wanted their own impressions. The chance to meet Sinatra was an opportunity to put your hand in the cage; with Elvis the attraction was more prosaic. He was the King, and who wouldn't want to meet royalty, who wouldn't want to be whisked into their orbit for a moment, however fleetingly? There were some – women, obviously – who had short- or long-term designs on Elvis, but most just wanted an anecdote: "I met Elvis and he was like THIS …"

As a lot of performers tended to be *allegro* on-stage and *moderato* when they're off, and as the general public – helped by the popular press – were beginning to understand this, so everyone was turning into an amateur psychologist, wanting their experiences to be the ones with the evidence of truth. Many of his fans simply wanted to know that Elvis was as "nice" and as well-mannered as they expected him to be. Others wanted more; in fact what many wanted was an experience that they could use as an example to show other people that the King was actually "nicer" than they expected. In fact it's surprising that the Colonel didn't cotton onto this as a way to exploit the salient attractions of his boy: which Elvis fan wouldn't have bought a white silk scarf emblazoned with the words, ELVIS – NICER AND BETTER THAN EVER?

Backstage, Elvis could be boorish and crass, but he was rarely offensive when there were "outsiders" around. He had genuine Southern charm, even if he could be a bit gruff. I know someone who spent time with Sinatra in his dotage, when he was in the business of hosting rather than entertaining, and the tale he told was grim to say the least. He was paying a visit to Sinatra's huge home in Palm Springs. Addled by drink, and perhaps by his already encroaching Alzheimer's, in conversation Sinatra proved to be dismissive of all and sundry. Offering my friend a drink, he pointed to his black waiter and said, "This coon will bring you anything you like," before launching into a tirade about the "Jewish-run" record industry, controlled by thieves and "kikes." The denouement of this meeting was signalled by the arrival of Sinatra's wife, Barbara, who entered the room wearing a bright red dress.

"Hey Barbara," shouted Sinatra at the top of his voice. "You look like a blood clot."

They then all decamped to a nearby Mexican restaurant, where Sinatra fell asleep mid-burrito.

Initially, Sinatra thought Elvis was something of a rube, or in Rat Pack vernacular, a "Clyde" – a geek, a jerk, a loser ... a civilian. Clydes were those ordinary Joes who had no future and no sparkle, those everyday, unworldly guys who were content to spend their lives on the margins. Either that or they were try-hards, those guys who wanted to be cool but who would obviously never be. Sinatra would always say he preferred the Beatles: "At least they're white." He was far more enthusiastic about other performers who came in his wake. In the mid-Seventies, when asked about the mania surrounding Barry Manilow, Sinatra simply said, "He's next."

For most, the sheer physical fact of an encounter with Elvis overrode any subjective or critical interpretation. The act of meeting Elvis was just too overpowering, like meeting the Pope or a President. With Elvis, all one needed to be swept away was a handshake and a "Pleased to meet you ma'am, good to meet you sir," delivered in that marinade of a voice. Elvis was surrounded by people employed to protect, guard, transport, feed and flatter, so all he had to do was stand and talk – uninterrupted and without argument. No one would contradict Elvis, while everyone laughed at his jokes. In this respect he probably thought he had genuine comic talent, as whenever he made a mildly ironic comment about something happening in his orbit, the acolytes – the Memphis Mafia – would collapse in hysterics, as though he had just told the funniest joke in the world.

The meet-and-greets were the only time in the day when Elvis got to meet anyone outside his own bubble. There was the concert of course, but then the concert experience was always exactly the same, with Elvis going through the motions, and his audience doing the same. Surprises weren't encouraged, either by Elvis or his audience, as what they wanted was what was advertised. The meet-and-greets were where Elvis could gauge the reaction of those who had had no previous experience of his world or his act, yet these events were becoming as predictable as the concerts themselves, as the exchanges were almost always identical. Elvis expected sycophancy and little else. He could express curiosity out of politeness – usually with those he considered to be simply "plain folks" – yet as he had such little genuine curiosity about the world, these exchanges usually went nowhere.

Often, when women went backstage to meet him, the exchange was exactly as it would have been if it had happened back in the late Fifties, when Elvis was a teen pin-up. They would giggle, blush, kiss him on the cheek, maybe hug him, and then cover their face with their hands, amazed at being in such close proximity with their idol. Like their hero, they were stuck in the past, encased in aspic, happy to relive their adolescence in the most complicit way possible.

"I went to a New York concert in the early Seventies and I may as well have not existed," recalls a (male) American university lecturer based in London. "The show was all about the women. Sure, there were a lot of men in the audience but we all felt like spectators. Not spectators at a show, but spectators at the relationship between Elvis and all the women in the audience. It was astonishing. I loved the show but after a while began to question why I was there in the first place. I think a lot of men actually wanted to see Elvis, to see what he was like and to tell other people about it; whereas women

needed to see him in a completely different way. It ticked a
different kind of box."

The comedian Steve Martin met Elvis once, backstage
at the Las Vegas Hilton. Martin had been opening for
Ann-Margret, who was in cabaret there, and he had been
performing the kind of surreal magic tricks that later made
him such a star on *Saturday Night Live* (one of the highlights
of his show was sticking his tongue through a piece of tissue
paper, as though it was some kind of sorcery). After her run
was over, she was due to be followed by Elvis, and as the King
knew her and liked her, he decided to take Priscilla to see one
of her final shows. "So, the show is over and we're all in our
dressing rooms," says Martin. "I look down the hall and I see
this beautiful woman coming towards me, and it's Priscilla.
I've no idea it's her, but it's Priscilla. She peels away and then
suddenly there's Elvis behind her – he's all dressed in white,
he's got this black hair and this huge diamond buckle that
celebrates his appearances at the Hilton Hotel. He looks great.
And he sees me, and stops and says, 'Son, you have an oblique
sense of humour.'"

This cracked Martin up, not just because of the way Elvis
pronounced it, managing to make the word sound incredibly
exotic, but also because he used it in the first place.

One wonders how much longer Elvis would have lasted in
Vegas. By 1977 he had already been performing in the desert
for eight years, and was well and truly sick of it – sick of the
dust, the broken neon, the stale smell of last night's Frascati
and the incessant unwanted attention. Had he lived, he
would surely have moved on, perhaps by creating his own
theatre, as Andy Williams and others were to do in Branson,
Missouri, or his own theme park, à la Dolly Parton. A TV
series was already being discussed – who's to say it wouldn't

have become the longest-running variety show in the history of American television? Alternatively, the Colonel could have been forced to sort out his passport issues, allowing Elvis to tour the world, playing all those places he'd only read about in magazines. Who knows how invigorated he might have been by jet-setting around the world, experiencing the delights of London, Paris or Rome. Who knows how fulfilling this would have been, and how travel might have affected his creativity, and his desire to incorporate his experience into his music. Perhaps he would have played stadiums; after all, Elvis was bigger than Led Zeppelin, the Eagles and Fleetwood Mac put together. Why play the Hilton every night when you could play Shea Stadium? Then again, solace might have beckoned instead, and he could have retired from performing, retreating into the relative privacy of the recording studio to create great gothic concept albums, and country and western extravaganzas – triple albums full of overwrought cover versions, telling the story of America through popular song. Or maybe he would have renounced it all and properly got God. Elvis the dutiful preacher would have been the greatest attraction in the known world. Who wouldn't have gone to church to hear Elvis sing gospel?

Elvis was a big church man, and he took his religious studies seriously. Of course he compartmentalised them, and his beliefs would never dovetail with his debauched lifestyle, yet he was a believer and a follower, and extremely susceptible. Which is one of the many reasons he was so popular, especially in the southern states of the US. Women had started to bring their sick and disabled children to Elvis concerts in the hope that he could heal them, hoping to be fortunate enough to have them touched by Elvis himself.

Even though Elvis was a believer, the religious community in Tupelo, the Mississippi town where he was born, was not especially proud of Elvis. Or at least, not until he died. Many from his parents' generation just could not grasp what they considered to be "poor white trash" making something of himself. After his death, however, fans started to send money to the city, to enable them to do something in his memory. This money was eventually used to build the Chapel at his birthplace, but more importantly, it awakened the city fathers to the fact that Elvis was now a tourist draw.

Elvis played his last concert in Vegas on December 12th, 1976. Five days before, he wrote a note almost a song lyric in his suite at the Hilton expressing how he felt "so alone sometimes" and that he "would love to be able to sleep." The verse ends with the refrain asking for help from the "Lord" and the pitifully weary sentiment that I have "no need for all of this."

David Dalton and Lenny Kaye described the finale to one of his early Seventies performances: "He hits his stride on 'You've Lost That Lovin' Feelin',' touching height with 'Bridge Over Troubled Water.' From there, the only place he can possibly go is 'The Battle Hymn Of The Republic' … the kind of show-stopper reserved for a state hero and/or national monument.

"After that, he sets about to deliberately cool things down. First a melancholy 'Funny How Time Slips Away,' with Elvis walking around the stage, singing to different parts of the hall; a forthright 'I Can't Stop Loving You,' which continues the message portion of the farewell; finally, into probably his most lovely song, 'Can't Help Falling In Love.' And then, when it's over, he takes his cape, spreads it across his shoulders, and with arms outstretched, kneels to the audience, head bowed in grateful salute. They are his, he theirs. This is the supreme moment. For royalty, there can be no others."

By the end of his Las Vegas years, Elvis had become a melancholy baby, and happiness seemed to be in short supply. Although most performers will say that the stage is one of the few places that can bestow happiness, and that losing themselves in performance is a state of bliss, for years Elvis gave the impression of sleepwalking through his sets, disdainful of his audience, and unhappy in himself. Performing didn't appear to be a release, or indeed a vehicle for catharsis; often it looked like a chore. Occasionally a fog of incoherence would envelop him, and he would start rambling, his monologues interrupted by laughing and the occasional hearty cough. People were still so nervous around Elvis, and if they were sitting in front of him tended to laugh at anything he said, so he could have probably turned his act into a light entertainment combination of stand-up comedy and mawkish crooning. Some said he already had. If Elvis couldn't find peace on stage, he could certainly find it at home, as Graceland was his one place of solace. Here he was in control, here he was calm. Outside the grounds, the only other place he could find happiness was Hawaii. Both Hollywood and Las Vegas offered too much noise, too much temptation, and too many people. Hawaii was somewhere he could disappear to, somewhere so far away that hardly any non-service American had been there. When he first started visiting the islands, they had yet to be turned into tourist resorts, so Elvis could wander the beaches without being continually stopped for autographs and photographs.

Elvis loved Hawaii, and had a twenty-year love affair with the islands and their people. Of course, he didn't tour abroad – the "Colonel," who had no passport, and no desire to get one, made sure Elvis stayed in the US – and always vacationed in North America. Hawaii was as far away as he could get from

Memphis. From his first visit in 1957 to his final vacation in March 1977, Elvis visited the islands regularly. Not only did he make three movies in Hawaii (*Blue Hawaii, Girls! Girls! Girls!* and *Paradise, Hawaiian Style*), but he also came to Hawaii for live performances, the most famous being the show on January 14th, 1973, that was telecasted worldwide as *Elvis, Aloha From Hawaii – Via Satellite*. In 1969, having just returned from yet another holiday there, Elvis suggested he and the family continue on to Europe. The idea was dropped immediately when Parker argued that Elvis's European fans would be insulted if he were to travel there as a tourist before performing there. They went to the Bahamas instead.

Hawaii was the very first place Tom Parker was stationed after he enlisted in the US Army back in 1929. There being relatively little tourism at the time, the islands were proper tropical paradises. So in November 1957, just as *Jailhouse Rock* was opening in movie theatres across the US, Parker decided to finish Elvis's current tour in Hawaii rather than Los Angeles, convincing his charge that this would be an exotic vacation as well as work. With days to kill, Elvis and his entourage sailed to Honolulu on the U.S.S. *Matsonia*, taking four long days to travel the 2500 miles. On November 10th he played two shows at the Honolulu Stadium (3pm and 8.15pm); for his last performance of "Hound Dog," he jumped off the stage and sang standing just feet in front of the audience. During the intermissions that day, the Colonel gave a masterclass in hawking to locals charged with moving through the audience selling photographs: "Take whatever bill they hold up, and don't give nobody no change."

The dressing room that Elvis used is still in the auditorium, a concrete box with a chair, a sofa and a vanity mirror and nothing else. And it hasn't been used since Elvis sat here in 1973. For the Hawaiians, Elvis's appearance was like Valentino, Sinatra and the Beatles all deciding to play a concert on Waikiki Beach.

Although much of Elvis's Hawaiian work suffered from a crisis of imagination, not all was as anodyne as his critics like to make out. The 1961 song "Blue Hawaii" is so quintessentially "Elvis" that it's difficult to think of it being recorded by anyone else, yet it was originally a hit for Bing Crosby, initially for the 1937 Paramount Pictures film *Waikiki Wedding*, starring Crosby and Shirley Ross. Crosby rerecorded the song in 1956 for an album of the same name, but it will always belong to Elvis – hook, line and surfboard. What's ridiculous is that barely five years after inventing rock'n'roll, Elvis was covering a song that Crosby popularised the year Elvis burst into the public consciousness. An equivalent would have been the Sex Pistols covering Elvis's "Way Down" in 1982, without any hint of irony.

Most of Elvis's thirty-three movies were below par – during "Rock-A-Hula Baby" in the 1961 film *Blue Hawaii* he appears to be dancing with two feather dusters, household implements that, it has to be said, displayed marginally better theatrical skills than some of his co-stars – but they are not without merit, not without their own appeal. The Hawaiian films in particular may not be very good, but they still have a strange attraction, and immense charm.

On paper, little was expected of any of Elvis's films. If you looked through the "forthcoming attractions" column in *Variety* or one of the trade papers in the Sixties, you would often just see "ELVIS MOVIE," like someone might mention a James Bond film – not that an Elvis movie was ever in the same league as a Bond film.

Here, for instance, is the synopsis of Elvis's first Hawaiian film, 1961's *Blue Hawaii*: "Elvis returns to Hawaii after two years in the Army" – did you see what they did there? – "determined not to do what his mother wants, which is to take a job in the family pineapple business, settle down and marry a girl of his own social position.

"Instead Elvis gets a job as a guide in a tourist agency where his sweetheart, Joan Blackman, works, and his first assignment is escorting around the island four pretty schoolgirls, chaperoned by Nancy Walters. One of the schoolgirls, Jenny Maxwell, develops a crush for Elvis and continuously throws herself at him, causing Elvis some trouble with his sweetheart. Everything is resolved in the end, when Elvis marries Joan in a colourful boat wedding and they soon hope to open their own travel agency."

Honestly, could you imagine Carl Perkins, John Lennon, Mick Jagger, Keith Richards, Jim Morrison, David Bowie, Joe Strummer, Kurt Cobain or Liam Gallagher aspiring to open their own travel agency? The storyline of his next Hawaiian film, 1962's *Girls! Girls! Girls!* was just as anodyne, as was the narrative of 1966's *Paradise, Hawaiian Style*: "Elvis and his buddy James Shigeta start a helicopter charter service in Hawaii" – obviously – "Elvis has three gorgeous girls – Linda Wong, Marianna Hill, Julie Parrish – steering customers to his charter service, and business is so good Elvis hires Suzanne Leigh as a secretary. While taking a girlfriend for a ride in his helicopter, Elvis loses control and doesn't regain it till the careening chopper has forced an automobile into a ditch. The driver of the car is John Doucette of the Federal Aviation Agency and Elvis is grounded until further notice.

"Elvis finds that James Shigeta and his daughter Donna Butterworth had a crash landing, and Elvis flies to the rescue. The newspapers have reported the rescue, and the aviation board may cancel Elvis's flying licence permanently. Elvis goes to see John Doucette and explains everything, and the FAA agent assures him that because of the mitigating circumstances of the rescue he will not lose his licence."

It was as though Elvis was appearing in movies scripted by Enid Blyton.

The *NME*'s Alan Smith had this to say about *Paradise, Hawaiian Style* in 1966: "It all bored me to tears. I sat watching the same old situations and listening to the same old songs, and I thought: 'In heaven's name, can't they think of anything original and new?'

"This is my own opinion as a reviewer, and I'm sorry to hurt the feelings of those staunch Elvis fans who are by now reaching for pen and paper, ready to accuse the *NME* of having a permanent hate against their idol. However, surely even they would like to see him in a film with a really strong story line and a good dramatic acting role?

"The songs feature accompaniment by the Mellowmen and the Jordanaires, and include the title song; a pleasant mid-tempo number called 'Queenie Wahine's Papaya,' the catchy 'You Scratch My Back' (which has a beat something like Herman's 'This Door Swings Both Ways'), and a fastish" – "Fastish"? – "tom-tom traditional song, 'Drums Of The Islands.'"

Meanwhile, in the Sixties, Hawaii began to develop its own musical lingua franca, a kind of Polynesian Populuxe dreamworld exemplified by Martin Denny, the King of Exotica. This was exotic mood music, an unapologetic cocktail of Hawaiian melodies, Latin rhythms and all-American sentiments. Exotica was described as apple pie with a hint of mango, a kind of subversive alternative for the suburbanites who weren't interested in joining the counter-culture. "If you've ever tried half a papaya and put a scoop of passion fruit in it, it's a marvellous taste," said Denny. "My music is like that, an exotic fruit salad." His music was a mesmerising and often surreal marriage of quiet jazz and psychedelic sound effects: finger cymbals, bamboo sticks, congas and sea birds. Exotica also used the theremin, a wooden box with two antennae – one controlling the volume, the other controlling the pitch – invented in New York in the Thirties by the Russian Leon Theremin. One of the earliest electronic instruments, sounds were created by the radio waves excited by the wire antennae. It became a staple of many a sci-fi soundtrack; used to great effect by Les Baxter, Clara Rockmore, Samuel Hoffman and Robert Moog in the Fifties and Sixties, and by Captain Beefheart and Tangerine Dream in the Seventies, it also came back into fashion in the Nineties, used by Portishead, Tricky and Jamiroquai. Robert Moog, who invented the legendary analog Minimoog synthesizer in 1971 – thus changing the face and form of modern electronic music – experimented with theremins from an early age. He built his first model at the age of fourteen, wrote many articles on how to construct them, incorporated those ideas into his own work, and eventually began producing the machines commercially.

The theremin, like the work of Les Baxter and Martin Denny, helped give Hawaii a genuine sense of otherness, and the islands soon became the default destination of choice for hip young suburbanites who thought they were above the likes of Palm Springs, Miami Beach or Las Vegas. Consequently, Elvis's presence there helped preserve his allure, giving him an exotic quality that was actually beyond him. While he didn't understand it, he appreciated the fact that he was part of a semi-ironic world that didn't detract from his mainstream appeal.

This fed directly into "tiki" culture, the mid-century style that influenced restaurant design and cocktail bars, resulting in places such as Trader Vic's – Cantonese cuisine and exotic rum punches, with a kitsch decor of flaming torches, rattan furniture, flower leis etc. Here, there was carved teak and Halloween orange everywhere. Exotica and tiki became popular tropes in Hawaii, allowing a whimsical style to develop alongside an un-ironic one. And how did you "do" lounge? How did you join the cocktail nation? Easy: "First, develop an attitude of richness over riches, of swankness, suaveness and strangeness to set yourself apart from the horde of uniformity. Secondly, find or create the proper lounge atmosphere. Set up an overall theme, such as Polynesia or outer space, while blocking out the outside world by covering windows and removing inside clocks. Enhance this theme through undulating drapes and sensuous textures, such as silk or velour throw pillows."

"Hawaii was artificial, and kind of perfect," said David Bailey, who photographed the islands a lot in the late Sixties and early Seventies. "I like rawness, and a sense of adventure, and Hawaii was the last place on earth for any adventure. Every night at six o'clock they'd have a shower in the gardens to cool down the evening. I always took my camera, but there was nothing there to photograph. Everything was too sterile, too plastic. Tahiti was more interesting because it was French, and raw, but Hawaii was too antiseptic. It's incredibly beautiful but I just didn't want to photograph it. There's nothing there, and there never will be."

Nevertheless, Hawaii became a home-from-home for Elvis, and he treated the place as his own back garden. He shared his love of the islands with the world through movies, concerts and songs. "I think it began with the movie, *Blue Hawaii*," said Hawaiian DJ Tom Moffatt. "People got a chance to see a Hawaii that they'd never seen before. A lot of people were attracted to Hawaii because of Elvis and all of a sudden they're seeing the most beautiful place in the world. Elvis and *Blue Hawaii* opened up Hawaii to the world."

It's easy to say that Hawaii is where the emasculation of Elvis began. Certainly the overgrown boy wandering aimlessly through *Blue Hawaii* wasn't the sexual whirling dervish of 1954. When Elvis had started, he had flaunted himself with mascara and glitzy outfits, showing himself off as a kind of heterosexual Liberace. The guitarist Chet Atkins even once said that he "couldn't get over that eye shadow," saying that watching Elvis "was like seein' a couple of guys kissin' in Key West." Well, Atkins was no doubt pleased by Elvis's appearance in *Blue Hawaii*, as he looked completely hetero, but also completely neutered. Even the sex scenes looked like episodes from a sitcom, but then that was the point. All of Elvis's movies were designed for teenagers and were released when they would be most likely to go to the movie theatres, namely the holidays – spring break, summer and Christmas.

His Hawaiian films were little but trailers, acting largely as glorified advertisements, helping put Hawaii on the international tourism map. But by the time it came to film *Paradise, Hawaiian Style* the expectations were so low that the Colonel even tried to get the Beatles to sing a song with Elvis during the finale. Unsurprisingly, they wanted nothing to do with it. The Colonel loved a gimmick, and in 1972 he announced that Elvis would perform a show in Hawaii that would be broadcast worldwide via satellite. He had seen Richard Nixon live by satellite from China, and thought that if it was good enough for the President, then it must be good enough for Elvis, too. The show would start just after midnight in Hawaii, in order for the live performance to be viewed during prime time in Australia, New Zealand, Japan, Korea, Thailand and the Philippines, and seen by the thousands of

US servicemen in Southeast Asia. The following night the concert would be shown in twenty-eight European countries via a Eurovision simulcast, while NBC would air it in the States. So half a billion people would see Elvis run through his 23-song set. It was during the satellite show that Elvis reinvented himself as Captain Marvel, having commissioned a special $10,000 diamond-encrusted superhero cape to wear during the performance.

Elvis's last trip to Hawaii was in March 1977, four months before his death. The islands had become a familiar escape, and he still loved going, yet his body had given way to such an extent that he no longer felt comfortable on the beach, or indeed in the heat. "We played football," recalled one local, "and it was sad, very sad. Elvis was overweight and just unable to function normally. I guess it was all that medication they said he took. Somebody'd throw him the ball and he'd catch it and start running and he couldn't stop. He was just unable to control his own body. One time he ran right into a cyclone fence and cut his hand."

During this trip there was talk of Elvis coming back to Hawaii for another documentary feature, but in reality it was never going to happen. In his deluded state, at the time of his death he was contemplating many things – not least a world tour – and he often talked of starting the tour (a tour the Colonel would probably have never allowed) in Honolulu.

August 16th put paid to all that.

Like a lot of Americans, Elvis thought that if he had been to Hawaii then he didn't need to go anywhere else in the world that wasn't America. He continues to be held in such affection there that the only non-World War II books and artifacts in the gift shop at the Pearl Harbor Visitor Center celebrate his time there. When I visited, having just spent two hours at the site, taking a boat ride out to see the remains of the *U.S.S. Arizona*, this seemed more than a little incongruous, but perhaps no more opportunist than the commemorative Pearl Harbor coffee mugs that sat next to them on the cabinet displays. Elvis still hangs over the islands like a mist, and his name comes up in conversation all the time. I certainly heard his name mentioned more often that Barack Obama's, and he was born there.

Up on the North Shore, the countryside around Ekahi Beach Park ("Pipeline"), Waimea Bay and Waimea Valley hasn't changed in the forty years since Elvis was last here, and the lush, exotic jungle is the place of dreams, the place imagined in *The Blue Lagoon*, *Avatar* or *Jurassic Park*. Breathtaking, beyond beautiful, this is the place the Caribbean wishes it was. This is where surfers come to ride the biggest waves, and where photographers come to capture them as they leap over the water like bronzed, dazed superheroes. You'll see baby turtles, old hippies, young Japanese couples and thousands of American men who appear to have based their vacation look on Hunter S. Thompson.

Elvis: What Happened, the book written by three of Elvis's former employees – bodyguards Red West, Sonny West and Dave Hebler – that detailed his self-destructive lifestyle, his fondness for firearms and most alarmingly his drug misuse, appeared a couple of months before his death. The media interest surrounding its publication only exacerbated the rumours that Elvis was now a fully fledged addict. As many said at the time, the book was a gift for the ghoul inside all of us. It told of Elvis's introduction to amphetamines, his graduation to downers, the inevitable and constant flow of women, his childish obsession with guns, and his belief that he possessed supernatural powers. "He will read and he will get hopping mad at us because he knows that every word is the truth and we will take a lie detector test to prove it," said Sonny. "But just maybe, it will do some good."

Elvis was incensed by the book, and the effect he feared it might have on his business, and his public profile.

"They said I was all fucked up. I'm not fucked up by no means. On the contrary, I've never been in better condition in my life. I got a daughter and a life. I love to sing. After all, what profiteth a man if he gains the world and loses his own soul?"

Elvis's fascination with guns was well known. He liked to carry them on his person, often loaded. Alice Cooper remembers meeting Elvis at the Las Vegas Hilton in 1971, where he was performing: "He had the penthouse – this was when he was at the top of his game. I had always been a fan as a kid, so I jumped at the chance to go upstairs and meet him. When I got to the lift I found it was me, Liza Minnelli and the porn actress Linda Lovelace."

On arriving at the penthouse, Cooper was immediately frisked for guns by the King's security team. "I don't know why they bothered – when we got inside the place was full of guns," says Cooper. "Elvis took me into the kitchen, opened a drawer, and pulled out a loaded pistol, telling me to put it to his head. I recognised it straight away, a snub .32. I didn't know what to do. I had this gun in my hand and was expecting one of his security to come in any second, see me holding a weapon and shoot me dead. A little voice in my left ear was telling me, 'Go on, this is history, kill him, you'll always be the guy who killed Elvis.' In my other ear was another voice saying, 'You can't kill him, it's Elvis Presley – wound him instead, you'll only get a few years!' A fraction of a second later Elvis did a flying kick on the gun, and sent it flying, before tripping me and pinning me to the ground by my neck, announcing, 'That's how you stop a man with a gun.'"

Nobody much cared about the guns, though, which in the South was just like collecting cars, or mistresses. It was the revelations about his drug intake that were truly shocking, even to those who were relatively close to Elvis in the music industry. They obviously knew he had weight issues, and knew he dabbled with drugs, but nobody apart from those in his employ really understood just how addicted he had become.

"I talked to him about drugs," said Red. "I said, 'You don't need this stuff.' He said, 'Nuh-uh. You're wrong. I do need it.' And that's when I threw my hands up and said, 'I've done all I can do.' And I was gone shortly thereafter."

Before they wrote the book, they all tried to curry favour with Elvis, not that it worked. They would have much rather been back at Graceland than be forced to sell themselves like this, but they figured it was the only currency they had. "He'd fired his bodyguards and they came to me and asked if I could talk to him, see what was wrong, and I tried but he wouldn't answer the phone," said Tom Jones. "Somebody would answer and say, 'Yeah, I'll tell Elvis that you called and he'll get back to you,' but he never did. He didn't want to be reminded that he wasn't Elvis Presley any more."

Elvis became more and more depressed, and was dreading the upcoming tour. This would be the first time that his audience would see him looking so overweight, now with the knowledge of what the book contained. He knew he had been busted, and was petrified about how his fans were going to react. "You could see the, 'God, I don't know if it's worth going on' mentality," said David Stanley. He was kind of dreading the tour – he kept thinking, 'They're gonna think this, they're gonna think that.' He was just really confused.

"The last time I saw Elvis, he said good-bye to me. He was crying. 'I love you.' He hugged me. 'I'll never, ever see you again. The next time you see me, it'll be in a higher place and a different plane.'"

Elvis liked to be melodramatic, and even though Stanley thought little of it at the time, time was what Elvis didn't have.

Elvis had long had an alarming daily schedule, rising in the afternoon, and going to bed in the early hours of the morning. He'd been doing this for years, staying up later and later after concerts, taking as much ownership of the night as possible.

He would often sleep for days on end, asking the various doctors who supplied him to knock him out. He would fall asleep in his nine-by-nine-foot, double-king-size bed, the world outside kept hidden by the black fake suede panels stuck over all the external windows of the room.

Every night before retiring he would take an exhaustive cocktail of drugs, some swallowed, some injected, that would send him off to sleep. There were three batches, known as "attacks"; one included a manila envelope containing eleven pills and three small disposable syringes loaded with Demerol. A study of Memphis prescription records shows that in the last three years of Elvis's life, his personal physician Dr. George Nichopolous prescribed over 19,000 sedatives, amphetamines and narcotics for Elvis. Presley was a walking, mumbling drugstore.

After taking his first batch of drugs, sitting up in bed, Elvis would eat two or three large cheeseburgers, complete with fries, followed by five or six generous banana splits. He was said to be very fond of Fool's Gold Loaf, a hollow loaf filled with a jar each of peanut butter and grape jelly and a pound of bacon. Elvis also loved ugly steak – chicken fried steak with green beans, mashed potatoes and crowder peas – as well as banana pudding, pecan pie, watermelon and buttermilk biscuits. According to his staff, Elvis only once cooked for himself, inventing a new dish in the process. Once, late at night at Graceland, instead of waking one of his cooks, Elvis decided to fix himself a meal. He first generously spread peanut butter on a slice of bread, and then added a slice of synthetic American cheese. Asked why he had concocted such an unappetising dish, Elvis replied, apparently bemused by the question, "Because I was hungry."

He would then sleep. A few hours later he would slowly begin to wake, a sign that an aide had to administer more drugs, having taken Elvis first to the bathroom. As the cocktail of drugs destabilised many of the bodily systems that normally control muscles like the anal sphincter and the bladder, the aide was often too late, finding that Elvis had soiled himself both front and back.

Then there would be Attack Three.

By the time the abominable cocktail of drugs was on the closing laps of a grand prix around his dilapidated circulatory system, it was time for another go.

"At the end, Elvis had a trailer in the back of Graceland where a full-time nurse lived, Tish Hinsley," said Vernon's stepson David Stanley. "And in that trailer was a drugstore. Every night about twelve or one, we'd give Elvis what we called Attack One. It was a package of eleven drugs, including three shots of Demerol, and then Elvis would eat. And you had to stay with him for that, because sometimes he was so stoned that he'd choke on his food. Then, after he fell asleep, you'd have to sit there and watch him. And three or four hours later, he'd wake up and take another package of drugs which we called Attack Two. After several more hours of sleep, Elvis would wake once again and take Attack Three. This would be the same contents of attacks one and two. So you're talking, by the time you got done – let's just call it eleven sleeping pills per attack – that's thirty-three. Let's call it three shots of Demerol per attack – that's nine shots. And some people would say, 'Well, golly, that's six months' worth.' That was a nightly dose."

On properly waking later in the afternoon Elvis would self-medicate, grabbing a handful of Dexedrine, putting cotton wool balls doused with liquid pharmaceutical cocaine up his nose, before eating his breakfast – scrambled eggs, crispy fried bacon, sausages and butter-soaked biscuits, washed down with a gallon of strong coffee. Just as Hollywood was about to embrace the organic craze, Elvis had moved back in time, demanding to be fed white trash food at all times of the day. Elvis's diet always reminds me of a *New Yorker* cartoon by Ed Koren, depicting a middle-aged couple having dinner in a restaurant with their teenage daughter. The daughter is saying to the waitress: "And exactly how is the peanut-butter-and-jelly prepared?"

He went through periods of intense constipation. As his colon had been so damaged by his drug intake, he resorted to taking enemas. Constipation turned out to be one of the contributing factors to his death. Elvis's world was a world of extremes – up, down, awake, asleep, off, on, in, out.

He almost never socialised, and would never be caught by the paparazzi at parties. He entertained at home, at Graceland, with his stooges, the Memphis Mafia, and that was about it. Elvis would often arrange for the local cinema to screen a film for him late at night; on his very last day he asked an aide to find him a print of the film *MacArthur* to watch the following night, before he went off on tour. A big Monty Python fan, he had loved *Monty Python And The Holy Grail* – he was particularly fond of the line, "Your mother was a hamster and your father smelled of elderberries" – so much that he bought a print (this being before the days of video cassettes) and had watched it five times already.

Graceland (to pronounce the word correctly, you need to stress the first syllable, swallow the second *a*, and drop the *d*), his white-columned, eighteen-room suburban mansion, was his hideaway, his salvation, and while it was usually swarming with people (Elvis didn't like to be alone, even if he rarely left his home), it felt safe. The best-known feature inside was the tiki-style Jungle Room, which looked like something out of a movie. Housed in an extension built in the mid-Sixties, it featured an indoor waterfall, fur armchairs, a green shag-pile carpet and a wooden bar carved with animal and totem figures.

The room's excellent acoustics meant it was often used for rehearsals and recording. Elvis was obsessed with sound quality, and used to regularly update the sound system at Graceland. He also tried to create his own version of "surround sound" in his private jet, the "Lisa Marie", by having fifty-two speakers installed. When he listened to a piece of gospel music, for instance, he wanted to feel as though the singers were there in the room itself, rather than just their voices coming through the speakers. He may not have been able to write music, but he knew how he wanted it to sound. You could say that Graceland looked as though someone had tried to replicate the Sir John Soane's Museum in London by spending a small fortune in Woolworth's. But that's unfair, very unfair. It was Tardis-like, though, and so cluttered it looked as though Elvis had moved from a house twice its size while still trying to keep the same amount of furniture.

Elvis had bought the jet for the sole purpose of touring abroad, yet every time Elvis brought the subject up, the Colonel would find a new excuse to nix it. Tax issues, financing problems, security risks, production details – you name it, the Colonel could say it was a potential problem and that Elvis would be mad to consider it. What no one knew at the time was that Parker was in fact an illegal alien, born Andreas Cornelis van Kujik, and that if he had flown out of the country he wouldn't have been let back in again.

In the last months the King was trapped inside a nightmare from which the only escape was to never wake up. Bloated, heavily in debt and sexually impotent, he was unconscious more often than he was awake.

"Like myself, you may possibly agree that Elvis really has sold his soul for rock'n'roll," wrote Todd Slaughter, the president of the Elvis Presley Fan Club, early in 1977. "Elvis has given his all in exchange for the love he'll never receive; money he can never spend; and immortality he will never live to appreciate. Like Disney, Presley will bequeath this world his heritage ... [In the mean time] he'll continue to sing his way through the saga of his life, admitting to all that he has 'One Broken Heart For Sale.'"

CHAPTER EIGHT

Don't Be Cruel

"He will always be our King: forever, irreplaceable, corrupt and
incorruptible, beautiful and horrible, imprisoned and liberated"
– Dave Marsh, *Rolling Stone*

Almost as soon as the ambulance was summoned to
Graceland, rumours of Elvis's demise began to reach Memphis
newspaper offices and radio and television newsrooms. Jaded
local reporters took a wait-and-see attitude, however, having
heard such rumours before. Over the years, many crank
callers had declared that Elvis had been killed in a car or
plane crash, or that he had been shot by the jealous boyfriend
of an infatuated fan. Once, someone even reported that Elvis
had drowned in a submarine, off the coast of Hawaii. Yet
the newsroom of *Memphis Press-Scimitar* was struck dumb
immediately when a trusted source confirmed that this
time the news was for real. Memphis radio station WMPS
made the first official announcement via announcer Dan
Sears whereas WHBQ became the first TV station to halt
its regular broadcasts with an announcement of the tragedy.

Aged only forty-two years, the news of Elvis' death was
an earthquake shaking the emotional foundations of a
generation around the globe whose own identity and essence
had been given form by Elvis, popular music's first true idol.
His demise was one of the century's hugest media moments.
Television, print and radio coverage broke all bounds, not
stopping after a few days but carrying on for several weeks,
often longer.

As the news spread, radio stations immediately started to play his records; most organised tributes, others simply played listeners' requests. ABC and NBC immediately produced late-night tributes; CBS, the only network not to follow suit, had its lowest evening ratings in years. On the ABC special, Chuck Berry was asked how Elvis would be remembered by other musicians. True to form, Berry managed to be playfully churlish: "Oh, boop, boop, boop. Shake your leg. Fabulous teen music. The Fifties. His music." In Berry's eyes, Elvis was just a white boy who had stolen the black man's music. *His* music.

In Britain, BBC radio chose at first not to interrupt its programming. Radio 2 presenter Ken Bruce remembers the day vividly: "In 1977, I was a staff announcer for BBC Scotland and was on a radio news reading shift on the day the news came through. As I recall, we were broadcasting a programme from London at the time, and Radio 4 decided not to break into the programme to make the announcement. Our newsroom took a different view, possibly because our duty editor was a huge Elvis fan, and so it fell to me to fade out the programme and announce the death of the great man to Scotland, half an hour before the rest of the nation knew."

Over on Radio Luxembourg, a couple of minutes after newsreader Mark Wesley broke the news, programme director Tony Prince cleared the schedules in honour of the man who had had such an effect on music broadcasting: "Ladies and gentleman, this is Tony Prince. Elvis Presley has died in the United States of America. Well maybe you know, maybe you don't know, that this radio station was the first radio station in Europe to ever feature the man and his music. Maybe you also know that I am probably one of his biggest fans in the world. I met him twice, I've interviewed him twice; I've introduced him live on stage in Las Vegas. And I just had a little cry downstairs because it's like losing a father to me. For some it's really deep down inside and I know that many of you will be feeling the same way. For the next four hours on Luxembourg: in memory of the King. Elvis is dead. His music will live on for ever."

The obituaries the next day were long and exhaustive. Some would have been prepared way in advance, but you could tell that others were written on the hoof, mainly by those whose lives had been so affected by Elvis's own, twenty years previously. In fact many of the obits were simply written by fans.

The *Commercial Appeal*, Memphis's biggest daily paper, carried a more than fitting tribute, hailing Elvis as "an American cultural phenomenon who will never be fully understood." Elvis may have been the most famous man in the world, but he was also a local hero. In the eyes of most Memphians, that was far more important.

"Memphis always saw Elvis as a son, a boy-made-good in the tough world of entertainment … He was the entertainer who magnetized the nerve system of the young and to touch him was to be sanctified …

"He could not help but reflect openly his love of family, his comfort with old friends, his preference for the environment in which he grew up. Sometimes he was just another Humes High School kid grown up to big-car status …

"He was an asset to Memphis in more ways than fame. A tourist attraction, yes. But also a symbol. His rock'n'roll style, his easy physical grace, his modulated drawl, his glance of recognition as he passed you on the street, made him fit the surroundings.

"If he was proud to tell others that he was from Memphis, Memphis was proud to have him claim it as his home."

The newspaper for Elvis's birthplace, the *Northeast Mississippi Daily Journal*, carried the headline "The King Is Dead: Entire Nation Mourns Death Of Tupelo's Own Elvis Presley," accompanied by a photo of the bloated singer looking positively demented.

Legendary pop journalist Lester Bangs wrote an obituary for New York's *Village Voice*. "I got the news of Elvis's death while drinking beer with a friend and fellow music journalist on his fire escape on 21st Street in Chelsea … We knew a wake was in order, so I went out to the deli for a case of beer … I passed some Latin guys hanging out by the front door. 'Heard the news? Elvis is dead!' I told them. They looked at me with contemptuous indifference. So What. … Not for everyone was Elvis the still-reigning King of Rock'n'Roll, in fact not for everyone is rock'n'roll the still reigning music. By now, each citizen has found his own little obsessive corner to blast his brain in: as the Sixties were supremely narcissistic, solipsism's what the Seventies have been about, and nowhere is this better demonstrated than in the world of 'pop' music. And Elvis may have been the greatest solipsist of all."

The *New Yorker*, in its August 29th issue, ran an imaginary letter from a man who was thirteen in 1956, the year when Elvis became "Elvis." Elvis at the time was still low culture, and the "Talk Of The Town" piece was beautifully arch. The writer starts by describing Elvis's voice on "That's All Right," his 1954 breakout single: "Elvis Presley's voice is like a high, sharp shiver. There isn't any part of the song not covered by a thrilling energy. This is a significant American song, sung by a significant American man … He didn't know what he was about, but he was protected for a while by his naiveté and by his simple energy. He cut through gruesome layers of self-consciousness, although they closed in on him later

... I saw a television newscast about Elvis and it made me mad, because the newsman who conducted it was exactly the kind of nineteen-fifties guy – full of false inflection and false authority – who was completely blown away by Elvis; and there he was again, full of false inflection and false authority still, condescending to him."

In the UK, the *Guardian* announced: "The King is dead and there will be no replacement." The *Times* delivered a measured response. "A new art form, a youth revolution were not among the objectives of Presley or his promoters," wrote Philip Norman. "He was launched in the middle Fifties as a moneymaking confection with a life, possibly, of six months. It was inconceivable that the catchpenny excesses of the moment – the slicked hair and shaking torso; the guitar, flashed and flourished and spun – would create a style to fascinate millions of young people for twenty years afterwards. ... That he himself never did or said anything remotely outrageous, significant or even interesting has only added to the purity of his myth.

"He leaves behind clubs and associations dedicated to impersonating his voice and his appearance, and unable to believe him guilty of even the smallest aberration. What lay behind the music was never clear – if indeed, there was anything at all. But, merely by innuendo, he is assured of his place in history."

By the weekend, the British tabloids were ready to unleash their own brand of ghoulish sensationalism. The *News Of The World* led with "He Knew He Didn't Have Long To Go," while the *Sunday Mirror* lifted the lid with "Elvis – His Idea Of A Night Out Was A Tour Of The Undertakers." In the *Sunday People*, under the headline "Elvis Was My Lover – By Diana Dors," the former British movie starlet described assignations in her Beverly Hills mansion: "there, amid the orchids and the gardenias, we would make love. He was the nearest thing I've ever known to Heaven." Jimmy Savile, 35 years before being outed as a pathological paedophile, claimed that "The Elvis I Knew Was No Junkie" – presumably because the children's TV presenter didn't know him at all.

All the papers carried exhaustive articles on the women, the drugs and the loneliness that had brought the King to his knees. A piece in the *Daily Mail*, entitled "The Empty Throne Of The King Who Died Afraid And Alone" and built upon F. Scott Fitzgerald's fragile premise that "the rich are different," rambled on for three pages about Elvis's obsession with "dark fantasies" without really explaining what these were.

The *Daily Express* even quoted a notable punk, the Damned's Brian James, whose reflections were tame compared to the idle thoughts of some of his peers: "I felt bad when I heard the news, but for us he died ten years ago. His death marks the end of an era. And it's about time." Almost as a riposte, London's *Evening Standard* carried a leader column under the heading "He Was The One" which concluded: "Presley's death, like his life, is inevitably attended by much that is ersatz and professionally staged – an extravagance of kitsch of every variety. But there is no mistaking the real shock, bereavement and desolation on thousands of those faces pressed against the gates of his house and queuing sadly for the memorial services. Will they cry like that for Johnny Rotten?"

The closest equivalent in the US was the notorious *National Enquirer* magazine.

According to Iain Calder, its longtime editorial director, Elvis's stepmother – his father's wife Dee Stanley Presley – showed up at the *Enquirer*'s Memphis hotel rooms a few days after the death, offering to sell her story. So too did his last girlfriend, Ginger Alden. The magazine pulled off one of its biggest-ever coups two weeks after the funeral, when it published a photograph of Elvis lying in his coffin. The *National Enquirer* paid $18,000 for the image, which was taken with a small camera hidden by one of the viewers – probably Elvis's cousin Billy Mann – who'd filed through Graceland during the mourning period. The issue, black-bordered, with the picture plastered between huge headlines, sold a record six and a half million copies.

At that time, the *NME*, Britain's biggest music paper, was selling over a quarter of a million copies a week. Its editors had been due to put Elvis Costello on the cover of their next issue. After the tragic news of the 16th, however, they swapped Elvises.

The cover photo on the 48-page, 18-pence, August 27th issue was a vintage 1956 shot of the boy on stage, surrounded by the words "Elvis Lives: Remember him THIS way." The news piece inside stuck to the original official line, and seems almost quaint now: "Elvis Presley's sudden death last week, at the age of forty two, leaves a mystery that will remain unsolved for all time. No one will ever know exactly what killed him. Officially he died from a heart attack, but doubtless this was the final result of numerous contributory factors."

The piece went on to claim that at least half of the estimated "7,000 million dollars" that Elvis had earned, had, thanks to his lavish lifestyle, disappeared. Three separate obituaries focused on Elvis's incendiary effect on a generation, and his gradual slide into mediocrity and embarrassment. His demise was already a fabulous parable that lent itself to grandiose retelling – the narrative arc that withers and dies.

"Stardom kills," wrote Charles Shaar Murray. "It wreaks an awful destruction on all but those with the utmost strength and inflexibility and those with the utmost humility and self-knowledge. And the kind of stardom that was visited upon Elvis Presley was simply more than he could handle … Maybe, if he'd have been able to see into the future, he'd've preferred to stay a truck driver. As it was, we turned him into what he became, but *we* didn't have to pay the price."

For Mick Farren, "Without Elvis Presley history would certainly have been different. Jagger might have become an estate agent, Dylan a rabbi, Lennon a bricklayer or Johnny Rotten a judge. He probably was one of the tiny handful of artists who actually affected the course of human affairs."

In the words of the paper's assistant editor Neil Spencer, "For much of the world Presley came to represent the American Dream … For me personally, he'll always be a cut out photograph on the bedroom wall of a short-trousered welfare state schoolboy; a distant unreal voice on the juke box, suggesting a promise of something more vital and colourful than the drab reality of 1950s Britain could ever provide. But like others before him … what Presley found at the heart of the American Dream was disillusionment and death."

Headlined "D.P. Costello of Whitton, Middlesex, it is your turn to be The Future of Rock & Roll," the huge profile of Elvis Costello that was initially meant to be that issue's cover story was largely responsible for springboarding Costello to critical stardom.

"It's been a rough old week for Elvis Costello," wrote star writer Nick Kent in the slang-heavy style of the period. "Last weekend he was right up there in the playlists with his 'Red Shoes' single – a tentative third-time lucky – a cosy Top 30 cloister for the album and even the national press getting hot-to-trot with the Costello form for 1977.

"And what happens? Some other geezer sharing Costello's maiden name sloughs off the mortal coil and all the 'tastemakers' consider it irreverent to even make mention of this young-blood's very existence.

"Result: the man who would be king's career is in a right two-and-eight for the whole week of August 13–20. A grievous impasse after such a mercurial lift-off ..."

Even the *NME* gossip column was full of Presley tidbits, recounting the story of *Daily Mail* movie critic Margaret Hinxman, who, distraught at the BBC's extensive coverage of Elvis's life and death, was heard to remark, "I just couldn't believe it. I mean, if he were Joan Crawford or someone ..."

Usually filled with advertisements for denim waistcoats, clogs and novelty T-shirts, the *NME* classifieds were this week overflowing with Elvis memorabilia, notably cheap posters and T-shirts covered in the already ubiquitous slogan "ELVIS LIVES."

Word of the death of Elvis arrived in metropolitan Australia at approximately 7.30 in the morning of the 17th of August, too tardy to hit the morning press.

The following day, the Melbourne daily the *Age* announced that RCA Australia had already by chance nominated August as Elvis Presley Month and had supplied record stores with extra copies of his albums. "Melbourne ... she ain't nothin' but a town agog," ran the editorial. "The death of Elvis Presley, the 'King' of Rock, left most people all shook up rather than crying all the time. City record shops reported the greatest surge in buying of Elvis' records for many years ... At Allans Music in Collins Street (Melbourne City) one window was redecorated by 9.15am with Elvis records and a big portrait poster, all draped with a black ribbon. Radio got into the act from the moment the news teleprinter announced the shock tragedy just before 7.30am ... Stan Rofe, Melbourne's forty-year old 'daddy' of the DJ's, "Heard it over the air" at the breakfast table ... and stopped eating there and then. 'I just felt I didn't want to go to work, but then I thought they would need me to help do a tribute,' he said."

For the hundreds of thousands of Elvis obsessives in Australia, his death felt somewhat special, as the time difference meant they almost imagined they had the event to themselves. If you were an Elvis fan, indeed if you were anyone's fan, all you ever wanted to feel was special, and the fact that Australia felt isolated meant that it was easier for those fans to feel that way. Far from feeling disconnected, those who cared about Elvis – and there were a lot of them – felt somehow privileged, as though he had died all over again in Australia.

According to Ralph, a mechanic who was just seventeen when Elvis died, "When the news came through, it felt as though it should have been on an old-fashioned newsreel, like the kind they used to have in the war. When Elvis died, we were so far away from it that he may as well have died on another planet. Which in one way I suppose he did."

And as in every other country where the King was worshipped from afar, his devotees went out and bought all his records again, some to hear them, some to feel a connection, some just to make some sort of contribution to the narrative – "Hey, you know, as soon as he died I had to go and try and buy a copy of *50,000,000 Elvis Fans Can't Be Wrong*."

Could 50,000,000 Elvis fans be wrong? Of course they couldn't.

Most *Rolling Stone* readers probably saw Elvis as little more than an overweight Vegas nightclub throwback, with no relevance to the modern music scene. He was all the way from Memphis, and a mighty long way down rock'n'roll. When he died, however, the magazine's founder and editor

Jann Wenner decided to scrap a completed edition that was about to be printed in favour of an issue devoted to the King. It was the right decision. The September 22nd issue, with a vintage photograph of Elvis on the cover, and one simple cover line – ELVIS PRESLEY 1935–1977 – sold more copies than any other in the magazine's history.

Tributes inside included the following from celebrated rock critic Dave Marsh: "Elvis was the king of rock and roll because he was the embodiment of its sins and virtues: grand and vulgar, rude and eloquent, powerful and frustrated, absurdly simple and awesomely complex. He was the King, I mean, in our hearts, which is the place where the music really comes to life. And just as rock and roll will stand as long as our hearts beat, he will always be our King: forever, irreplaceable, corrupt and incorruptible, beautiful and horrible, imprisoned and liberated. And finally, rockin' and free, free at last."

The critic Greil Marcus, who wrote extensively about Elvis, was on vacation in Hawaii – Elvis's favourite destination – when he got a call from the magazine, asking him to write an obituary.

"What kind of joke is that?" he said.

"*Rolling Stone* isn't the *New York Times*, we don't keep obits on file," he was told.

He didn't accept the news of Elvis's death at all, not in any way, but at the same time he knew it was true. He went down to the hotel bar and ordered a Jack Daniel's, straight from Tennessee, "just like Elvis Presley's first 45s."

When he ordered another, the barman suggested he try a far more appropriate drink: "A Blue Hawaii. You know, the movie?"

Marcus stuck to his bourbon.

Rolling Stone had just moved from San Francisco to New

York, to 745 Fifth Avenue to be precise, and on August 16th the staff had just put the finishing touches to its 248th issue. The first to be produced in the city, it was a celebration of Manhattan, with a special cover by Andy Warhol depicting feminist and mayoral hopeful "Battling" Bella Abzug.

Producing the issue had not been an especially pleasant experience, as most of the furniture and office furnishings had yet to be delivered from the West Coast, and many of the staff were feeling homesick. The weather outside was hot and sticky, and the new air conditioning had yet to be installed, testing people's patience in the extreme. To round things off, a diligent although not especially accomplished saxophone player was practising next door, and all the *Rolling Stone* staff were party to the results through the open windows.

New York was at its most intense. The streets were full of people, as often the streets were cooler than people's homes. The cinemas were full, too, thanks to their air conditioning, and so too were restaurants. Anywhere cool was popular. Even soccer games. The previous night the New York Cosmos had treated 77,691 fans, the largest crowd that had ever watched an event at Giants Stadium or attended a soccer match in the US or Canada, to an exhibition of magic. For weeks now, the city had resembled something from a pulp thriller, all hot and frustrated in the daytime, and all noir and complicated at night. The city was so hot it made you dizzy. So hot that some downtown tenants had taken to standing on chairs under their ceiling fans, having put towels under door slats to trap the cool air inside. When you went to Central Park, so many people were sitting on the grass that it looked as though a concert was about to start. People were actually sick of going out, as for the first time in years, the town felt dangerous as soon as the sun went down. Times Square and the streets around it in midtown felt like an unpoliced and irreligious no-go zone full of hookers, pimps, muggers and panhandlers. This was *Last Exit To Brooklyn*, in real time, and in 3D.

Just as the *Rolling Stone* team were preparing to leave the office for the day, keen to get out into the park and cool off, the shocking news came through that, one thousand miles away in Memphis, Elvis had died. Details were sketchy, but the salient fact kept being repeated. Elvis Presley, the King of Rock'n'roll, was dead. He had been found unconscious in his bathroom, his pyjamas around his ankles, with one hand in a jar of Goober Grape and the other clutching the Bible. At least that was what they were hearing …

Peter Herbst, a young news editor, walked into Jann Wenner's office to find him slumped behind his metal desk, red-faced and obviously distraught. He looked as though he had been crying for quite some time.

"It's a cover," blubbed Wenner, wiping his face with a handkerchief, and trying to regain his composure.

Herbst looked confused, as Wenner was still crying so hard he couldn't hear what he was saying.

"It's a cover!" repeated Wenner, this time raising his voice as he brought his head up from the table. Herbst then understood, as the rest of the staff soon would, that Wenner was going to scratch the issue they'd just put to bed, and produce a new one devoted entirely to Elvis. Fuck New York; it was now all about Memphis. Wenner knew that for many, Elvis had been the spark that had fired them into adolescence, that in Elvis they had found someone to believe in; and that in rock'n'roll, as they had learned it from him, they had found a way of life that they wouldn't have swapped for any amount of money, because it was, and would be forever, endlessly rewarding and fulfilling. It was only natural that they would feel a certain hollowness inside, wasn't it? Actually, a certain hollowness?

What was he thinking? They probably felt as though their guts had been ripped out. Wenner knew that, perhaps more than the deaths of Joplin, Hendrix or Morrison, this was the one that was going to properly mark out the rock'n'roll years, the boy from Tupelo who torpedoed the old, square America with his libidinous air-humping and godless country blues, a man who remade the world so that the Beatles might rock, and the Rolling Stones may roll.

Jann Wenner was a rock'n'roll enthusiast, a man who made an industry out of a passion. In love with the idea of rock as a force for change, a force for good and a force for cultural emancipation, he said that Elvis embodied rock'n'roll in a towering way. He didn't move the genre forward or give it a social conscience like John Lennon, but he was rock'n'roll incarnate.

So, in New York, at the offices of *Rolling Stone*, a new magazine was called for, and they had four days in which to do it.

Tired, sticky and hot, and looking forward to a few days off, the staff initially protested, but they also knew that not only would Wenner not change his mind, but also that he was right not to. An ad-hoc features meeting was convened, and they rapidly planned the replacement Elvis issue: journalists were packed off to Tupelo, Mississippi, to Memphis's Forest Hill Midtown Cemetery, and to Los Angeles, where one star writer Ben Fong-Torres was sent to interview Elvis's former bodyguards, the men responsible for *Elvis: What Happened?* Only a few weeks ago, these men had been compared to tabloid lowlife, but now Wenner needed them; they, in return, were happy for the publicity. A few days later Wenner also bought in a piece written by Caroline Kennedy, who was one of the few "reporters" invited to the funeral. The former president's daughter was interning at the *New York Daily News* at the time, but for some bizarre reason the paper rejected her piece; Wenner simply got someone to rewrite it.

The *Rolling Stone* team didn't sleep properly for the best part of four days. They were kept going by a running buffet of sandwiches, beer and selections from Elvis's Sun sessions blasting away on the stereo, one of the few office staples that had found its way from San Francisco.

According to the magazine's biographer, Robert Draper, "Staffers worked for four days straight, catnapping on cots when a spare hour could be scrounged, doing their best to ignore the fatigue and that merciless saxophone noise screeching in their ears and the humidity that dragged across their faces like a cat's tongue … When it was done and the presses rolled, Peter Herbst held an early copy of No. 248, the Elvis issue, in his hands, and looked out his window at Central Park, and – like Wenner – cried. They had served the King well. 'It was definitely the most emotional moment I had in journalism,' he said. 'And for the magazine, it was one of the last great moments.'"

The whole thing was a magnificent production, more than worthy of the team who put it together, and more than worthy of the man it celebrated. In addition to the various tributes, all elegantly written, and all crafted from the heart, a 1971 concert review by John Landau was reprinted as a memorial. However, one contribution didn't make it into the issue. Wenner had contacted the magazine's London stringer, and asked if he could solicit some opinions about Elvis's death, either from a rock luminary or from some of the new groups who were making waves at the time, notably the punk rockers. Eventually, after a day or so, the writer managed to secure a quote, although it wasn't the sort they had expected, or indeed the type they were used to at *Rolling Stone*.

In the end an actual punk luminary was found, in the

shape of John Lydon, a.k.a. Johnny Rotten, who said, when asked if he could sum up Elvis's passing in one pithy sentence, "Fuckin' good riddance to bad rubbish."

My word. Those from Elvis's generation were of course much kinder. Roy Orbison reminisced about his last meeting with the King, backstage in Vegas the previous December. "Had a *fantastic* visit, almost two hours, from the time he came off to the time he went back on. We talked about the early days. We talked about the people we admired – each other – and people who tried to really perform, from the heart, with soul, as opposed to trying to make commercial records. I hope people remember the impact – it's not only historical fact, but it's lingering fact."

Paul Simon was also quoted at length, recounting the first time he had ever heard Elvis, back in '54 or '55. "I was in a car and heard the announcer say, 'Here's a guy who, when he appears onstage in the South, the girls scream and rush the stage.' Then he played 'That's All Right Mama.' I thought his name was about the weirdest I'd ever heard. I thought for sure he was a black guy.

"Later on I grew my hair like him. Imitated his stage act – once I went all over New York looking for a lavender shirt like the one he wore on one of his albums. I did stop liking his music pretty early, though. I felt wonderful when he sang 'Bridge Over Troubled Water,' even though it was a touch on the dramatic side – but so was the song."

Bruce Springsteen was understandably reverential. "I could not imagine that guy dying. He was so incredibly important to me, to go on and do what I want to do. When I heard the news it was like somebody took a piece out of me ... To me, he was as big as the whole country itself, as big as the whole dream. He just embodied the essence of it and he was in mortal combat with the thing. It was horrible and, at the same time, it was fantastic. Nothing will ever take the place of that guy. Like I used to say when I introduced one of his songs: 'There have been a lotta tough guys. There have been pretenders. There have been contenders. But there is only one King.'"

The magazine was about to celebrate its tenth anniversary, an anniversary that would not be remembered for its celebration of how the counter-culture had moved into the mainstream, but for a commemorative issue marking the death of the man who had made *Rolling Stone* possible in the first place. Elvis had been on the cover once before, in 1969, with an image from his black leather live comeback, and he would be again, in 1981, on the occasion of Albert Goldman's scandalous biography. In 1992, during the magazine's 25th anniversary year, Albert Watson photographed Elvis's gold lamé suit to create one of the most iconic covers of the decade. Two years later that same suit made another appearance on the cover, this time worn by cartoon characters Beavis and Butt-head, and it was there once again six months later, adorning Jerry Seinfeld.

By the time the originally scheduled New York issue hit the newsstands a few weeks later, it felt a little flat. Wenner had bought an ad on the back page of the *New York Times* to announce their arrival, yet the copy-line looked almost apologetic. "We're new in town," it read. But then so what? *Rolling Stone* was a rock'n'roll magazine, right, and wasn't Elvis dead? Suddenly everything was different, and so many things had changed. The US counter-culture always felt like a coastal thing, a West Coast explosion, a California bubble that had little to do with New York. Sure, the Woodstock festival might have taken place in upstate New York, but it never felt that way. New York was too tough for hippies, who were given short shrift in its stores and bars, and now that Elvis had died, now that the rock'n'roll era was over, what use was *Rolling Stone*? When Wenner moved the magazine east it didn't so much feel like the beginning of something, as the end. If you want to point to a time, a date, that the first era of rock'n'roll truly ended, it was August 16th, 1977.

Elvis was also mourned by those in the country music industry, who had taken him to their hearts because of his innate passion for the genre. If truth be told, until Elvis came along, only a few artists, such as Eddy Arnold, had managed to shake off the perception of country as a regional thing. Elvis opened the door for country singers like Marty Robbins, Sonny James, and Johnny Cash, and helped to expose their music to a broader market.

In the *Country Music Review* in October 1977, Martin Hawkins wrote that: "There are those who argue that Elvis caused irreparable harm to country music by igniting the fires of rock which threatened to engulf the country music industry of the mid-Fifties. But that is just not so. Pure country music died with the very beginnings of the recording industry if you take that argument to its logical roots. And even in the early Fifties Eddy Arnold, Red Foley and the other 'country crooners' were deliberately setting out to merge country with the rest of the popular music industry.

"The fact is that the emergence of Presley and of rock music probably did more to publicise and revitalise country music than to harm it, and arguably was more beneficial in the long run than the creation of Nashville as a recording centre."

In the wake of Elvis's passing, dozens of "one shot" tribute magazines were produced, along with a dozen more cash-in paperbacks, some extolling his virtues, others exploiting the knowledge that he was a heavy drug user. His films started to reappear on television, too, and instead of being broadcast in the middle of the afternoon, they were now scheduled in the evening, often as part of "Elvis Nights" or themed mini festivals. Elvis was an industry built for television, and after his death, television didn't forget to remember that.

Perhaps echoing what Colonel Tom Parker was already thinking, one Hollywood executive commented on hearing of Elvis's death, "Good career move." In revenue terms this would turn out to be true, as Elvis would earn more money dead than alive.

They say there are no second acts in American life, but Elvis's was going to be bigger than his first.

RCA immediately set about releasing old records and new packages of previously recorded material alike, fanning the flames of the fire as well as keeping it stoked. By the end of the year, six Elvis albums were high in the US charts. They were soon followed by the likes of *Legendary Performer Volume 2*, *Elvis Sings For Children And Grown-Ups Too*, *Our Memories Of Elvis*, *Elvis: A Canadian Tribute*, *The Elvis Medley*, *A Golden Celebration* and dozens and dozens more.

A month after the singer's death, Ronnie McDowell's song "The King Is Gone" climbed to No.13 in the *Billboard* chart. McDowell went on to make a career out of Elvis: in 1979 he provided the vocals for the TV movie *Elvis*; two years later he appeared in another TV movie, *Elvis And The Beauty Queen*; and he was also the voice of Elvis in the mini-series *Elvis And Me*.

Anyone who had ever spent more than ten minutes with the King tried to get a book deal. Most succeeded. One of the most imaginative was Ilona Panta, a psychic who claimed that God personally chatted with her about Elvis and whose book

Elvis Presley: King Of Kings asked the question, "Will you be ready when Elvis returns?" Almost as impressive was *A Presley Speaks* by Elvis's uncle Vester, the official gatekeeper at Graceland, priced at $10 in paperback and $25 for the deluxe boxed version, which came complete with an engraved cover and a rather fetching white satin scarf wrapping, the kind you could drape around your neck as you sang Elvis songs to yourself in the bathroom mirror.

Even J.D. Sumner (nicknamed Jim Dandy), who had been in Elvis's backing band since 1971, decided to cash in, recording a truly appalling and rather macabre spoken-word single, "Elvis Has Left The Building" – a great title for a dreadful record. The denouement consists of Sumner intoning, in his deepest, most funereal voice, "Elvis has left the building, but he will always be around."

For the remainder of 1977, and much of 1978, Elvis appeared to own the US. His records were never off the radio, his films were never off the television, and the papers and magazines just couldn't get enough of him. For visiting tourists, it was as though they were in the United States of Elvis. Not that anyone seemed to mind. After all, he was modern-day royalty, the King, and this was his kingdom.

The country even smelled of Elvis. Leather. Pomade. Elvis's favourite Parisian cologne. The dogwood trees around Memphis. A shellac 78rpm Sun single. Elvis was in the air.

Across the Atlantic, rock'n'roll impresario Jack (*Six-Five Special, Oh Boy!*) Good, who had previously managed such early UK rockers as Tommy Steele, Marty Wilde, Billy Fury, Jess Conrad and Cliff Richard, decided with Elvis's corpse still warm to revisit his past, and put the King's story on stage. His musical *Elvis* opened at the Astoria Theatre in London's West End in November 1977, with Elvis portrayed by three actors.

Tim Whitnall was the young Elvis; Shakin' Stevens was Elvis in the Army and Hollywood; and PJ Proby was Elvis in his Las Vegas years. Live musical accompaniment was provided by rock'n'roll revival group Fumble. The week before the show opened, *Time Out*, then one of the country's hippest magazines, carried a magnificent cut-out mask of Elvis on its cover, with the tag-line: *In the future, everybody will be Elvis for 15 minutes.* The next year, it won Best Musical at the Evening Standard Drama Awards.

In Japan, the radio and TV news reporters who announced Elvis's death actually cried on air. For years Elvis had been an icon in Japan; he was just what they needed, someone initially outrageous, but ultimately anodyne. "He's a kind of healer," said Ayako Maeda, a professor of English literature at Yokohama's Ferris University, in 2002.

Elvis was adored in Japan. When the *Aloha From Hawaii Via Satellite* show had gone live at 12.30am on the morning of Sunday January 14th, 1973, the time in Japan was 7.30pm on the Saturday night, and it came as the climax of a nationwide "Elvis Presley Week." His popularity in Japan was made clear when the station broadcasting the show announced the next day that Elvis had captured nearly a forty per cent share of the audience – and this in a highly competitive six-network market – breaking all Japanese television records.

The first time I went to Japan, in 1982, I made sure to visit Tokyo's famous Yoyogi Park, which was where all the rockabilly gangs hung out on a Sunday morning. I went with a friend, a translator and a hangover, but I wasn't disappointed. They had all congregated by the Meiji Jingu shrine near Harajuku Station, all young men from fifteen to thirty, perfectly dressed in greaser Americana honed to the last finest detail, even the brands of handkerchief inserted down the pockets of their Levi jeans – their molls all dressed in Fifties pencil skirts and looking suitably demure. They all looked immaculate, and had done since they first started congregating, the weekend after Elvis died, five years earlier. Most were simply copying the Elvis style as other groups would copy punks, mods or rockers, but a few were doing it as part of a family tradition. A worship of Elvis was being passed down from father to son. One young man I spoke to – who was eager to tell my translator as much as possible about his life – said he'd been encouraged to worship Elvis as much as his father had. "Elvis has always been big in our family. He is a family tradition. We have much respect for Elvis. He is King. He is the King."

Tokyo's fashion tribes (or "kei" in Japanese) would soon become as much a feature of the city as its shopping districts and Michelin-starred restaurants. Punks, mods, goths, neo-hippies, new romantics, and dozens of variations of the above would meet either in Yoyogi Park or Takeshita Dori, a street that was once to Tokyo what Carnaby Street was to London. By 2010 there were Dolly Kei ("Little Bo Peep meets Hans Christian Andersen"), Loli Kei (Lolitas), Gosurori (goth Lolitas) and Gyaru-Ohs ("girl men"). There are still rockabillies today, although they now prefer to be known as "Rollers," their thinning hair bullied into receding quiffs.

The commercial exploitation of the departed Elvis started within moments of his death. As soon as Colonel Parker received the news, he called Vernon Presley and painstakingly explained that as literally thousands of people would now be trying to cash in on the tragedy, they must all take care – saliently by allowing Parker to control Elvis's estate.

Given the green light by the frankly bewildered and grief-stricken Vernon, Parker called Harry "The Bear" Geissler, the president of merchandising company Factors, Inc. They agreed to open negotiations on the Elvis Presley souvenir rights as soon as possible. One of the first collectables they sanctioned was three limited edition pewter figurines representing three different aspects of Elvis's career: the early years, the movie years, and the Vegas years. Why anybody would want them is unfathomable, yet they sold, in large numbers. The same year, Limoges of France were commissioned to create an official commemorative plate. Truly hideous, it nevertheless sold for $25, and people loved it. Some enterprising soul also started producing vials of clear liquid that was marketed as Elvis's sweat. That sold too.

The Colonel even bottled his dead client. Not long after Elvis's death he authorised the Frontenac Vineyards in Paw Paw, Michigan, to produce 120,000 bottles of a white wine with a picture of Elvis on the front and a commemorative poem by the Colonel on the back. There were also decanters, called "Elvis 77," "Elvis 55" and "Elvis 68." Irony number one was that the $30,000 the Colonel made in royalties made him, line for line, one of the highest-paid published poets in the US. Irony number two was that Elvis hated wine.

Everyone wanted a piece of Elvis, and no stone was left unturned, no angle ignored. Memphis promoter Buddy Montesi purchased Elvis's Mississippi ranch and began to sell seven-inch chunks of the fence. "My plan was to sell it an inch at a time to the fans. We made up certificates of transfer, individual deeds, the whole shot. If we sold an acre at five dollars a square inch, we could've made a bundle."

At Graceland itself, the merchandise continued to climb the walls, and small mountains of it accumulated on the other side of the highway, where it sat, its custodians sitting on upturned boxes, waiting for another dollar. By the second anniversary of Elvis's death there was an entire shopping mall opposite the mansion, selling thousands of different Elvis products, most of them wildly inappropriate: teddy bears, ashtrays, racquet balls, coasters that looked like the Sun record label, hound dog slippers, guitar-shaped hairbrushes, TCB keychains, pennants, flags, slim coffee-table books, Christmas tree decorations, black nylon ties covered in white musical notes, plastic drinking cups, T-shirts, polo shirts, calculators, wall clocks, sparkly socks, wristwatches, posters, postcards, cigarette cards, belts, belt buckles, pen knives, sunglasses, pocket mirrors, wallets, bumper stickers, windscreen stickers, even "dirt from Graceland", "Elvis breath" and "Elvis sweat."

CHAPTER NINE

God Save The King

"Who am I talking to? I'm just talking to you, Momma. And one of the boys – he's still here. Somebody's always watching me so I don't get in any trouble" – Elvis Presley

It was the idea of Elvis that we were mourning, as much as the man himself. This was common. In 1959, British pop artist Peter Blake started a painting called "Girls With Their Hero." A pictorial depiction of hero worship, it featured a small group of screaming teenage fans shouting, crying or holding their heads, surrounded by the ephemera of fandom – images of Elvis from magazines, posters and advertisements. As Blake put it in 1960, "This is a straight representation of sixty comments on Presley ... I've never actually seen him in the flesh and don't particularly go for his type of music ... but I'm a fan of the legend rather than the person." A year later Blake painted a self-portrait – one of his most famous works – in which he not only wears an Elvis badge, but also holds an Elvis fan magazine.

Elvis was a popular subject for pop artists. Andy Warhol used his image hundreds of times; he even produced fifty portraits of him in one day. Warhol's life-size painting "Double Elvis (Ferus Type)" from 1963, using an image from one of Elvis's early Hollywood films, *Flaming Star*, epitomises his obsession with fame and the public image. "It was thrilling to see the [Los Angeles] Ferus Gallery with the Elvises in the front room and the Lizes in the back," said Warhol. "Very few people on the [West] Coast knew or cared about contemporary art, and the press for my show wasn't too good. I always have to laugh, though, when I think of how Hollywood called pop art a put-on! Hollywood? I mean, when you look at the kind of movies they were making then – those were supposed to be real?"

Elvis as an image refuses to die. The fashion industry, which likes to go out of its way to claim that it is never starved of ideas, continues to use Elvis as a trope in the same way it uses tartan, leopard-skin, Savile Row, camouflage, fluorescents, punk or gender play. There are few male twentieth-century icons as formidable or as enduring as Elvis, and in fashion – although they will always claim otherwise – proven ideas are never left to fester for long. The Elvis we all know from 1956 is as much of a fashion cliché as Marilyn Monroe or Grace Jones, which is why the industry loves him so much.

Elvis lives.

A year after Elvis's death, the critic John Berger posed the question, "Has the camera replaced the eye of God?" He argued that the decline of religion corresponded with the rise of the photograph, in which case: "Has the culture of capitalism telescoped God into photography?" To judge from the way in which Elvis's image ricocheted around the world in the year after his death, it would be easy to say the answer was "yes." In death, Elvis very quickly became an icon, a cult hero worshipped for his image as much as his talent, worshipped for the accident of being born at the same time as his followers, adored for being the first teenage pop star.

He is astronomical in more ways than one. Take the term "Elvis year," denoting the year in which a product, person, or phenomenon peaks in popularity. It first appeared in a piece by Gareth Branwyn in *Wired* in 1995, which described 1993 as having been the "Elvis year" for the children's character Barney the dinosaur.

After his death, money swirled around Elvis like the proverbial seagulls around a trawler. Still beloved, Elvis makes more money in death than he ever did alive, and is just as popular. Punch "Elvis Presley" into your Google bar and you immediately get 29 million results.

Every year up to 600,000 visitors pass through Graceland, the Locus Sanctus, the holy place, a tourist honey pot that continues to dignify itself as the Lourdes of America. It's been called an unabashed temple of vulgarity, and is still one of the most "individual" homes in North America. When Japanese prime minister Junichiro Koizumi visited the US in 2006, he asked President George W. Bush if he could visit Graceland. Lisa Marie and Priscilla Presley agreed to give a private tour. Describing the experience as being like a dream, Koizumi launched into singing one of Elvis's songs.

I visited Graceland in 1994, on a road trip across the US, and had all the traditional, almost clichéd responses: I couldn't believe how small it was, or how tacky it was inside, and couldn't really imagine how anyone could live in such a claustrophobic space. I went outside and stared at the grave for a while, painfully aware that since *This Is Spinal Tap* this was a pilgrimage that was difficult to make without smiling, or giggling, and then left the grounds sooner than expected. After a short time I'd had enough. I also did Beale Street, the motels with the guitar-shaped swimming pools, Sun Studios and all the rest. I'd marvelled at and then been appalled by all the Elvis merchandise, and left town with a predictably generic response to the experience. Like visiting Vegas, I figured, Graceland was something I probably didn't need to do twice in one lifetime.

A couple of decades went by, however, and I found myself wondering whether if Vegas could reinvent itself, could

Graceland? I knew that the management had streamlined the Graceland experience, gentrified parts of the surrounding area, and run many of the daggy souvenir stallholders out of town.

For years, I had had an obsession with North American kitsch, and would find convoluted ways to visit the Catskill resort hotels, Coney Island, Atlantic City, and all the other examples of faded Fifties grandeur, when the thought of suburban America stretching its wings and creating a modern world out of Tupperware, chrome and neon was still rather exciting. Obviously Las Vegas was the holy grail of twentieth-century American kitsch, and the idea was to spend some time there having driven down from New York, through Philadelphia and Washington, and picked up Route 66 en route to Los Angeles. As quintessential road trips go, it is one of the best, as well as one of the longest – at least in the States.

It was the long stretch of the road through New Mexico, Arizona and California that conveyed to me the strongest sense of what it must have been like to make the great crossing in the Thirties; towns out here finished before they began, fading away into scrub. Arizona in particular was a moonscape of monstrous proportions, Route 66's two-lane blacktop cutting through it like a charcoal arrow. Towards Winslow a raggedy little section of the old route was still flanked by telegraph poles that staggered over the horizon like old men looking for the sea. Just outside Winslow I found another holy grail, a real one this time. The sun was falling in the sky, promising a rich, dark sunset as I sped along the highway to Two Guns. In the distance the Juniper mountains cut across the horizon like tears of pale blue tissue paper. As I gunned down towards them, I looked to my left and saw a deserted Drive-In, standing forlorn in the dirt, casting shadows that stretched all the way back to town. Here was the true spirit of Route 66 in all its faded glory. Like the highway itself, the Tonto Drive-In was a totem of America's glorious past, a testament to the new frontier, the freedom to travel, and the Populuxe automative dream of the Fifties, when a car was still every American's birthright. This deserted cathedral, which had probably screened every one of Elvis's movies, stood stoic and proud in the burnt sienna sunset, and was quite literally the end of the road.

The thing is, having driven through Texas, New Mexico and Arizona, by the time I got to Vegas, and having fallen in love with the landscape – with the exponential sky and the unblemished desert – I hated the place. Sure, when you went downtown you still felt the last echoes of Rat Pack glamour, but the vast steel and glass new hotels along the Strip only made me feel as though I were in an extravagant but oh-so cheap video game. How, having trekked across the southern states, could they build this monstrosity in the middle of God's own kingdom?

Graceland at least possessed some dignity, if only because of its previous owner. Graceland was Elvis's Mount Vernon, a thirteen-acre plantation mansion that became a kind of rich man's Bethlehem, decorated with lots of mirrors and white furniture. Here, the King really was King, while Gladys and Vernon became more than Memphis royalty, they became the city's own Jesus and Mary.

So how did Graceland feel in 2013?

When I approached Graceland nineteen years after my previous visit, having immersed myself in Elvis's world for the preceding six months, I was determined to take things a little slower. As I walked through the gates I started softly singing the Paul Simon song, "The Mississippi Delta was shining like a national guitar …," surely one of the most evocative lines ever written for a pop song.

This time, Graceland was a revelation. Far from being a black velvet Valhalla, it's something of a design classic, albeit an accidental one. Sure, it's so themed and so over-designed and so dense that some parts inevitably feel a little naff, but the house was last touched in 1975, and I defy anyone to find a house that was last renovated in 1975 and not feel that it's a little vulgar and unrefined. Graceland isn't especially tacky; it's just very particular. There are certainly some rooms that look kitsch – some deliberately so (the pool room in the basement, for instance), some not (when Elvis decided to make the extension at the back of the house an homage to Hawaii, he bought all of the furnishings for what would become known as the Jungle Room in less than thirty minutes, although it's not known if he had his eyes open for the entire time) – and the clash of design styles is overwhelming at times, but after all, this was the home of a rock star, and not all rock stars are blessed with innate good taste. I've been in the homes of many performers, and by dint of the fact that most are so wealthy they inadvertently possess many things of great worth, they also tend to surround themselves with the outlandish, the arch and the extreme. In this context, Graceland has always been judged harshly. For instance, Elvis's TV room in the basement is a riot of yellows and blues, and full of chrome and glass, yet if Mr. Freedom's Tommy Roberts had lived here in the Seventies, or had it been designed by Elio Fiorucci or Ettore Sottsass, or created by the German artist Tobias Rehberger, the room would be regularly featured in *wallpaper** magazine.

Graceland is treated as a joke by people who haven't even been there, who hear about its embarrassing ambitions from anecdotes that become more grotesque and exaggerated each time they're told. For years Graceland has been a punchline, a way to illustrate that Elvis was really just good-looking white trash who got lucky.

That does him a disservice.

The Graceland management has also done a spectacular job cleaning up the area. Having bought up the real estate, Elvis Presley Enterprises has transformed the strip opposite the house from what once looked like a third-world approximation of Atlantic City, replacing the low-rent souvenir shops with a state-of-the-art admissions building and a series of museums and shops that gives the whole area the feel of a theme park, and not at all in a bad way. I remembered the Graceland experience as being a kind of camp rite of passage; now it's like visiting Universal Studios. Some of these new mini-museums are little but shopping opportunities, not that you feel aggrieved by that. You also get to see Elvis's vast car collection (including his purple '56 Cadillac Eldorado, his '73 Stutz Blackhawk and his '71 Mercedes) as well as dozens of his jumpsuits, and get to climb aboard his two private planes. The only mildly disquieting thing about Graceland is the fact that on the audio tour you're still solemnly informed that Elvis died of heart failure.

Memphis these days is a city of museums. Besides the Cotton Museum, the Fire Museum, the Memphis Pink Palace Museum and the Art Museum, you can visit the National Civil Rights Museum (housed in the Lorraine Motel, where Dr. Martin Luther King was assassinated), the Rock'n'Soul Museum ("The only museum with groupies"), the Stax Museum of American Soul Music ("Nothin' against the Louvre, but you can't dance to Da Vinci") and Sun Studios, which looks today much as it did when Elvis recorded "That's All Right" back in 1954. The city feels more alive than it has since the economy collapsed in 2008, with major business development (FedEx is based here), growing service industries, good new restaurants, a flourishing art scene, and a sense of renewed Southern pride. While it's still the recipient of billions of "poverty dollars" – metropolitan Memphis ranks among the US's poorest urban areas – the city is growing.

Yet its defining characteristic is Elvis. The tourist board might try to push the blues of Beale Street, barbecue culture and the city's (admittedly brilliant) basketball team, the Memphis Grizzlies, but it's Elvis's town. The man has been completely overwhelmed by his own iconography. In fact Elvis had been overwhelmed by his own iconography almost as soon as he became famous. Being in Memphis reminded me a little of being in pre-glasnost Moscow, where every flat surface was covered with an image of Lenin. Obviously these days those flat surfaces are covered in broken neon signs advertising luxury goods companies, but before the break-up of the Soviet Union, Lenin's omnipotence was constantly reinforced by a visual smorgasbord of grandiose headshots: the kind of political iconography that these days is reserved almost exclusively for North Korea.

Walk around Memphis, and it's as though Elvis never died. He is as omnipresent and as ubiquitous as the former leader of the Union of Soviet Socialist Republics. His is the first face you see when you arrive at the airport, the last face you see when you turn off your bedside light in the hotel. His face adorns walls, billboards, hotel walls, coffee shops and strip malls. Not even Lenin had his face on a breakfast menu or a lip salve.

Elvis's death even precipitated a mass migration to Memphis, like the dustbowl surge to California in the Thirties. So many people moved to the city that you could almost imagine the tourist board had planned his execution.

Graceland's first floor has long been one of the most talked-about enigmas in the entertainment industry. It holds many secrets, and as it is completely private, and has never been open to the public, nor photographed or filmed, it has been bathed in an almost mythic glow. It is practically the only aspect of Elvis's life – and his death – that remains a secret. A secluded sanctuary where he lived and loved, it remains out of bounds for most of the Graceland employees. While it's inconceivable that some of the staff don't surreptitiously make their way upstairs to gawp at Elvis's bedroom, as well as the place he died, the only people officially allowed on the first floor are Priscilla and Lisa Marie.

What a sanctuary Graceland was, a place where Elvis could disappear. As Priscilla remembers it, "Memphis was playtime. He was truly a free spirit, and a kid at heart. We'd watch movies at all hours of the night, roller-skate, go to the fairgrounds, go on roller coaster rides. We'd race go-karts up and down the front drive. We'd play badminton in the summer and have snowball fights in the winter. These were his ways of relaxing."

Millions of Elvis tourists pass the staircase to the first floor during their tour; every single one sees the guard posted at the bottom of the stairs. A second guard stands vigilant at the top, like a doorman, looking after a door that is never opened, a door to a world that remains closed to all. As the house is quite small, the heavy double doors guarding Elvis's bedroom were originally padded for soundproofing, so the staff couldn't hear any of his libidinous activities (or lack of). These days they remain chained and locked.

Numerous celebrities have pleaded for a private tour. Reputedly, all have been declined including President Clinton. "No fan has ever breached the security of the [first] floor of

Graceland," said Bob Carlson, from Graceland Museums. Many have tried to breach security and wander up the stairs, pretending to be lost, or just dim, but all have been stopped. The only Elvis fan to have made it upstairs is lifelong fanatic Nicolas Cage, who married Lisa Marie in 2002, in what might be considered a unique approach to flouting the Graceland rules. It's been claimed that during the week of the 25th anniversary of Elvis's death, he sat on the King's "throne," composed himself in the prone posture in which Elvis died, stretched out on the King's bed and even tried on one of his leather jackets. This sounds unlikely, and is almost certainly not true, yet it illustrates just how hallowed the first floor of Graceland has become, and how silly stories spring up like unwanted weeds.

Both the bedroom and the bathroom are said still to look exactly as Elvis last saw them. That might seem fanciful, but Graceland staff insist that nothing has been touched. The bedroom still holds his pyjamas, his underwear, his socks and shoes, his shirts, sweaters and sunglasses, his jumpsuits, gloves and house slippers – all are preserved, just in case the King makes an unexpected visit. If you were to walk into the bathroom you'd see his cologne (he was wearing Brut on the day he died), toothpaste (his favourite was Crest), hair dye, deodorant, towels, enema and constipation medication, cotton balls, combs, brushes, hair gel, body lotion and various make-up vials and brushes.

As the blurb for a book by Gregory L. Reece, *Elvis Religion: Exploring The Cult Of The King*, puts it: "From Graceland to Las Vegas, from fans to impersonators, from novels, films and popular music to internet websites, outsider art and tabloid conspiracy theories, the cult of Elvis Presley has, since his death, become ever more imaginative." Elvis became an object of obsession for people needing to fill a void in their lives.

There are those who have painstakingly catalogued every different jumpsuit that Elvis wore in concert during the Seventies. In Holly Springs, Mississippi, thirty miles southeast of Graceland, a man called Paul MacLeod claimed to have taped (on VHS, using six VCRs) every TV programme that mentioned Elvis since the King's death. His home, Graceland Too, held nearly sixty thousand newspaper clippings that he said substantiated "the King's unparalleled influence on international pop culture at large and in the universe."

Someone has even compiled a definitive list of the prefixes that Elvis used before the first line of "See See Rider" – including "Yeah," "Well," "Whoa" and "Oh" … Not a day goes by when he isn't mentioned in the news: take the woman in Australia who shot her husband for incessantly playing "Burning Love"; the Uzbekistani pop star who opened an Elvis-themed café in Tashkent; the documentary *Schmelvis: In Search Of The King's Jewish Roots*; the Finnish Elvis who performs all his songs in Latin; and the tree in Derbyshire that grew into the shape of Elvis's profile.

One fan travelled all the way to Louisiana to see the shop where Elvis came with his mother to buy a bike.

Rarely a month goes by without yet another story concerning Elvis's whereabouts, reinforcing the idea that he's not actually dead, and has been in hiding since 1977. He's been spotted driving a truck, working in McDonald's, and was even spied on film as an extra in an airport queue in *Home Alone*. Tennessee is cobwebbed with Elvis shrines designed to appeal to the Presley pilgrim, everything from Elvis memorabilia shops, car museums and plaques saying "Elvis pelvised here." Meanwhile, every clairvoyant in the state claims to still have him under contract.

A woman called Gail Brewer-Giorgio even published a book called *Is Elvis Alive?*, accompanied by a cassette tape of what she said was a posthumous phone call from Elvis. Not only was it a bestseller, it was translated into five different languages.

Elvis is always popping up in the least likely places. Take the following extract from *Elvis After Life – Unusual Psychic Experiences Surrounding The Death Of A Superstar*, by Raymond A. Moody Jr., which is the testimony of a Georgia policeman called Harold Welch, about his wayward son:

"I had a dream about Elvis Presley … He told me he had some information about Tony … He said, 'I'm worried about Tony, sir. Tony is a fan of mine. He's out there in Los Angeles and I can't get through to him.' … He said, 'Look, Tony is staying in a rooming house.' Then I saw, or Elvis showed me, a scene. There was a short street with a drugstore on the corner and a short-order diner across from it. Suddenly, Elvis and I were right there on the street … Elvis kept trying to point out things to me so I would recognise them … He said, 'Look man, you gotta look at this. This is important, man.' He showed me an old house. It was run-down. Seedy looking. Elvis said, 'Man, your son is on drugs. You gotta get him some help.'" Welch flew to LA, found a street like the one he'd seen in his dream, and eventually found his son. The book also contains four cases of people who experienced premonitions shortly before Elvis's death.

Barmaid Elizabeth Prince revealed in July 1993 that she had lived with Presley from 1978 to 1981 in Atlanta, Georgia. They had met when he played at a naval club lounge and a romance developed. "He proved to me a thousand ways that he was Elvis," she insisted. Although their relationship was over, she still spoke to him regularly on the telephone. In August 1983, window cleaner John Carter ran into Elvis in a queue outside a Burger King – of course – in Encino, California. "He was a little fatter, a little more stooped and the hair wasn't slicked back – it was shaggier and greyer. But it was him." The *Daily Sport* revealed in 1988 that a blue suede rubber booted Elvis was secretly working as a fishmonger in a Hounslow, Middlesex, poissonnerie, specialising in Hound Dogfish. In August 1989, the *Sunday People* tracked Elvis down to a secret farm hideaway near Birmingham. Elvis, the report revealed, had faked his death to avoid a Mafia hit team. He was now living quietly as a horse breeder, under the name Johnny Buford. Elvis was also seen working in the grocery section of a Palm Beach supermarket in 1992. The witness, journalist Ed Anger, recalled: "I overheard this guy humming 'Love Me Tender' while he was filling the cantaloupe bin." When questioned, the shop assistant confirmed not only that he was indeed Elvis, but that the object in his coffin was in fact a wax dummy.

The writer Chet Flippo once had the good fortune to visit Graceland in the company of Jerry Lee Lewis. No great Elvis fan – the last time he'd visited Graceland, when Presley was still alive, he had been arrested at the gate with a gun in his car – Lewis had mellowed to such an extent that he had agreed to be a guest on a radio broadcast live from the King's former home. After the show was finished, he said to Flippo, "Yeah, they makin' all this damn money off damn Elvis Presley. I don't even know whether he's dead or not. I thought he was, anyway. If that sonofabitch comes back alive, I'm gonna kill myself."

Elvis continues to defy our expectations of how dead rock stars are meant to behave. This was also true in life. In his 21-year career he didn't grant a single proper full-length interview. He therefore remains a fascinating enigma, one whose primal motivating forces will probably never be known. Elvis's death continues to grow as much as his life, as it acquires breadth and scope and meaning.

Tellingly, as Gilbert Rodman points out in his book on the posthumous world of the King, *Elvis After Elvis*, when the US tabloids finally managed to attract mainstream media attention for one of their silly "UFOs Ate My Sister" stories – the *Star*'s 1992 exposé of Bill Clinton's alleged affair with Gennifer Flowers – many commentators saw Elvis as the obvious benchmark by which to judge the paper's scoop. As one tabloid writer put it: "This is bigger than Elvis, because for the first time the rest of the press has to come to us. They think we're trash but they do the same things we do all the time. They just hate to admit it."

Bigger than Elvis.

Bigger than Elvis? As Elvis is larger than life, he has proved to be too much for mere mortals, which explains why there have been so few biopics. He is alluded to often, and he appears as a cypher, or in character in many films, but actually representations are few. In 1979 John Carpenter directed a TV movie, *Elvis*, in which Kurt Russell gave such a convincing performance he was nominated for an Emmy. "Elvis is simply too big for a biopic" commented impresario Sally Greene. "People are scared of tackling him. He is bigger than a biopic."

He can still hijack the media on a slow news day, especially in the US, and whether he is spotted at a supermarket, or inspired someone to change their name, or been the subject of a regional fun-run, the news still makes way for Elvis. The King has traction.

When Kirsty MacColl released her single "There's A Guy Works Down The Chip Shop Swears He's Elvis" in 1981 – "With your mohair suits and foreign shoes, News is you changed your pick-up for a Seville ..." – it was soon covered by Norwegian singer Elisabeth Andreasson for her country album *Angel Of The Morning*, complete with new Swedish lyrics: "Killen ner' på Konsum svär att han är Elvis" ("The guy down Konsum swears he's Elvis"). American singer Mandy Marie Luke also included it on her 2009 country album *$600 Boots*, with a reworking of the title to "Thrift Shop." Elvis works all over. Wikipedia's "list of songs about or referencing Elvis Presley" contains nearly two hundred of the damn things, including such enticing prospects as "A Century Of Elvis" by Belle And Sebastian, "Elvis Ate America" by Passengers, "Apparition In Las Vegas" by Pete Atkin, "DisGraceland" by Alice Cooper, "Dead Elvis" by the Doug Anthony All Stars, "Elvis On The Radio, Steel Guitar In My Soul" by the KLF, "I Saw Elvis In A UFO" by Ray Stevens, "Let's Let Elvis Get Some Sleep" by Pat Minter, "A Growing Boy Needs His Lunch" by the Dead Kennedys and – naturally – "I Met Elvis At The Nudybar" by the Bones.

Elvis has been claimed by everyone, even the Scots. Almost unbelievably, there are various Elvis tartans. In 2004, after it was discovered that his roots could possibly be traced back to Lonmay in Aberdeenshire, an official Lonmay tartan was designed, made up of blue, grey, green and yellow. Designed by Mike King, the kilt even comes with a sporran engraved with thistles and a bald eagle, representing the Scottish and American link. "I am very proud of this Presley of Lonmay tartan as I bought his records when I was younger and am a fan," said King. "We used blue to represent the nearby town of Peterhead – the Blue Toon – as well as grey for the skies, green for countryside grass, and yellow for local cornfields." The Scottish Register of Tartans also lists the "Presley of Memphis" tartan, designed by Brian Wilton and based on the "American" tartan in the colours of the US flag, which "discreetly introduces Elvis Presley's favourite colour pink plus a gold band to represent his legendary number of gold discs."

Pink Floyd's Nick Mason has an entire shooting outfit made from the Lonmay tartan, and also commissioned hat makers Lock & Co to produce a set of shooting caps.

Elvis has even been co-opted – finally – by the jazz community. Until 2007, Elvis had about as much to do with jazz as he did with astro-physics. Cyrus Chestnut's *Cyrus Plays Elvis* changed all that. Some jazz greybeards said that joining the dots between the two "required enough torturously twisted geometry to have given Euclid a headache," but the record was generally well received.

You can see a version of Elvis any day of the year, in any place you like. An average day on eBay offers over ten thousand Elvis items in over two thousand categories. Almost as soon as he died, Elvis impersonators started to multiply, cropping up in the least likely places, from Lancashire working men's clubs to Home Counties Chinese restaurants. They started appearing with some regularity in Las Vegas, and were even spotted in brothels in Taipei. "If life was fair, Elvis would be alive and all the impersonators would be dead," said Johnny Carson on *The Tonight Show*. Back in the day, Elvis was a form of righteous chaos, a whirlwind of twentieth-century inevitability: first there was shocking Elvis, then celluloid Elvis, supper-club Elvis and finally gilded Elvis. And it is the jumpsuited gilded Elvis that the *Elvi* tend to favour. The top notes were easy to copy: a black wig and sideburns, a playful lip curl and a version of the Blue Aztec jumpsuit. Tribute artists were suddenly everywhere, often combining the image with an unexpected pastime, like roller-skating or couriering.

Within six months, wedding chapel *Elvi* were as common as door-to-door salesmen. Even the slightly flat vibrato could be learned. It was the ease with which tribute acts could copy such a seemingly indefatigable talent that appealed to them: in truth, all anyone needed was a sequinned white jumpsuit with elephantine bellbottoms and a high collar with shoulder-wide wings, girder-sided sunglasses and an array of gargantuan rings on their fingers. Thus Everyman could become Superman.

Warren, a work colleague of mine, got married on a whim in Vegas a few years ago. When he called the first Elvis chapel on his list, he was told that not only was there no room at the inn, but that he might find it difficult getting an Elvis at such short notice, as most had just left for an Elvis convention in Florida. He eventually found a spare Elvis at the Graceland Wedding Chapel, which proudly displayed a list of celebrities who had chosen to tie the knot there. They included Jon Bon Jovi, Billy Ray Cyrus, Aaron Neville and various members of such groups as Def Leppard, Kiss, Deep Purple and the Thompson Twins. "I thought it was hilarious that they gave you a list of who had got married there," said Warren. "Especially when they got to Lorenzo Lamas, as they had to put *Falcon Crest* in brackets afterwards." The Graceland Wedding Chapel is still a going concern, still keen to get thee wed, still offering customised Elvis-themed vows: "We offer fresh flowers, silk flowers, digital photography, limousine service, DVD recording technology and ceremonies broadcasted over the internet to make your wedding in Las Vegas memorable and an event to be cherished for your entire life. So whether you are looking for a Traditional Ceremony or our signature Elvis Wedding in Las Vegas, we are here to serve the needs of all."

As was Elvis, when Elvis was alive. In a tribute written for *Rolling Stone*, Bono hailed the King as follows: "Out of Tupelo, Mississippi, out of Memphis, Tennessee, came this green, sharkskin-suited girl chaser, wearing eye shadow – a trucker-dandy white boy who must have risked his hide to act so black and dress so gay. This wasn't New York or even New Orleans; this was Memphis in the Fifties. This was punk rock. This was revolt. Elvis changed everything – musically, sexually, politically. In Elvis, you had the whole lot; it's all there in that elastic voice and body. As he changed shape, so did the world: He was a Fifties-style icon who was what the Sixties were capable of, and then suddenly not. In the Seventies, he turned celebrity into a blood sport, but interestingly, the more he fell to Earth, the more godlike he became to his fans."

We want old Elvis, and we want young Elvis. In 1992, in an unprecedented move by the Postal Service, US citizens were invited to elect a King by choosing which image of Elvis to use on a stamp. The choice lay between two thematically distinct portraits: a watercolour of the youthful Elvis by Mark Stutzman, or a more mature "Vegas" Elvis painted by John Berkey. Pre-addressed ballots were distributed in post offices around the country and in the April 13th, 1992, edition of *People* magazine. America spoke, loudly, returning nearly 1.2 million ballots: more than three quarters of voters, including the presidential candidate Bill Clinton, preferred young Elvis. The Elvis stamp was dedicated at Graceland a fraction after midnight on January 8th, 1993 which would have been Elvis's 58th birthday. It remains the most popular US commemorative stamp of all time, inviting the thought that the cult of Elvis is rather closer to a religion than anyone previously imagined.

As Mick Farren once said, Elvis arrived at a moment

in history when a period of extreme political and sexual repression was starting to break apart, and was immediately adopted as a global and highly organic symbol of individual freedom. Mediated by television, he was the conduit of all that was young, loud, brash and new. Not that he was rewarded for his vision. Struck down in middle age by the same demons that were affecting all the counter-cultural heroes around him, he was worshipped by a generation who didn't really know what to do with him. Other than worship him, of course.

Yet Elvis remains hallowed, impervious, ballooning in stature by the year. Even though his creativity seemed to gutter almost immediately, the flame of inspiration was so strong that it still burns. The late great Lester Bangs, never one to mince his words, said as much so many years ago. "The only credible explanation is that Elvis was from another planet, like in Superman or the New Testament. There was always something supernatural about him. Elvis was a force of nature. Other than that he was ... a big dumb hillbilly coupla points smarter than his mule who wandered out from behind his plough one day to cut a record for his sainted mother and never came back, which he probably woulda forgot to do even if he hadn't been whisked up. Why shouldn't one physical corpus be capable of containing these two seeming polarities simultaneously? Especially if he's from outer space?"

In 2013, Mimoco, the company known for its Mimobot flash drives made to resemble geek-friendly characters like Boba Fett, Captain Kirk and Batman, added a figure from a completely alien sphere of pop culture, Elvis. Why he suited the tech audience wasn't clear, but Mimoco covered their bases by offering a choice between a limited edition *G.I. Blues*-era Elvis or the jump-suited 1973 *Aloha From Hawaii* Elvis.

Was this Elvis 2.0?

Elvis 1.0 was a perpetual shadow for David Bowie for over forty years. Having once misguidedly thought that they were somehow aligned because they shared the same birthday, Bowie had to live with the fact that when January 8th came around every year, the papers would always be full of Elvis, always mentioning his name first. Even when Bowie was probably the biggest star on Earth, in 1983 and 1984, when he was on the cover of every magazine in the world, it was still Elvis who grabbed the headlines ("Rock'n'roll legend Elvis Presley, who died seven years ago …") However Bowie finally won out in 2013, when he decided to release his comeback single "Where Are We Now?" on his 66th birthday – and as he hadn't released a record since 2003, ten years earlier, this was actually a proper comeback – all the press attention revolved around him. All of it. After all, the media had only assumed Bowie was dead; Elvis really was.

I am reminded of Elvis at least twice a day, as I walk in and out of my house. On the stairs leading into my hall I have a framed black-and-white print of the famous picture that Scottish photographer Albert Watson took in 1992 of Elvis's $10,000 gold lamé suit, the one made by Nudie's of Hollywood in 1957. Watson cleverly put the suit on a hanger, automatically giving it museum status, while it also looked as though it had just come back from the cleaners. It might seem perverse to photograph one of the most famous outfits in rock'n'roll history in monochrome, yet the treatment gives the image, and the suit, a pathos that you simply don't get from looking at the original suit.

Watson's photograph looks like a memorial, which is why I like it so much. Watson is famous for his portraits of everyone from David Bowie to the Rolling Stones, from

Tupac Shakur posing with a pistol to Kate Moss squatting in the nude, from sailors in Beijing to convicts in Louisiana, but for me this simple, elegiac portrait of Elvis's trademark suit stands out above all the rest. Elvis is nowhere to be seen, but he is here, all here.

The Colonel and Nudie Cohn were great friends. Before exploiting Elvis, Parker had managed country singer Hank Snow, for whom he commissioned some exotic rhinestone outfits from the tailor. Snow had also briefly been Elvis's manager, and actually introduced the boy to Parker, but as soon as Parker saw how popular Elvis was becoming, Snow was marginalised.

Parker hadn't forgotten the suits he'd had Nudie make, though, and towards the end of 1956, he hatched a plan for him to make a very special suit for Elvis. At the time Elvis was the Golden Boy, so Nudie decided that what he needed was a Golden Nudie Suit. Instead of a cowboy cut, he opted for a modified hep-cat tuxedo style with a shawl collar and cuffs covered in rhinestones. True to form, Parker spun a gimmick from the commission, branding it "The $10,000 suit" when in fact it had cost just north of $2000 ("Hey, $9500 was pure profit," joked Nudie).

Elvis, perhaps predictably, hated the suit. He didn't think it was too flashy; it was simply too heavy. He wore it for photo sessions, but only four times in concert – on March 28th, 1957 in Chicago, and then again in St. Louis, Toronto and Tupelo. He then started wearing the jacket with black trousers, as the lamé pair were too constricting.

The suit is on display today in the Hall of Gold at Graceland, a testament to all that was real about Elvis, and testament to all that was not.

Whenever I think of Elvis, I always think of the Samuel Charters novella, *Elvis Presley Calls His Mother After The Ed Sullivan Show*. It ends like this:

"No, Momma, we didn't get cut off this time either. I just had something to discuss with the boys. You know, like you told me to do, I always have Gene or Junior sleeping in the room with me ... Anyway, I know I won't walk off anywhere in my sleep tonight. After all that dancing they had me do in those rehearsals – and then after I got all ready they didn't show it anyway! ... Listen to this, Momma, what you are hearing is the truth ... when I get into my bed tonight, I'm going to stay right in it and not get up for one minute. And you know I mean every word I'm saying.

"Who am I talking to? I'm just talking to you, Momma. And one of the boys – he's still here. Somebody's always watching me so I don't get in any trouble."

CHAPTER TEN

A King's Ransom

Elvis's greatest songs, his greatest performances.
His fifty greatest recordings

1. "That's All Right" (Arthur Crudup), 1954

"That's All Right," Elvis's first commercial single, was the record in which Sam Phillips proverbially "captured lightning in a bottle." Consequently, it has become the lodestar of rock'n'roll, the song by which every other rock song should be judged. It would be wrong to say that before this there was nothing – there was jump blues, R&B, hillbilly, urban swing, Ike Turner and even Bill Haley – but this was the line in the sand, the vortex through which the teenage demographic came of age. Written and originally performed by the blues singer Arthur Crudup – *not* a rock'n'roll name – "That's All Right," lasting just one minute and fifty-seven seconds, was one of the defining moments of the twentieth century. When the recording session was done, bass player Bill Black said, "Damn. Get that on the radio and they'll run us out of town."

When asked what style the track was, Elvis's guitarist Scotty Moore responded: "I cannot tell you. It wasn't even really the lack of a drummer. I guess it was just a combination of several different styles rolled into one. I was a big fan of Merle Travis, of Chet Atkins with his thumb and finger styles, and a lot of the blues players – it was just trying to roll different sounds together, and that's what came out … I just did everything I could, you know? … I played everything I knew. I wasn't even looking for an individual style, and probably, I'd never have known that I had one if I'd stayed in a five- or six-piece group, but by pulling it down to a trio like that, you naturally had to do more. So that was how I developed the combination rhythm and a few notes type thing – we were forced into it really, I guess you could say."

"That's All Right" was also the first proper rockabilly record. After it came out, Elvis was known as "the Hillbilly Cat" and "the King of Western Bop," until he became public property a few years later.

It's also the record that has the ability to make you forget all others, that forces you to banish the gentrified pop that came in its wake, as well as the raggle-taggle blues that came before it. This is the rock'n'roll sticky fly trap. "That's All Right" is one of those things that just can't be argued with, a pop-cultural milestone whose importance only escalates with age.

Though the acetate of Paul McCartney's first band, the Quarrymen – owned by the man himself – is still probably the rarest record in the world, a Sun acetate of "That's All Right" that surfaced in 2013 would run it a very close second. It's one of the two-sided acetates – backed with "Blue Moon Of Kentucky" – that were sent to the WHBQ, WMPS and WHHM radio stations. John Heath bought it for $6000 in 2004 from a retired English teacher in the Memphis area. She had acquired it from her mother's friend, who had once worked for a Memphis radio station.

"The sound went straight up your spine," as country star Waylon Jennings put it. "It just climbed right through you."

Billboard's response? "A potent new chanter who comes thru with a solid performance."

Oh, and pretty much invents rock'n'roll as we know it, creating something that had never been heard before, and setting himself free in the process.

David Lynch saw its impact as "Like being hit with a truck filled with happiness. It was a thrilling truck, and you know, I sort of wish everybody could experience that feeling. You've heard these stories. So many musicians when they heard Elvis for the first time, they just slammed their head with their fist and just said, 'Damn! This is it!' And it was just suddenly so obvious. It wasn't there, and then it was there. And it had this unbelievable power, and it just screamed out, and everybody and his little brother lit up like a Christmas tree. It was unbelievably beautiful. I just, inside, felt this thrill, this love of the sound. It was like grabbing onto an electric wire."

The following other Sun songs are also indispensable: "Just Because," "Trying To Get To You," "Good Rockin' Tonight," "Baby Let's Play House," "When It Rains It Really Pours," "Blue Moon" (a thirty-two-bar pop classic that Elvis turns into an eerie sixteen-bar blues), "You're A Heartbreaker," "Blue Moon Of Kentucky," "Tomorrow Night," "I Don't Care If The Sun Don't Shine" (just listen to the extraordinary way Elvis pronounces kiss as "kist") …

2. "Mystery Train" (Little Junior Parker and Sam Phillips), 1955

Recorded in July 1955 as his noble farewell to Sun, "Mystery Train" was Elvis's cover of a fairly nondescript 1953 song by Little Junior Parker, and serves as further empirical evidence that Elvis really was the man who turned old rhythm and blues records into brand new rockabilly ones. Songwriter Doc Pomus described it as sounding like somebody coming up from the swamp, and it still does, with Elvis standing there, water and viscous fluid dripping from his curled lip and his satin shirt, his eyes tracing every inch of your baby's body, as he moved from burbling baritone to whining tenor in a heartbeat.

One man this record inspired was the great Johnny Burnette, a pioneer of wildman rockabilly who made records so fiery, so sparse, they sounded almost elemental, as though nothing could have possibly come before them. Burnette's stuff was field music, bashing out a rhythm with two big sticks, a fuzzy guitar and a raucous yell. Collars up, lip curled, grease in hand: "Lonesome Train," "Honey Hush," "Drinkin' Wine Spo-De-O-De" – oh Lawdy!

3. "Heartbreak Hotel" (Mae Boren Axton, Tommy Durden and Elvis Presley), 1956

"Heartbreak Hotel" was based on a suicide note; Sam Phillips originally called it a "morbid mess," and the demo vocalist Glenn Reeves thought so little of the song that he wanted his name to be kept from Elvis. The first take of Elvis's own recording attempted to mimic the "slapback" sound of Sun, with little success. When it was rerecorded, however, the lumbering blues started to work, with Elvis's slurred vocals sounding almost desperate. "His phrasing, his use of echo, it's all so beautiful," said Paul McCartney. "As if he's singing it from the depths of hell." It turned out to be his first national number one, selling over two million copies.

4. "Don't Be Cruel" (Otis Blackwell and Elvis Presley), 1956

Elvis swings through "Don't Be Cruel," a prime example of late-period western bop, with a completely understated performance. In a word, it was loping. Sam Phillips, who no longer had anything to do with Elvis's career, had to pull his car over to the side of the road when he first heard it on the radio. "I thought, they have finally found this man's ability … The rhythm was right, and it was moving along just right, it had that absolute spontaneity, and yet Elvis still had command."

5. "Hound Dog" (Jerry Leiber and Mike Stoller), 1956

"Hound Dog" was originally recorded by Big Mama Thornton in 1953. Elvis's version was jauntier, based in part on a spoof take on the song by Freddie Bell & The Bellboys, whose act he had seen in Las Vegas. When he performed it on *The Milton Berle Show* he added his half-speed coda, thrusting his groin into the heart of middle America, and sent the rest of the country into something of a panic. It ended up selling seven million copies. According to songwriter Mike Stoller, who, along with his partner, had initially considered Presley to be something of an idiot savant, "I heard the record and I was disappointed. It just sounded terribly nervous, too fast, too white. But you know, after it sold seven or eight million records it started to sound better."

6. "All Shook Up" (Otis Blackwell and Elvis Presley), 1956

If you believe the story that Otis Blackwell was inspired to write the lyric of "All Shook Up" by an excited bottle of soda, after his publisher challenged him to write a song about "anything," then you'll also believe that it marks one of the first examples of pure "pop" writing. Not only is it a song about "nothing," it is also a song literally about "pop."

At the end of *Grease*, when Olivia Newton-John undergoes a complete transformation to become a rock chick, it was originally planned that Olivia and John Travolta would sing a version of "All Shook Up." Movie songwriter John Farrar had other ideas, and came up with "You're The One That I Want" instead. Which obviously wasn't the same thing at all.

7. "Love Me" (Jerry Leiber and Mike Stoller), 1956

Even back then, back at the very dawn of rock'n'roll, when commitment and sincerity were of paramount importance,

Elvis treated "Love Me" as a bit of a jape. Look at him performing it on TV at the time and he'll have a smirk on his face, either winking at his band or at a girl in the audience. It was corny, it was schmaltzy and it was old-fashioned ... and yet ... and yet it was sexy. Leiber and Stoller wrote it as a parody of country and western, but it quickly became a standard of the genre. And as soon as Elvis covered it, the song became his and his alone. He performed it on his 1968 comeback TV special, and throughout his tours of the Seventies, and every time he did, the women in the audience would whoop and holler and pretend to swoon. This was their adolescence he was playing with, and they loved it. He would slowly sing, "Treat me like a fool ..." and then wait for the screams and the giggles, wait for the women in the audience who had wet themselves to the song the first time around to leap up in their seats and start applauding. He would look down with lidded eyes at his girls in the front row, give them a lopsided grin and maybe twitch one leg. And they loved it. This was their song, their moment, and it wasn't for sharing. All eyes would be on his, in case he glanced their way, and made them feel – oh-so-fleetingly – like they had done back in 1956. Elvis knew the power of the song, and although he'd always found it a bit tacky, he'd perform it with passion if not necessarily with commitment. David Lynch understood its power too, and got Elvis-aficionado Nicolas Cage to sing it to his squeeze Laura Dern in the 1990 thriller *Wild At Heart* (a.k.a. *The Wizard Of Elvis*), causing her to go into paroxysms of desire.

8. "Jailhouse Rock" (Jerry Leiber and Mike Stoller), 1957

Having already written "Riot In Cell Block #9," Leiber and Stoller were the perfect team to write Elvis's "crime song" – "Jailhouse Rock." After Elvis successfully covered "Hound

Dog," the Colonel offered the writers a deal. According to Jerry Leiber, "We did about four or five movies, and each one was sillier than the last. We were getting cross-eyed from trying to keep our interest up. And then we ran into a problem with Colonel Parker, who was a colonel like I'm a ballet dancer." That said, when Elvis sings, "If you can't find a partner use a wooden chair …" he sounds as though he's coming to burn your house down. By the time of 1962's "She's Not You," which Leiber and Stoller wrote with Doc Pomus, Elvis's records were beginning to sound so familiar that they all sounded like Christmas.

9. "Young And Beautiful" (Aaron Schroeder and Abner Silver), 1957, Jailhouse Rock

Aaron Schroeder wrote over 1500 songs, including seventeen for Elvis, of which five reached number one ("A Big Hunk O' Love," "Good Luck Charm," "I Got Stung," "Stuck On You" and "It's Now or Never"). He liked to say, not always in jest, "I don't read music – that's why I make so much money." In the late Sixties Schroeder negotiated the music rights for Hanna-Barbera's animated productions, and ended up writing the theme song for *Scooby-Doo, Where Are You!* in 1969. Surprisingly, it was never covered by Elvis.

10. "Too Much" (Lee Rosenberg and Bernard Weinman), 1957

"Too Much" was first recorded in 1954 by Bernard Hardison as an R&B record. By tinkering with its backbeat, Elvis turned it into a slow fuck against the wall, but in the whitest way possible.

11. "Crawfish" (Ben Weisman and Fred Wise), 1958

Originally designed as a vehicle for James Dean, Elvis's fourth – and best – film, *King Creole*, found him working with Walter

Matthau and the man who directed *Casablanca*, Michael Curtiz. Certainly the sexiest song ever sung about seafood, "Crawfish," Elvis's duet with a fish pedlar in the French Quarter of New Orleans, is one of his best performances, while the slow, aching blues is so cool that it was always referenced by Joe Strummer as being his favourite Elvis track. Elvis looked like Jimmy Dean and sang like no one on earth – certainly like no one on Bourbon Street. The title track is also a belter.

12. "Wear My Ring Around Your Neck" (Bert Carroll and Russell Moody), 1958

One of the most generic Elvis songs there is, "Wear My Ring Around Your Neck" is guaranteed to stop any self-respecting Teddy Boy "creeping," and get them swinging their partner around the dancefloor. Unfortunately the song was notable for breaking a string of ten consecutive number ones for Elvis, peaking at number two.

13. "Hard Headed Woman" (Claude DeMetrius), 1958

Elvis had released over fifty different singles by the time of this twelve-bar knockabout, yet "Hard Headed Woman" was so popular that it became the first rock'n'roll single to earn the RIAA designation of Gold Record. Close your eyes and you'll hear Bill Haley, Chuck Berry and a whole mess of blues.

14. "A Big Hunk O' Love" (Aaron Schroeder and Sidney Wyche), 1959

A classic chunk of rock'n'roll, "A Big Hunk O' Love" featured in some of the King's shows in Las Vegas. It was recorded in Nashville on June 10th, 1958 during his solitary studio session in the midst of his two years of army service.

15. "(Now And Then) There's A Fool Such As I" (Bill Trader), 1959

A country song written in 1952, "Fool Such As I" had a surprising amount of traction. It was even recorded by Bob Dylan, once in 1967 and again in 1973. Elvis's version remains the one we all know and love.

16. "Stuck On You" (J. Leslie McFarland and Aaron Schroeder), 1960

"Stuck On You" was Elvis's first hit single after his two-year stint in the US Army. The song itself was so good that you couldn't tell it marked the start of a slow inexorable slide to oblivion.

17. "Girl Next Door Went A' Walking" (Bill Rice and Thomas Wayne), 1960

Besides "Girl Next Door Went A' Walking," Elvis's first post-Army album, imaginatively entitled *Elvis Is Back!*, also included "The Girl Of My Best Friend," "Such A Night" and "Reconsider Baby," all Presley classics. Other similar songs that use his oft-mocked "uh-huh" style include "Treat Me Nice" and "I Got Stung."

18. "What's She Really Like" (Sid Wayne and Abner Silver), 1960

In the movie *G.I. Blues*, Elvis briefly sings "What's She Really Like" while he's in the shower. The full-length version, with instrumental accompaniment, appears on the soundtrack album. For his sins, Wayne also wrote "Do The Clam," from *Girl Happy*, one of Elvis's most lamentable films. Even in Elvis World – that extraordinary alternative universe – that must count as a sackable offence.

19. "It's Now Or Never" (Wally Gold, Aaron Schroeder and Edoardo Di Capua), 1960

"It's Now Or Never" was adapted from the Italian standard "O Sole Mio." Written in 1898, it was brought to worldwide attention by Mario Lanza, of whom Elvis once recalled: "I had records by Mario Lanza when I was seventeen, eighteen years old. I would listen to the Metropolitan Opera. I just loved this music." Tony Martin had a hit with an English-language version in 1958, "There's No Tomorrow." Elvis heard that while he was stationed in Germany, and decided to commission some new English lyrics as soon as he left the Army. Gold and Schroeder then wrote the song in twenty minutes, the best twenty minutes' work they ever did; the single went on to sell over twenty million copies, spending five weeks at number one in the US alone. His voice soaring, his confidence at a peak, Elvis suddenly sounded for all the world like a Neapolitan tenor. Lady whisperer Barry White later recalled that he heard this song while he was in jail for stealing tyres, and fell in love with it so much that it convinced him to pursue a career in music.

Pop critic Paul Morley once suggested that a song can be thought of as being a pop "great" only if you can envisage Elvis singing it. This is one of those songs.

20. "Are You Lonesome Tonight?" (Lou Handman and Roy Turk), 1961

Elvis had such a thirst for schmaltz that he was almost a dipsomaniac, and would regularly dip into the past to find songs that he considered to be standards. When he came out of the Army, he may have been aware he needed to revitalise his rock'n'roll chops, but he also wanted to expand his musical horizons, and broaden his musical talent. Before managing

Elvis, the Colonel had looked after the crooner Gene Austin; as "Are You Lonesome Tonight?" was one of Austin's most popular songs, it's believed that Parker asked Elvis to record it as a favour. As ever, Elvis could have said no.

Over a third of the song is spoken rather than sung, and live, Elvis had a tendency to rework the lyrics: on August 26th 1969, while playing a show at the International in Vegas shortly after his return to live performance, Elvis switched a line to, "Do you gaze at your bald head and wish you had hair?"

The song verges on the edge of parody so many times, and always reminds me of the TCB oath written by Elvis on a plane journey from Los Angeles to Memphis in 1971: "More self-respect, more respect for fellow man. Respect for fellow students and instructors. Respect for all styles and techniques. Body conditioning, mental conditioning, meditation for calming and stilling of the mind and body. Sharpen your skills, increase mental awareness for all those who might choose a new outlook and personal philosophy. Freedom from constipation."

21. "Blue Hawaii" (Leo Robin and Ralph Rainger), 1961
Nick Cave, Leonard Cohen, Scott Walker, you can all eat your black hearts out; "Blue Hawaii" proves that Elvis could have easily guested with the Velvet Underground. Bing Crosby first recorded the song in 1937, while David Byrne gave us his own version on 2008's *Big Love: Hymnal*. The film itself is pretty dreadful – shocker, right? – but the soundtrack is actually quite good, including a ridiculously syrupy track called "Hawaiian Sunset," which if it had been written by Burt Bacharach and originally sung by Dionne Warwick or Dusty Springfield would have been covered thirty times by now.

22. "Can't Help Falling In Love" (Hugo Peretti, Luigi Creatore and George David Weiss), 1961, Blue Hawaii

Some say the Andy Williams cover is better, has more poignancy, but then there are also those who prefer Pepsi to Coke. "Can't Help Falling In Love" is loungecore before loungecore knew it existed. According to critic David Bret, this was regarded as Elvis's own personal *hymne à l'amour*, representing his most important love affair, the one he conducts with his fans to this day, even from beyond the grave.

23. "Surrender" (Doc Pomus and Mort Shuman), 1961

You only have to listen to the first two bars of "Surrender" – one of twenty-five songs that Pomus and Shuman wrote for the King – to imagine how easy it would have been for Elvis to become embroiled in the James Bond films. Does "The James Bond Theme" sound a little similar to "Surrender"? Play this over the opening credits of *Dr. No*, *From Russia With Love* or *Goldfinger* and simply imagine Elvis in a midnight blue tux walking onto a large yacht in St. Tropez, or seducing Shirley Eaton in a Florida hotel room …

24. "Little Sister" (Doc Pomus and Mort Shuman), 1961

With arguably the finest guitar-driven intro of any record released in the last sixty years, "Little Sister" ranks among the greatest of all rock'n'roll records. With echoes of British bands such as Johnny Kidd and the Pirates (especially "Shakin' All Over") and the Shadows, it demonstrates – yet again – Elvis's ability to tackle a style and improve upon it. "Little Sister" was actually a double A-side, coupled with "(Marie's The Name) His Latest Flame." That makes it not just one of the best rock'n'roll singles of all time, but simply one of the best singles ever.

25. "Suspicion" (Doc Pomus and Mort Shuman), 1962

Setting paranoid lyrics against a chirpy bossa nova, "Suspicion" is melodramatic Elvis at his best. It was successfully covered by Terry Stafford two years later, although the best cover was actually the rather more blithe version by the Bonzo Dog Doo-Dah Band, whose singer Viv Stanshall was a huge Elvis fan. It included a spoken passage that, had he considered it, Elvis might even have got away with: "Darling, if you love me, please show me some proof of your good intentions. I'd like it on my desk on Monday morning at the very latest. I know this might seem silly, but I want to be absolutely positive. If you have been deceiving me, well, it's time you got a boyfriend ..." On the record he says "well, it's a neat bit of jiggery-pokery."

Elvis was Stanshall's thing. Stanshall could spend days dressed as Elvis, playing out his own little personal homage. He would impersonate him on stage, where he would wear a gold lamé suit, and play songs that had been deliberately written in his style. One, "Death Cab For Cutie," was a send-up of one of the teenage tragedy or "death songs" from the early Sixties, featuring a girl who takes a doomed journey against her lover's wishes. Stanshall and co-writer Neil Innes stole the idea from the title of an American pulp fiction crime magazine, and the song became popular due to its inclusion in the Beatles' 1967 television extravaganza, *Magical Mystery Tour*, in which Stanshall performs it with a stripper from the infamous Soho sex club, Raymond's Revuebar. Accompanied by two guitarists, a saxophone player and a drummer, Stanshall lopes onto the stage, sporting a Zapata moustache, an open-necked shirt and his lamé suit, a modish pocket square sprouting out of the breast pocket. He pumps his arms in slow motion as he mimes a sprint towards the microphone stand.

26. "Good Luck Charm" (Aaron Schroeder and Wally Gold), 1962

A living room walking blues that was a cliché before it was even released, "Good Luck Charm" is nevertheless one of Elvis's most endearing songs, the kind of tune that Ringo might have sung had he been asked to.

27. "Return To Sender" (Winfield Scott and Otis Blackwell), 1962

If you're going to flap your knees like a drape-jacketed penguin, then "Return To Sender" is the song to do it to. Whenever the BBC runs a clip of Teddy Boys dancing in the aisles, they either use this or Bill Haley's "Don't Knock The Rock."

28. "Viva Las Vegas" (Doc Pomus and Mort Shuman), 1964

Before it became too arch for words, "Viva Las Vegas" was already unintentionally ironic. At the time, the film it came from tried to paint Vegas as a city of fast money, fast women and even faster blackjack dealers, as though we were all somehow unaware of this. Perversely, in the fifty-odd years since it was originally recorded, the song has taken on a new resonance, a new integrity – just listen to Bruce Springsteen's 1992 version. As the city itself becomes more preposterous, so the song becomes more authentic.

29. "You're The Boss" (Jerry Leiber and Mike Stoller), 1964, Viva Las Vegas

This is one of those Elvis rarities that is rarer than hen's teeth: a genuine duet, this one sung with Ann-Margret. It's a great song, and sexy to boot, sung by two people who shared the same bed in real life as well as on screen, and it glides along like a snake on a scorching New Orleans sidewalk. "We both felt a current, an electricity that went straight through us," Ann-Margret wrote about their on-off-on relationship. "It would become a force we couldn't control." The master of this was released recently; not only has it been cleaned up so Elvis and Ann-Margret's voices are now properly separated to left and right channels, but it's also seventeen seconds longer (and funnier).

30. "Crying In The Chapel" (Artie Glenn), 1965

Elvis just couldn't help dipping into the past. Wary of covering anything too contemporary, whenever he had a crisis of confidence, he would trawl the charts from the Fifties, trying to find a song his mama would have liked. So it was with his cover of Glenn's "Crying In The Chapel" from 1953 (when it had been one of the most covered songs of the year, the best version being by Sonny Til & The Orioles). Elvis recorded it in 1960 for inclusion on his gospel album *His Hand In Mine*, but then held it back until it was released in 1965 as a special "Easter" single.

It was the success of this song, which reached number three in the US and number one in the UK, that made Elvis accept an invitation to meet the Beatles. Their own success, in Elvis's mind at the expense of his own, had until then made him wary of meeting them. The event, on August 27th at a Frank Lloyd Wright house in Beverly Hills that Elvis rented from the Shah of Iran, wasn't what anyone involved had hoped for. Elvis thought the Beatles rude and silly, while they thought he was dull, and surrounded by sycophants: as Ringo expressed it, "Elvis would say, 'I'm going to the loo now and they'd say, 'We'll all go to the loo with you.'"

31. "Tomorrow Is A Long Time" (Bob Dylan), 1966

The sessions that produced the songs that ended up on the

1967 Grammy-winning gospel album *How Great Thou Art* also produced this extraordinary version of Bob Dylan's "Tomorrow Is A Long Time." Elvis recorded other Dylan songs – "Blowin' In The Wind," "Don't Think Twice, It's All Right" and "I Shall Be Released" – but this was the most successful. His version was based on another cover by the folk singer Odetta, whose particular take on the song was sparse and bluesy, and appeared on the 1965 album *Odetta Sings Dylan*. Dylan once said that Elvis's version was his personal favourite cover of his work. Ever.

32. "A Little Less Conversation" (Mac Davis and Billy Strange), 1968

"A Little Less Conversation" was a minor hit from a minor movie, *Live A Little, Love A Little*. A 2002 remix by Junkie XL, however, which was inspired by the original song's inclusion in the 2001 film *Ocean's Eleven*, became a worldwide smash, topping the charts in nine countries. Bizarrely, the original has also been used in various political campaigns, including those of Vermont Governor Howard Dean, Democratic presidential nominee Senator John Kerry, Republican hopeful Sarah "Chauncey Gardiner" Palin, as well as George W. Bush, who used it for his successful reelection bid in 2004.

"The Edge Of Reality" (Bernie Baum, Bill Giant and Florence Kaye), 1968

If Jimmy Webb had tried his hand at writing an existential psychedelic ballad, "The Edge Of Reality" could have been it. In the film *Live A Little, Love A Little*, Elvis walks through a slightly naff dream sequence dressed in an electric-blue satin suit that seems as though it had originally been designed as a pair of pyjamas, looking about as uncomfortable as he ever had done in a movie (and that's saying something).

Once again, it would have made a great Bond theme song, whether sung by Matt Monro, Tom Jones, Shirley Bassey or Elvis himself. The same team also wrote "(You're The) Devil In Disguise."

Elvis was never a great fan of the counter culture. Even though he was addicted to prescription drugs, he went out of his way to disparage the hippie movement, and anyone who was in the vanguard of anti-American protest. In 1970 he famously asked President Nixon for a Bureau of Narcotics and Dangerous Drugs Special Agent badge – although Priscilla later claimed he only wanted it so he could transport his drugs and guns without being arrested.

That was the thing about Elvis: no matter how cool he was, during the Sixties he became increasingly square. Given his antipathy towards jazz, it was ironic that he would be labelled with the genre's anodyne put-down (if you had to be "there" or "square," by this point Elvis certainly wasn't anywhere close to "there"). He would always be Elvis, but towards the end of the decade he started to look a little like Herman's Hermits, a bit long in the tooth and narrow of trouser. His seemingly innate hipness had modulated into a burgeoning naffness that he himself would have been unable to identify or acknowledge. Elvis didn't mind some of his men wearing their hair long, but he would never consider it himself. Longhairs were freaks'n'weirdos, and not the sort of men who would be tolerated at Graceland. Elvis was nothing if not a good old boy … Ultimately, Elvis had very little curiosity about the world; he certainly only had a small ration of insurrection. When he joined the Army and was sent to Germany, seven East German boys were jailed for "worshipping Elvis" and for making skin-tight blue jeans their "uniform of the day." Private Presley was driven to verbal intervention: "Man," he informed an interviewer, "those Commies across the border are really squares, wouldn't you say?"

34. "Let Yourself Go" (Joy Byers), 1968

When it was released, the movie *Speedway* looked as anachronistic as the Beach Boys or Herman's Hermits, pop products fighting for their lives in a world smelling of patchouli and Moroccan. Ten years later, *Grease* would seem full of warm nostalgia and fond memories; in 1968, Elvis just appeared to be pressing the same old button on the jukebox. Appearing at Woodstock might have been worse for his reputation, and more public, but appearing in old-fashioned schlock like this was almost as damaging. Still, "Let Yourself Go" was a great song, and one that deserved better context. Elvis performed the song in his 1968 TV comeback special, but as the scene was set in a brothel, it was removed at the request of the show's primary sponsor, the Singer Corporation.

35. "Rubberneckin'" (Cory Jones and Bunny Warren), 1969

"With all due respect to Elvis Presley," said Paul Oakenfold, who remixed "Rubberneckin'," from the movie *Change of Habit*, in 2003, "I don't think 'Rubberneckin'' was a classic. It's not 'Heartbreak Hotel.'" Oakenfold's remix came a year after Junkie XL's "A Little Less Conversation," for another Presley compilation, *Second To None*. "There are classics, and I personally would never touch a classic. Initially, I was like, well, I don't know if I could do this [but] the challenge was to keep the integrity of Elvis and make sure it wasn't cheesy; keep what was initially there, the arrangement or structure, but give it more of a current feel. It's done in a way that I believe works ..." and which sold in huge numbers.

36. "Long Black Limousine" (Vern Stovall and Bobby George), 1969

Singing is a perishable skill, yet Elvis largely remained in control of his voice, right up until the end. Just listen to "Long Black Limousine." Elvis often added a little too much sugar to melodramas such as this, but on this occasion he let the song speak for itself. Full of sadness, full of pathos, this was bleak. Forget miserabilist paeans like Ricky Nelson's "Lonesome Town," Portishead's "Sour Times," R.E.M.'s "Everybody Hurts," Bruce Springsteen's "Highway Patrolman" or Jeff Buckley's "Hallelujah" – this might not be the sound of despair, but it's a damn fine portrait of tragedy. A lot of Elvis songs featured emotions unworthy of commemoration, but this was a simple story of a life gone wrong, a body returned home for burial. It would have been perfect for the Rolling Stones, shoved onto side two of *Sticky Fingers* or *Some Girls*, with Jagger singing in his comedy Southern twang. The song has also been covered by the Grateful Dead (appallingly), Merle Haggard (generically), O.C. Smith (averagely) and dozens more people who thought they could add a little more depth, a little less light. None of them is a patch on Elvis. One of the things that makes the song so durable is the *Weltschmerz*, and while it is hardly a festival of spiritual despair, it is one of the unlikeliest songs Elvis ever sang.

What started out as a melodramatic country morality tale, became, in Elvis's hands, a slow sombre blues. Stovall and George's odyssey is lyrically similar to early Sixties "death" songs such as "The Leader Of The Pack," "Teen Angel" and "Dead Man's Curve," yet it is fundamentally much darker, and grander in scope, and could have been written by Lee Hazelwood or indeed in more recent times by Nick Cave. In fact it's perhaps the darkest song Elvis ever considered, using a treatment that doesn't even hint at redemption. In hindsight, of course, it's also full of pathos, as it echoes the narrative arc of Elvis's own life.

When Elvis chose to cover a song, he usually amplified the arrangement by making it more grandiose and melodramatic; with "Long Black Limousine" he pared it down, making it more gothic in the process. There is a post on one of the many websites devoted to the song, which is adapted from an old uncredited piece in *Rolling Stone*:

"It is quite a song ... Elvis never sang with more passion; he was bitter, and of what other recording by Elvis Presley can you say that? Of course, Elvis was no fool; he knew the song was about him, the country boy lost to the city if there ever was one, but he sang as if he liked that and loathed it all at once. He contained multitudes. His singing cut through the contradictions, blew them up. William Carlos Williams might say that 'the pure products of America go crazy,' but you might also say that the crazy products of America are pure, or something like that. When the stakes are as high as they always were in Elvis's case, the neat phrase is not to be trusted; always, it will obscure more than it will reveal."

37. "In The Ghetto" (Mac Davis), 1969

Having spent a decade wandering somnambulantly through a series of increasingly silly films, the King probably knew by the end of the Sixties that he wasn't the monarch any more, even though he would always be rock'n'roll royalty. After the huge success of his 1968 TV special, Elvis stepped back from making pop for a while, and recorded *From Elvis in Memphis*, a record steeped in the South. The album was an eclectic mix of country and soul, but the killer track was the final song on side two, a message song about poverty, politics and struggle. "In The Ghetto" was pop social commentary of the first water, written by Mac Davis – who had originally intended calling it "The Vicious Circle" until he realised that nothing rhymes with "circle" – and deliberately chosen by Elvis. He was so determined to make it work that it took 23 takes until he felt he'd done the song justice.

"With 'In The Ghetto,' he was just really into it," said guitarist Reggie Young, who played on the record. "I remember it being stopped a few times – he just wanted to do it better. It was like he was finally doing a song with some meaning to it, with some soul – it would have to turn him on. By this time he was really enthused about what he was doing, he really cared … Instead of it just being a party, you know, go to the studio and have a party, he was really trying."

"The Colonel was against it," said Priscilla. "He thought it was so risky and identified Elvis too closely with black America. He came close to talking Elvis out of releasing it."

38. "Almost" (Buddy Kaye and Ben Weisman), 1969
Elvis was continually criticised for his choice of ballads, as they were usually considered to be well below par. But when he got it right, he could define a song in the time it took him to record it. Weisman wrote more songs for Elvis than anyone, and knew the man well:

"I approached writing for Elvis differently than I did for any other artist. Elvis challenged my imagination. The songs had to have a combination of blues, country, rock and pop, sometimes gospel or swamp boogie, you name it. I lived my creative life walking in his musical shoes. And what shoes they were! Elvis had so much spirit. Beyond compare really. Elvis was a transformer, a rebel, like a meteorite, someone who only comes along once every few hundred years. He had that level of magnetism. Astonishing to be a part of it! And to write for him, to try and express what I knew he was going through as a man, throughout that whole journey. I feel very lucky."

39. "Any Day Now" (Burt Bacharach and Bob Hilliard), 1969
Unlike almost every entertainer of the Sixties and Seventies
you might care to mention, Elvis wasn't a great interpreter of
Burt Bacharach songs. He thought them too feminine, too
complicated. When he covered "Any Day Now," written by
Bacharach and Bob Hilliard in 1962, and originally performed
by Chuck Jackson in 1965, Elvis managed to eradicate much of
the nuance, creating a far more orthodox song in the process.
Incongruously, Elvis considered Bacharach to be slightly old-
fashioned, associating him with suburbia, faux sophistication
and the JFK years. Bacharach's finely calibrated melodies,
incessant key changes, and melancholy top-notes were
anathema to Elvis, who preferred more conventional narratives.
Elvis also had an issue with Hal David's metropolitan lyrics.

40. "Suspicious Minds" (Mark James), 1969
When Elvis recorded "Suspicious Minds," during the same
American Sound Studio sessions as "In The Ghetto," he made
it sound as though he had written it himself. He had told the
producer of his 1968 TV special that "I give you my word
I will never sing a song I don't believe in," and this time it
showed. As Q magazine once pointed out, towards the end
of the song, when he wheels back to the very first lines –
"We're caught in a trap, I can't walk out, Because I love you
too much baby" – he starts to repeat them as an endless,
infernal incantation. The song mirrors its meaning: everyone
locked in their own Shakespearean cycles of pain and failure,
doomed completely. It was recorded some time between four
and seven in the morning, on the fourth take, but it nearly
didn't see the light of day. The Colonel demanded a co-writing
credit for Elvis until RCA – knowing they had a smash on
their hands – persuaded him to back down.

Around this time, Elvis also started performing Tony Joe White's "Polk Salad Annie," a song that seemed appropriately swampy for him to cover in that it describes the lifestyle of a poor rural Southern girl and her family. It was also a favourite of Norman Mailer's. On the tenth anniversary of Elvis's death, when *USA Today* asked various notables to name their favourite Elvis song – Paul Newman chose "Hound Dog," while Carl Sagan couldn't make up his mind between "Little Sister" and "(Marie's The Name) His Latest Flame" – Mailer said, "I used to listen to it when I was jogging, and it was peppy and made running a little easier. It had that quality of his."

41. "Just Pretend" (Guy Fletcher and Doug Flett), 1970

Doug Flett has been a friend of mine for over thirty years. While he has had songs recorded by Aretha Franklin, Ray Charles, Frankie Valli, Joe Cocker and Tom Jones, and has recently enjoyed the fillip of having his song "Fallen Angel" included in the *Jersey Boys* stage show, nothing has ever beaten the thrill of having a song recorded by the King.

"I read an interview with Lisa Marie Presley and when asked about her favourite tracks of her father's work she named four, saying she liked the darker songs and 'Just Pretend' is one of the four," said Doug. "I'm pretty pleased about that as you might imagine. What we didn't know when we wrote the song was that Elvis and Priscilla had recently parted and if you listen to it with that in mind it's especially poignant." Another Fletcher/Flett song covered by Elvis is the magnificent "The Fair Is Moving On."

42. "I Just Can't Help Believing" (Barry Mann and Cynthia Weil), 1970, That's The Way It Is

Recorded by B.J. Thomas and released as a single in 1970, "I Just Can't Help Believing" went to number nine on the

Billboard Hot 100. It became an Elvis song, however, as soon as he released his own version a short while later – even though *Star Trek*'s Leonard Nimoy recorded his own interpretation, a challenging prospect in itself.

This is one of those songs that just sounds *great* on the radio, especially a car radio. While I have never really been in love with the car, per se, I have been in love with the idea of the road trip since I was still playing with Hot Wheels. I had no interest in trains, motorbikes or pushbikes – I wanted to sit behind the wheel of a Mustang, driving along the California coast, listening to Bobby Darin, the Regents, Buster Brown, Joey D and the Starlighters, and all the other songs on the *American Graffiti* soundtrack. OK, I'll admit that I once owned a Chopper, and just after the moon landing I spent at least six months wanting to be an astronaut, but then I've always been a fan of thermal micrometeoroid garments that offer limited shielding against particle radiation. Who hasn't?

Just a few years after I eventually learned to drive, I organised a road trip across the US with a friend of mine, Robin, a journey that would take us all the way from New York, Philadelphia and Washington down through the Blue Ridge Mountains, Nashville and Memphis before joining Route 66 and continuing on to LA, via Texas, Arizona, New Mexico and Nevada. And of course I made an individual mix-tape for every state, starting off on the Eastern Seaboard with lots of Bruce Springsteen and the E-Street Band, Bob Seger and the Silver Bullet Band, and Southside Johnny and the Asbury Dukes, before moving into the Southern States with plenty of Neville Brothers, Dr John, Allen Toussaint and of course, some Elvis, before joining the dustbowl motorway accompanied by fairly generic Seventies FM rock (the Steve Miller Band, the Eagles, Foghat, Boston etc).

I had failed to understand that the radio stations in the

States are built for long journeys, and that the soundtrack to my journey would be supplied whether I liked it or not. There was no need for me to make a cassette compilation that included "I Just Can't Help Believing" – or Steely Dan's "King Of The World," Robert Plant's "Big Log," or Neil Young's "Powderfinger," for that matter. They – and everything else I'd recorded for the journey – were on the radio every half an hour anyway.

"Good job you recorded this," deadpanned Robin as we trundled through New Mexico, after we'd listened to "Take It Easy" by the Eagles, "because they've only played it six times on the radio today."

43. "Kentucky Rain" (Eddie Rabbitt and Dick Heard), 1970

Riding high on the success of his 1968 NBC comeback special, Elvis headed into the studio in Memphis. Those recording sessions produced several notable hits, including "Suspicious Minds," "In The Ghetto" and the wonderfully maudlin "Kentucky Rain," about a man wandering the streets in search of the woman who left him. Like we didn't know …
This appears on the 2000 re-release of *From Elvis In Memphis*, while live versions are available on the box sets *Elvis Aaron Presley* and *Live In Las Vegas*.

44. "The Fool" (Naomi Ford and Lee Hazlewood), 1971

Recorded in Nashville instead of Memphis, and released in 1971, *Elvis Country (I'm 10,000 Years Old)* is actually one of Elvis's most cohesive albums, showing what Elvis might have achieved given more guidance. Working with a new band that included members of the original Muscle Shoals rhythm section, he cut 35 masters over five nights, forming the kind of studio relationship that Elvis hadn't had for years. There are many standout tracks, but "The Fool" by Naomi Ford and

Lee Hazlewood is one of the best, a rickety old rockabilly number originally recorded by Sanford Clark back in 1956, and given a sweet country treatment. Robert Gordon covered it magnificently in the late Seventies, and that's probably the definitive version, but Elvis's isn't far behind. The album also contains the lovely "Snowbird." According to *Mojo* magazine, "Passionate, wild, dynamic, *Elvis Country* sounds like it's tapped straight from the true soul of that once and future King. He'd never sing like this again."

45. "Always On My Mind" (Johnny Christopher, Mark James and Wayne Carson Thompson), 1972

By the time Elvis came to record "Always On My Mind" in 1972, it had already been a country flop for Brenda Lee earlier that same year. It became one of his biggest hits of the Seventies, a song that not only drew a line under his marriage to Priscilla – they had separated a few weeks before the session – but also brought the curtain down on his career. His voice had rarely sounded better. The song may have expressed resignation, but the voice was full of expectation and promise. "Always On My Mind" was famously covered by the Pet Shop Boys. When the band's Chris Lowe was asked about their song "Your Early Stuff" (composed of remarks made to them by cab drivers: "Those old videos look pretty funny, What's in it for you now, need the money?"), he said, "Funnily enough. I like the later stuff. I only liked Elvis when he went to Las Vegas. There's more emotion in the later work."

46. "Burning Love" (Dennis Linde and Arthur Alexander), 1972

A song in the style of Creedence Clearwater Revival, "Burning Love" is a modern take on an old genre, which of course was very Elvis. You can look at Elvis during this period and imagine what was going through Meat Loaf's head (and Jim Steinman's, come to that): a larger-than-is-traditionally-acceptable sex symbol singing souped-up rock'n'roll having been given a veneer of Seventies flash – like a Fifties Cadillac with a brand new engine. Excess and incongruity, basically. Had Elvis lived, it would have been marvellous watching him tackle "You Took The Words Right Out Of My Mouth" or "Bat Out Of Hell." That said, he would have had to stop smiling, as the whole point of Meat Loaf – and the reason we all bought into the idea – was that he took it seriously, something that Elvis rarely did towards the end. Even better, imagine Elvis putting himself in the hands of Jim Steinman, in the way that Johnny Cash did with Rick Rubin, listening to his beleaguered baritone wrapping itself around "I'd Do Anything For Love (But I Won't Do That)."

Steinman – who was essentially Meat Loaf's mentor and Svengali – had already made a nod to Elvis with his song "Two Out Of Three Ain't Bad," which had been inspired by a friend's suggestion that he needed a big ballad for the *Bat Out Of Hell* album. He took some lines from an Elvis hit – "I want you, I need you, I love you" – and put his own spin on them: "I want you, I need you, But there ain't no way I'm ever gonna love you … Now don't be sad, 'Cause two out of three ain't bad …"

As Steinman describes it, "To me [that song] was very country, by the way. I really heard it like the plains of Texas … I just heard it like a dusty plain. That was perfect to transfer to Meat Loaf who always had that in him anyway, that Elvis quality. I think there is a bit of Elvis, to say the least, in Meat."

47. "You Gave Me A Mountain" (Marty Robbins), 1973, Aloha From Hawaii: Via Satellite

Frankie Laine had a big hit with "You Gave Me A Mountain" in 1969. "Marty Robbins once told me that he'd been trying to bring 'You Gave Me A Mountain' to my attention for several years before he finally succeeded in November 1968. I wish he'd been quicker about it." Elvis wished he'd given it to him first, too, as this was the kind of melodramatic bombast he loved, a heads-down-see-you-at-the-end narrative, coupled with plenty of pathos. Having heard Elvis's near-operatic version, Robbins started performing the song in a similar way, and even began wearing embroidered white cowboy outfits.

48. "Moody Blue" (Mark James), 1977, Moody Blue
By the time Elvis recorded "Moody Blue," his professional career was so itinerant, so patchwork – and his albums such curate's eggs – that it was unusual to find much of worth. Written by Mark James – real name Francis Rodney Zambon – the songwriter responsible for "Suspicious Minds," "Moody Blue" was worth rather a lot. When Elvis recorded it in February 1976 in the Jungle Room at Graceland, he showered it with love and attention. He only performed the song live once, at a concert in Charlotte, North Carolina, on February 21st, 1977.

49. "She Thinks I Still Care" (Dickey Lee and Steve Duffy), 1977
Few fans took any notice of the early Sixties classic "She Thinks I Still Care," sitting on the flip side of "Moody Blue," and fewer still appreciated the sparse arrangement on which Elvis had insisted. This was his own interpretation of the *Plastic Ono Band* LP, stripping everything back to the bare essentials – twelve-bar guitar, floppy drums, rolling bass, an itinerant piano and a rich baritone owned by a drug-addled sex-symbol. His voice was completely undiminished by time. At an age when a lot of singers would be attempting to disguise their failings, or bend the songs to suit their range, Elvis picked up every song and put it in his pocket.

50. "Way Down" (Layng Martine, Jr.), 1977
When John Lennon died, his comeback single "Starting Over"
– a deceptively anodyne love song set to a loping rock'n'roll
backbeat – was already going down the charts, a victim of
uniform public lack of interest. Lennon hadn't released a
record for five long years, not since 1975, and he had found
it difficult to live up to expectations. Impossible, actually.
Of course when he was shot, the global outpouring of grief
involved the buying of the single, as well as its follow-up
"Woman" and the mediocre album they came from, *Double
Fantasy*, in vast, *vast* numbers.

Similarly, when Elvis died, "Way Down" shot back up
the charts like a fairground firework, all the way to number
one. As a result, we look back on Elvis's last single with
an affection coloured by memory and grief, a moment in
time, wrapped around a nondescript record defined by
quantitative logarithms rather than qualitative ones. "Way
Down" was better than almost any record Elvis had released
in the previous five years, but it wasn't "Mystery Train," wasn't
"Heartbreak Hotel," wasn't even "Burning Love." But it was
something, and in the absence of anything else it was the
something by which we would choose to remember him.

Chronological Bibliography

Operation Elvis, Alan Levy, Andre Deutsch, 1961

Elvis, Jerry Hopkins, Open Gate, 1971

The Great American Popular Singers, Henry Pleasants, Gollancz, 1974

Elvis: What Happened? Red West, Sonny West & Dave Hebler, Ballantine, 1977

Elvis Presley, Todd Slaughter, Mandabrook, 1977

Inside Las Vegas, Mario Puzo, Grosset & Dunlap, 1977

My Life With Elvis, Becky Yancey, WH Allen, 1977

Presley: Entertainer Of The Century, Antony James, Tower, 1977

My Elvis, Your Elvis, Gloria Straub, Random House, 1978

Elvis: The Truth, The Whole Truth & Nothing But The Truth, Emmett Jones, Willpower Fogle Books, 1979

Elvis '56: In The Beginning, Alfred Wertheimer, Cassell, 1979

I Called Him Babe: Elvis Presley's Nurse Remembers, Marian J. Cocke, Memphis State University Press, 1979

Elvis, Albert Goldman, Allen Lane, 1980

Elvis, The Final Years, Jerry Hopkins, Playboy Enterprises, 1980

Elvis We Love You Tender, Dee Presley, Billy, Rick & David Stanley, Delacorte Press, 1980

The Clash: Before & After, Pennie Smith, Plexus, 1980

Up And Down With Elvis Presley, Marge Crumbaker, New English Library, 1981

Gone Crazy And Back Again: The Rise And Fall Of The Rolling Stone Generation, Robert Sam Anson, Doubleday, 1981

David Bowie: An Illustrated Record, Roy Carr and Charles Shaar Murray, Eel Pie, 1981

Hellfire: The Jerry Lee Lewis Story, Nick Tosches, Delacorte Press, 1982

Elvis, Dave Marsh, Thunder's Mouth Press, 1982

Ice Cold Elvis: Here Comes The King One Last Time, Stephen Hathaway, Orick Press, 1982

Elvis: The Films And Career Of Elvis Presley, Steven Zmijewsky & Boris Zmijewsky, Citadel Press, 1983

Rock'n'Roll Confidential, Penny Stallings, Vermilion & Company, 1984

Automatic Vaudeville, John Lahr, Heinemann, 1984

Elvis And Me, Priscilla Beaulieu Presley, Century Hutchinson, 1985

The Big Room, Michael Herr & Guy Peellaert, Picador, 1986

The Moronic Inferno, Martin Amis, Jonathan Cape, 1986

Art Into Pop, Simon Frith and Howard Horne, Methuen, 1987

Elvis World, Jane & Michael Stern, Bloomsbury, 1987

Elvis After Life – Unusual Psychic Experiences Surrounding The Death Of A Superstar, Raymond A. Moody Jr., Bantam Books, 1987

Getting It On: The Clothing Of Rock'n'Roll, Mablen Jones, Abbeville Press, 1987

Are You Lonesome Tonight? Lucy De Barbin, Century, 1987

Elvis And The Colonel, Dirk Vellenga & Mick Farren, Delacorte Press, 1988

Is Elvis Alive? Gail Brewer-Giorgio, Tudor, 1988

The Wicked Ways Of Malcolm McLaren, Craig Bromberg, Harper & Row, 1989

Be My Baby, Ronnie Spector, Harmony Books, 1990

Amok: Fourth Despatch, edited by Stuart Swezey, Amok, 1990

Haircults, Dylan Jones, Thames & Hudson, 1990

Mystery Train, Greil Marcus, Penguin, 1990

The Rolling Stone Story, Robert Draper, Mainstream Publishing, 1990

Elton, Philip Norman, Hutchinson, 1991

England's Dreaming, Jon Savage, Faber & Faber, 1991

The Death Of Elvis: What Really Happened, Charles C. Thompson and James P. Cole, Delacorte Press, 1991

Dead Elvis, Greil Marcus, Doubleday, 1991

Elvis: The Last 24 Hours, Albert Goldman, St Martin's Press, 1991

Unseen Elvis: Candids Of The King, Jim Curtin, Victor Gollancz, 1992

Her Name Is Barbra, Randall Riese, Birch Lane Press, 1993

RE/SEARCH: Incredibly Strange Music, edited by Andrea Juno, Re/Search Publications, 1993

Graceland: The Living Legacy Of Elvis Presley, Mike Evans, Hamlyn, 1993

The Life And Cuisine Of Elvis Presley, David Adler, Crown, 1993

Coast To Coast, Andy Bull, Black Swan, 1993

Last Train To Memphis, Peter Guralnick, Little, Brown, 1994

Elvis: Rock'n'Roll Legend, Susan Doll, Publications International, 1994

A Biographical Dictionary Of Film, David Thomson, Knopf, 1994

Elvis + Marilyn: 2 x Immortal, Geri DePaoli, Rizzoli, 1994

Elvis By Those Who Knew Him Best, Roe Clayton & Dick Heard, Virgin, 1994

My Story, Ann-Margret, Putnam, 1994

The Elvis Encyclopedia, David E. Stanley, General Publishing Group, 1994

Elvis And The Memphis Mafia, Alanna Nash with Billy Smith, Marty Lacker and Lamar Fike, Harper Collins, 1995

Meaty Beaty Big & Bouncy! Classic Rock & Pop Writing

From Elvis To Oasis, edited by Dylan Jones, Hodder & Stoughton, 1996

Elvis, The Fifth Beatle, Steve Baren, Warlock Barnard Inc, 1996

Elvis! Steve Templeton, The Apple Press, 1996

Dear Boy: The Life Of Keith Moon, Tony Fletcher, Omnibus Press, 1998

The King Is Dead, Robert Holton, Katco, 1998

Careless Love: The Unmaking of Elvis Presley, Peter Guralnick, Little, Brown, 1999

Elvis Culture: Fans, Faith & Image, Erika Doss, University Press of Kansas, 1999

Elvis: Word For Word: What He Said, Exactly As He Said It, Jerry Osborne, Jerry Osborne Enterprises, 1999

Double Trouble: Bill Clinton And Elvis Presley In A Land Of No Alternatives, Greil Marcus, Faber & Faber, 2000

Spinning Blues Into Gold: Chess Records: The Label That Launched The Blues, Nadine Cohodas, Aurum Books, 2000

History Of The Twentieth Century, Martin Gilbert, Harper Collins, 2001

Elvis: The Hollywood Years, David Bret, Robson Books, 2001

Infinite Elvis, Mary Hancock Hinds, A Cappella Books, 2001

The Rat Pack: Neon Nights With The Kings Of Cool, Lawrence J. Quirk and William Schoell, Perennial, 2002

Elvis: A Celebration, Mike Evans, Dorling Kindersley, 2002

Elvis In Hawai'i, Jerry Hopkins, The Bess Press, 2002

Waking Up In Memphis, Andria Lisle & Mike Evans, Sanctuary, 2003

John Peel, Mick Wall, Orion, 2004

Blockbuster, Tom Shone, Simon & Schuster, 2004

The Colonel, Alanna Nash, Simon & Schuster, 2004

John Peel: A Life In Music, Michael Heatley, O'Mara Books, 2004

Everything Elvis, Helen Clutton, Virgin, 2004

A Man Called Cash, Steve Turner, Bloomsbury, 2004

Made In The UK: The Music Of Attitude 1977-1983, Janette Beckman, Powerhouse Books, 2005

Elvis By The Presleys, Priscilla Presley & Lisa Marie Presley, edited by David Ritz, Century, 2005

Margrave Of The Marshes, John Peel, Bantam Press, 2005

John, Paul, George, Ringo & Me, Tony Barrow, Andre Deutsch, 2005

Punk Diary: The Ultimate Trainspotter's Guide To Underground Rock, 1970-1982, George Gimarc, Backbeat Books, 2005

Strange Fascination: David Bowie, The Definitive Story, David Buckley, Virgin Books, 2005

Rockwiz: 1001 Songs, Tony Cresswell, Hardie Grant Books, 2005

Images Of Elvis, Marie Clayton, Parragon, 2006

The Elvis Impersonation Kit, Laura Lee, Black Dog, 2006

The Joke's Over: Memories Of Hunter S. Thompson, Ralph Steadman, Heinemann, 2006

Rolling Stone: 1,000 Covers, edited by Corey Seymour, Abrams, 2006

Elvis Religion: The Cult Of The King, Gregory L. Reece, Tauris, 2006

Seventies, Howard Sounes, Simon & Schuster, 2006

Me And A Guy Called Elvis, Jerry Schilling with Chuck Crisafulli, Gotham, 2006

Punk Rock: An Oral History, John Robb, Ebury Press, 2006

Elvis: Remembering August 16, 1977, Spike Collamore and Michael Best, Authorhouse, 2006

Albums: The Stories Behind 50 Years Of Great Recordings, Simon Smith & Tony Bacon, Outline Press, 2006

Elvis: Still Taking Care Of Business, Sonny West and Marshall Terrill, Triumph, 2007

Pop Art Book, edited by Nadine Kathe Monem, Black Dog Publishing, 2007

In Search Of Elvis, Charlie Connelly, Little, Brown, 2007

Sid Vicious: No One Is Innocent, Alan Parker, Orion, 2007

Babylon's Burning, Clinton Heylin, Canongate, 2007

The Elvis Encyclopedia, Adam Victor, Overlook Duckworth, 2008

Hang The DJ, edited by Angus Cargill, Faber & Faber, 2008

My Word Is My Bond, Roger Moore, Michael O'Mara, 2008

Hound Dog, Jerry Leiber & Mike Stoller (with David Ritz), Omnibus Press, 2009

The King And Dr. Nick, George Nichopoulos with Rose Clayton Phillips, Thomas Nelson Books, 2009

Route 19 Revisited: The Clash And The Making Of London Calling, Jonathan Cape, 2009

Elvis Religion: The Cult Of The King, Gregory L. Reece, I.B. Tauris, 2006

The Seventies Unplugged: A Kaleidoscopic Look At A Violent Decade, Gerard DeGroot, Macmillan, 2010

1001 Songs You Must Hear Before You Die, edited by Robert Dimery, Cassell Illustrated, 2010

Members Only: The Life And Times Of Paul Raymond, Paul Willetts, Serpent's Tail, 2010

A Rocket In My Pocket, Max Decharne, Serpent's Tail, 2010

Elvis My Best Man, George Klein with Chuck Crisafulli, Three Rivers Press, 2010

Starman, Paul Trynka, Little, Brown, 2011

One On One: 101 True Encounters, Craig Brown, Fourth Estate, 2011

The Man Who Sold The World: David Bowie And The 1970s, Peter Doggett, Bodley Head, 2011

Going To Sea In A Sieve, Danny Baker, Weidenfeld & Nicolson, 2012

Ride A White Swan: The Lives And Death Of Marc Bolan, Lesley-Ann Jones, Hodder & Stoughton, 2012

Bruce, Peter Ames Carlin, Simon & Schuster, 2012

First Class: A History Of Britain In 37 Postage Stamps, Chris West, Square Peg, 2012

Hello Again: Nine Decades Of Radio Voices, Simon Elmes, Random House, 2012

The History Of The NME, Pat Long, Portico, 2012

The Gentry Man: A Guide For The Civilised Male, edited by Hal Rubenstein, Harper Design, 2012

The Biographical Dictionary Of Popular Music, Dylan Jones, Bedford Square Books, 2012

Elvis Died For Somebody's Sins But Not Mine, Mick Farren, Headpress, 2012

Elvis All Shook Up, with an Introduction by Roy Blount, Jr., Sterling, 2012

The Train In The Night, Nick Coleman, Jonathan Cape, 2012

Hey Jo, Jo Wood, Harper Collins, 2013

A Prince Among Stones, Prince Rupert Loewenstein, Bloomsbury, 2013

Punk+, Sheila Rock, First Third Books, 2013

Hopper, Tom Folsom, It Books, 2013

The Soundtrack Of My Life, Clive Davis with Anthony DeCurtis, Simon & Schuster, 2013

I Dreamed I Was A Clean Tramp, Richard Hell, Harper Collins, 2013

My Way, Paul Anka, St. Martin's Press, 2013

Acknowledgements

"I was visiting a client in Washington, D.C. that day," says Ed Victor about August 16th, 1977. "For some reason, I brought my two sons with me on the trip; they were then thirteen and eleven. Although my trip there had an important business purpose, my client and I ended up talking about nothing other than Elvis' death. My sons were then old enough to appreciate what was happening, and they both still remember hearing the news." I'd like to thank Ed, whose original idea this was, along with Stephanie Sleap, James Mullinger, Paul McGuinness, Lucy Watson, Trevor Dolby, Tony Parsons, Bill Prince, David Bowie, Malcolm McLaren, Joe Strummer, Paul Simonon, Mick Jones, Burt Bacharach, Tony Bennett, John Barry, Shirley MacLaine, Doug Flett, Chris Charlesworth, Oliver Peyton, Anya Hindmarch, Nick Mason, Nik Cohn, Spas Roussev, Terry and Tricia Jones, Peter Blake, Bono, Warren Jackson, Margaret Walter, Robert Chalmers, Alice Morgan, Daniel Jones, Nils Lofgren, Holly Stevenson, Piers Morgan, Harold Tillman, Maggie Draycott, Isaac Tigrett, Jason Cowley, David Bailey, Alastair Campbell, Jessamy Calkin, Nick Kent, Andrew Lockett, Jimmy Page, Quentin Tarantino, Elton John, Tina Sinatra, Priscilla Presley, Lisa Marie Presley, Max Weinberg, Joanna Lumley, Simon Cowell, Keith Richards, Paul McCartney, Ringo Starr, Tony Elliott, Richard Young, Alan Bleasdale, Jo Vickers, Suzi Quatro, Ken Bruce, Chris Corbijn, Daniel Finkelstein and Tabatha Leggett, all of whom were tremendously helpful. Many thanks to the British Library and Central St. Martin's. Thanks obviously to

Sarah Walter, for her invaluable support, as ever, as well as to Edie & Georgia – who initially didn't think very much of ("Old, dead guy") Elvis at all, but who grudgingly got used to me playing "The Girl Next Door Went A' Walking" (one of the great, *great* Elvis records) at great volume, both at home and in the car (although there were always requests to turn Elvis down before I dropped them off at school, asking if I could turn over to Nick Grimshaw on Radio 1, or just turn the CD player off completely). Then there are huge thanks to Nicholas Coleridge and Jonathan Newhouse, for giving me the freedom to write the book in the first place. I always wanted the book to work in a micro/macro way (the minutiae, the epic sweep of Elvis's life), and in terms of detail, there is no greater "micro" book than *The King Is Dead*, Robert Holton's minute-by-minute guide to Elvis's funeral (or, as the book's blurb says, "A minute-by-minute drama of the funeral of rock'n'roll legend Elvis Aaron Presley, as told by the last man on earth to see Presley – funeral director Robert Kendall"). The book was invaluable, as were the following publications in their way: *Arena, Billboard, The Birmingham Post, Blitz, The Commercial Appeal, Conde Nast Traveller, Country Music Review, Creem, The Daily Express, The Daily Mail, The Daily Sport, The Daily Telegraph, Details, East Village Eye, The Economist, elvis.co.au, elvis.com, elvis.net, Empire, Entertainment Weekly, Esquire, The Evening Standard, The Face, The Financial Times, British GQ, The Guardian, i-D, The Independent, The Independent On Sunday, The International Herald Tribune, Jam!, The Los Angeles Times, The Mail On Sunday, Man About Town, Melody Maker, Memphis Press-Scimitar, Mojo, Music Week, New Musical Express, The New Yorker, The New York Post, The New York Times, Nova, The Observer, Paper, Popswap, Punk, Q, Record Mirror, Ritz, Rock's Back Pages, Rolling Stone, The Scotsman, Scotland On Sunday,*

Acknowledgements

Sounds, The South China Morning Post, Spin, Street Life, The Sun, The Sunday Express, The Sunday People, The Sunday Telegraph, The Sunday Times, The Times, Uncut, Vanity Fair, Viz, Vox, The Wall Street Journal, The Washington Post, Wikipedia, Wikiquotes, Wired, ZigZag. I have also enjoyed exploring the top and bottom drawers of dozens of Elvis websites (including the more than excellent *elvispresleymusic. com.au*), many of which are extraordinary in their obsession with detail.

Index

100 Club 6, 10
1977 2–29, 79

A
Adam and The Ants 80
The Adverts 56, 78, 86
Ginger Alden 32
Woody Allen 18
"All Shook Up" 264
"Almost" 280
"Always On My Mind" 285
American dream, the 41, 64,119, 221
American Graffiti 7, 13, 76, 283
Paul Anka 52
Annie Hall 18
Ann-Margret 273–4
"Any Day Now" 281
"Are You Lonesome Tonight?" 53, 269
Chet Atkins 204, 260
Australian "tour" 149–150

B
Burt Bacharach 281
David Bailey 136, 203
Danny Baker 81–2
Lester Bangs 217, 256

Baptist Memorial Hospital Memphis 30, 36
John Barry 184–7
The Beatles 148, 159–160, 274
Bill Belew 181
John Berger 239
Chuck Berry 18, 124, 190, 215
"A Big Hunk O' Love" 189, 267
Otis Blackwell 263, 264
Peter Blake 238
Blondie 111–12
"Blue Hawaii" 270
Blue Hawaii (film) 198–200, 203–4
"Blue Suede Shoes" 161
Marc Bolan 52
James Bond 184–7, 271
Bono 255
Bonzo Dog Doo-Dah Band 272
David Bowie 54–60, 114, 257
Marlon Brando 28
Richard Branson 100
"Bridge Over Troubled Water" 143, 159, 196, 229
James Brown 43
Johnny Burnette 263
"Burning Love" 55, 285
The Buzzcocks 21, 79, 98

Index

David Byrne 270

C

Nicolas Cage 247, 265
Alastair Campbell 66
"Can't Help Falling In Love" 196,
    271
John Carpenter 183, 251
June Carter 50
President Jimmy Carter 19–20,
    71
Johnny Cash 50
Samuel Charters 258
Chelsea School of Art 114
Cyrus Chestnut 253
Chrissie Hynde 90
The Clash 22, 86, 96, 98
President Bill Clinton 246
Eddie Cochran 92, 105
Sean Connery 186
Ray Connolly 140
cool 114–16
Alice Cooper 207
Elvis Costello 10, 107–9, 220–2
country music 231
"Crawfish" 266
Arthur "Big Boy" Crudup 120,
    124, 260
"Crying In The Chapel" 274
Tony Curtis 132, 186
Cyrus Plays Elvis 253

D

The Damned 219
Sammy Davis Jr. 47, 51, 163–4

day of Elvis's death 3, 214–37
James Dean 137, 267
Diana, Princess of Wales 8
disco 60
"Don't Be Cruel" 122, 156
Dr. Feelgood 26
Bob Dylan 50–1, 143, 268, 274

E

The Eagles 16
"The Edge Of Reality" 275
The Ed Sullivan Show 56, 64, 132
Elvis Aaron Presley 284
Elvis After Elvis 251
*Elvis, Aloha From Hawaii -Via
    Satellite* 198
*Elvis Country (I'm 10,000 Years
    Old)* 148, 284
"Elvis has left the building"
    (phrase) 1
*Elvis Presley Calls His Mother
    After The Ed Sullivan Show*
    259
*Elvis Religion: Exploring the Cult
    Of The King* 247
Elvis stamp 255
Elvis tartan 252
Elvis: What Happened? 75,
    206–7, 227
Joe Esposito 32, 38, 49

F

The Fall 87
Mick Farren 138, 221, 255
Farrah Fawcett 20, 46

Index

Flaming Star 238
Fleetwood Mac 15–17, 22, 53
Doug Flett 282
Chet Flippo 48, 250
"The Fool" 284
From Elvis In Memphis 279, 284

G
garage rock 21
G.I. Blues 268
Joao Gilberto 17
Girl Happy 268
"Girl Next Door Went A'
    Walking" 268
Girls! Girls! Girls! 198
"Golden Years" 54–5
Albert Goldman 37
"Good Luck Charm" 273
Graceland 31–3, 212, 237, 240–7,
    254
    crowds outside 39, 44
    wall around 45

H
Alex Haley 19
Bill Haley 124
George Hamilton 47
Richard Hamilton 31
"Hard Headed Woman" 267
Debbie Harry 93, 111
"Hawaiian Sunset" 270
"Heartbreak Hotel" 38, 53, 83,
    122, 139, 147,
Richard Hell 21, 106
Jake Hess 47

hippie movement 276
His Hand In Mine 274
"Hound Dog" 57, 139, 156, 159,
    162, 189, 264–5
"How Great Thou Art" 47, 275
Howlin' Wolf 121

I
Iggy Pop 54, 56, 63, 104
"I Just Can't Help Believing" 282
Lux Interior 122
"In The Ghetto" 279
"It's Now Or Never" 156, 269

J
Mick Jagger 31, 104
"Jailhouse Rock" 188–9, 265
The Jam 23, 79
Mark James 281, 287
Japanese rocker culture 234–5
Jim Jarmusch 91
jazz 276
Elton John 187
Mick Jones 93–4
Steve Jones 88, 103
Tom Jones 62, 208
"Just Pretend" 282

K
Robert Kendall 37, 42, 48
"Kentucky Rain" 284
B. B. King 50, 124
King Creole 92, 266
Evel Knievel 182

Index

L

Frankie Laine 286
Las Vegas 273
Led Zeppelin 18, 189
Brenda Lee 285
Robert E. Lee 48
Jerry Leiber 264–5, 273
John Lennon 52, 288
Let It Rock 81, 102–6
"Let Yourself Go" 277
Graham Lewis 27
Jerry Lee Lewis 190, 250
Liberace 182
"A Little Less Conversation" 275
Little Richard 50
"Little Sister" 271
Live In Las Vegas 284
Nils Lofgren 65
London
    as centre of punk 23
"Long Black Limousine" 49, 278
loungecore 271
"Love Me" 264
"Love Me Tender" 73, 176
Ray Lowry 94
George Lucas 13
Joanna Lumley 53
John Lydon (aka Johnny Rotten)
    10, 22, 88, 91–2, 95, 99,
    100–1, 229
David Lynch 262, 265

M

Kirsty MacColl 252
Greil Marcus 224

Dean Martin 121–2, 164
Steve Martin 194
Paul McCartney 24, 111, 147,
    261, 263
Malcolm McLaren 100-6
Neil McCormick 108
Ronnie McDowell 232
Malcolm McLaren 78, 81, 98
Meat Loaf 286
Memphis 91, 244–6
The Milton Berle Show 133, 264
Marilyn Monroe 102
*Monty Python And The Holy
    Grail* 211
"Moody Blue" 287
Keith Moon 70, 99
Roger Moore 160, 186
Scotty Moore 120, 129, 260
Paul Morley 269
"Mystery Train" 120, 262

N

Nag's Head, High Wycombe 4,
    8, 77
New Musical Express (NME) 24,
    26, 63, 109, 220, 222
New York Dolls 56, 105
George Nichopolous 35–6, 209
President Richard Nixon 19, 276
"(Now And Then) There's A Fool
    Such As I" 268

O

Paul Oakenfold 277
Roy Orbison 229

"O Sole Mio" 156, 269

P

Jimmy Page 189–190
Paradise, Hawaiian Style
    198–200, 204
Colonel Tom Parker 30, 43, 49,
    54, 135, 138, 140, 149, 198,
    235, 258, 266, 280
Tony Parsons 83–5
John Peel 82–83
Carl Perkins 50, 121, 161–2
The Pet Shop Boys 285
Sam Phillips 75, 119, 121, 144,
    260, 262, 263
"Polk Salad Annie" 282
Doc Pomus 262, 266, 271–3
Elvis Presley
    1968 comeback 57
    and black music 68, 123–5
    and Hawaii 197–205
    and Las Vegas 138–42, 164–80
    and Marlon Brando 28–9
    as fantasy lover for fans 66–9,
        171–9
    as sex symbol 60–2, 134–5,
        171–9
    as vocalist 147–8
    autopsy of 36
    daily schedule of 209–10
    drug use 209–11
    experience of meeting 190–4
    fascination with guns 207–8
    film career 183–7, 198–201
    final performance, Indianapolis
        2, 181–2
    golden Cadillac 149–150
    gyration of hips 160–1
    hairstyle 125, 132–3
    in Germany 276
    Las Vegas years 2
    Madison Square Garden press
        conference 1972 151–9
    obituaries of 216–28
    previous illnesses of 36
    reaction of British fans to death
        of 72–4
    reaction to death in New York
        225
    rumours, that still alive 248–
        250
    songs about 252
    understanding of the album
        format 146
Lisa Marie Presley 32, 33, 39, 44,
    240, 247, 282
Priscilla Presley 33, 39, 44, 182–3,
    240, 246
Vernon Presley 36, 42, 43, 50,
    158, 235
The Pretenders 90
Punk
    and Elvis 11, 25
    beginnings of 21–7
    ethos of intimacy in 26
    New York scene 111
Jimmy Pursey 82

Q

Suzi Quatro 53

R

The Ramones 21, 22, 26–7
"Ready Teddy" 56
Reg Presley 109–10
"Return To Sender" 273
"Riot In Cell Block #9" 265
rockabilly 109, 261
rock aristocracy 24
Rolling Stone 223–8, 230–1, 255
The Rolling Stones 86–7
Roustabout 69
Route 66 241–2
Roxy Music 114
"Rubberneckin'" 277
Rumours 15–7

S

Jon Savage 23, 101
Aaron Schroeder 266, 267, 268, 269, 273
Ridley Scott 15
The Sex Pistols 21, 56, 76, 82, 88, 98
    Elvis as an inspiration behind 101
Jan Shepard 28
"She Thinks I Still Care" 287
Sid (friend of author) 5–8, 76–7
Paul Simon 143, 229
Paul Simonon 93, 96
Frank Sinatra 51, 142, 164–7, 191–2
The Small Faces 56
Patti Smith 21
Ronnie Spector 70

Bruce Springsteen 63–5, 101, 229, 273
David Stanley 37, 49, 208
Viv Stanshall 272
Ringo Starr 104
Star Wars 13–15
Rod Stewart 52
Mike Stoller 264–5, 273
Barbra Streisand 138, 183
Jay Strongman 97
Joe Strummer 22, 86, 89–96, 99, 101, 267
"Stuck On You" 268
Sun Studios 119–121, 262
"Surrender" 271
"Suspicion" 272
"Suspicious Minds" 55, 60, 281
Swingeing London 67, 31

T

Talking Heads 26, 112–3
Quentin Tarantino 121
Bernie Taupin 187
Teds 88–9, 95–9
Television 112
Tennessee 248
"That's All Right" 120, 122, 217, 244, 260–3
"That's All Right Mama" 229
theremin, the 202
tiki culture 202–3
Time magazine 12
"Tomorrow Is A Long Time" 143, 274
"Too Much" 266

Feliks Topolski 134
The Troggs 109–111
Tupelo, Mississippi 195–6

V
Rudolph Valentino 68
Steve Van Zandt 63–4
The Velvet Underground 21
Sid Vicious 10, 99, 99–100
"Viva Las Vegas" 273
The Vortex 78, 79, 81

W
Andy Warhol 238
Ron Watts 4
"Way Down" 143–4, 288
John Wayne 46, 183
Sid Wayne 268
"Wear My Ring Around Your
    Neck" 267

Max Weinberg 65
Raquel Welch 69
Paul Weller 23
Jann Wenner 226–8
Alfred Wertheimer 125–133
Sonny West 75
Vivienne Westwood 102, 105
"What's She Really Like" 268
Barry White 269
Wild At Heart 265
Adrian Wootton 74

Y
"You Gave Me A Mountain" 286
"Young And Beautiful" 266
"You're The Boss" 273
"You've Lost That Lovin' Feelin'"
    196